Reflexivity in *Tristram Shandy*

Reflexivity in *Tristram Shandy*

An Essay in Phenomenological Criticism

James E. Swearingen

New Haven and London
Yale University Press
1977

Published with assistance from the
Louis Stern Memorial Fund.

Designed by Kate Emlen
and set in Baskerville type.
Printed in the United States of America by
The Murray Printing Company, Westford, Mass.

Published in Great Britain, Europe, Africa, and
Asia by Yale University Press, Ltd., London.
Distributed in Latin America by Kaiman & Polon,
Inc., New York City; in Australia and New
Zealand by Book & Film Services, Artarmon,
N.S.W., Australia; and in Japan by Harper & Row,
Publishers, Tokyo Office.

Library of Congress Cataloging in Publication Data

Swearingen, James E   1939–
   Reflexivity in Tristram Shandy.

   Bibliography: p.
   Includes index.
   1. Sterne, Laurence, 1713–1768. The life and opinions of
Tristram Shandy, gentleman. I. Title.
PR3714.T73S9   823'.6   77–5515
ISBN 0–300–02123–2

For
Wilba and James

There is not a more perplexing affair in life to me, than to set about telling anyone who I am—for there is scarce any body I cannot give a better account of than myself; and I have often wish'd I could do it in a single word—and have an end of it.

A Sentimental Journey

You could not discover the limits of the self, even by traveling along every path: so deep a logos does it have.

Heraclitus, "Fragment 45"

We shall not cease from exploration
And the end of all our exploring
Will be to arrive where we started
And know the place for the first time.

T. S. Eliot, "Little Gidding"

Contents

Preface

Ten years ago Martin Heidegger suggested in an interview with *Der Spiegel* that the overwhelming problem of the modern world is to understand the essence of the global movement of technology, with its peculiar assumptions about the existent, about the nature of truth, about the definitive character of man, and about the relation of being human to language.[1] To understand the anthropology implicit in that movement requires an unraveling that "can be prepared only in the same place in the world where the modern technological world originated. . . . It cannot happen because of any takeover by Zen-Buddhism or any other Eastern experiences of the world. There is need for a rethinking which is to be carried out with the help of the European tradition and of a new appropriation of that tradition." Heidegger observed furthermore that philosophy itself is not up to the task, its role having been preempted by the sciences, and that his own thinking "stands in a definitive relationship to the poetry of Hölderlin" who "points to the future" and "expects god."

The example of Heidegger's later essays on language and

1. "*Der Spiegel*'s Interview with Martin Heidegger on September 23, 1966," trans. Maria P. Alter and John D. Caputo, *Philosophy Today* 20 (Winter 1976), 268–84, esp. p. 281. By prior agreement the interview was reserved for publication until after Heidegger's death, which came in the spring of 1976.

poetry suggests that within the broadly defined realm of literary scholarship and criticism are both the texts which do that "rethinking" and the interpretive tools to engage in such an enquiry. For those who seek to make a "new appropriation" of the English tradition, Swift, Sterne, and Blake stand out as writers who "think ahead" by questioning the presuppositions and the aims in which the modern age is grounded. Whatever interest the following essay may prove to have in the local area of Sterne scholarship, its deepest impulse is to use the discipline of literary criticism as a means of meditating this peculiar destiny of modern life, through an examination of that crucial novel of the later eighteenth century, *Tristram Shandy*.

The project had its origin in my recognition that an intimate knowledge of *Shandy* offered a means of access to the esoteric reductions of Husserlian phenomenology. What followed was an effort to understand that peculiar nexus. In the spring of 1974, Edward G. Ballard of Tulane University allowed me to join his Heidegger seminar, and this intellectual experience focused many of the issues to which the present study is profoundly indebted.

Teachers to whom I owe older obligations are those at North Texas State University who were my early mentors—E. Garrett Ballard, William F. Belcher, Howard C. Key, and Martin Staples Shockley—and those at the University of Minnesota who guided and encouraged my studies in the eighteenth century—Robert E. Moore and Samuel Holt Monk.

For the leisure to complete this book I owe thanks to the Graduate School of Marquette University for a Summer Faculty Fellowship and to the Department of English for release time.

Steven Skousgaard, once my student, now my teacher, has read the manuscript carefully and saved me from a number of mistakes and imprecisions in the philosophical dimensions of the study. I wish also to thank Colleen Butch, for assistance in preparing the copy, and my editors at Yale University Press, Ellen Graham and Charles Grench, for their kindness and efficiency in seeing the manuscript through to publication. Finally, special acknowledgment is due to Jack Wages, whose friendship over the years has left me with obligations too extensive to recover and articulate; to Wilba Shaw Swearingen, who, beyond the intimate support of a wife, has brought the skills of enlightened librarianship to this project and offered guidance in what was at times new intellectual territory; and last, to James the younger, whose sense of humor has often saved us all from that "mysterious carriage of the body" calculated "to cover the defects of the mind."

J.E.S.

1

The Problem of Interpretation or Criticism under the Aspect of the Hobby-Horse

As Don Quixote lies sorely bruised from his brief encounter with the Yanguesan carriers, Sancho Panza gives the Asturian maid Maritornes an account of the perplexing question of who exactly the knight is. To her query, "What's a knight errant?" he replies, "I'll tell you, my girl, that a knight errant —to cut a long story short—is beaten up one day and made Emperor the next. Today he's the most unfortunate and poverty-stricken creature in the world; to-morrow he'll have two or three kingdoms to give to his squire."[1] Although Sancho has not fully understood either *what* or *who* exactly Quixote is, his interpretation is revealing. His account demonstrates the ludicrous posture of the knight-errant as he appears to a realistic world; it also shows how the act of interpretation is conditioned by Sancho's own good-hearted acquisitiveness and by the sedimentation[2] of experience which forms the context for the meaning that Quixote's experience can have for him at this early stage of their partnership. In this inadequate act of explanation there is a clue to the nature

1. Miguel de Cervantes Saavedra, *The Adventures of Don Quixote,* trans. J. M. Cohen, p. 119.
2. This archeological metaphor is used in phenomenology to stress the different and complexly interrelated levels or strata of consciousness which can be descriptively explained by means of reflection into the founding strata underlying any particular conscious act.

1

of interpretation as it is explicitly required by *Tristram Shandy* and as it will be examined in this chapter; but there is also a suggestion of the disintegration of ideals and reality in the cultural context of Quixote's adventures which bears comparison with the underlying occasion of Tristram's clarification of his "life and opinions." The nexus between Sterne's novel and that of his esteemed predecessor is a hero out of harmony with himself and his world, which is itself out of joint—a hero who undertakes a quest that culminates in recovery of himself.

Sterne signals the kinship of Tristram Shandy with Cervantes's great adventure story in a number of explicit passages. The earliest is the association of parson Yorick with the wandering knight, both of them misunderstood men of noble spirit. Yorick lives by a code that embraces the ancient kinship between wisdom and play, one that is beyond the comprehension of his parishioners; and that unfashionable combination draws their censure down upon his head. The close affinity between the characters of Yorick and Tristram, both of whom are masks for their author, gives the prototype of Quixote a broad application in Sterne's novel. Tristram's experience corresponds to Quixote's in several ways that justify the appellation of knight-errant.

Both are comic knights-errant, one trying to live by a purely literary ideal from the past, the other anticipating a radically reflective philosophic method of the future, and the occasion of their wanderings is a personal disorientation resulting from the problem of identity. Quixote has gone mad with reading romances of chivalry and forgotten who he is; Tristram lives in a world in which personal identity has been reduced to a *tabula rasa* and the "who" mistaken for a "what." As a result, both suffer a variety of adversities. Quixote's efforts to bring the refractory world into conformity with his ideals draws him out of his library and into the plain of Montiel to wander about in random search of wrongs to set right. In

Tristram's effort to account for himself and to understand the anomalies of his life from conception to consumption, he retires to his library to explore the fields of his own mental life according to no "man's rules that ever lived."[3] The adventures of both, one in the public world, the other in the private, ultimately lead to self-discovery. Don Quixote's illusion is eventually dispelled and he is reconciled to being who he is, simply Alonso Quixano the Good. Tristram Shandy's reflections lead through a combined archeology and teleology of the self to a clear understanding of the structure and processes of his own being.

The most significant parallel between these two knights-errant is the ontological riddle of their characters, their ambiguous status as fictive or real. Although Quixote is really a creation of Cervantes's imagination, the story is ostensibly copied from an Arabic manuscript by Cid Hameti Benegeli, which leaves open the question of whether Quixote or Quixada or Quesada or whoever he really is, is a historical person or a fictional character. There is the further complication of the Don's awareness of himself as simultaneously real and fictional: he knows in advance how his story will be written; he hears of himself as a character in a book; and he even has to try to live up to his own reputation as a character. These complications are calculated to undermine confidence in Quixote's real ontological status and to give him a vitality that extends beyond the boundaries of his story.[4]

Whereas the figure of Quixote cannot be entirely contained by Cervantes's story, in Sterne the ambivalence emanates from two directions: both the reader's status and Tristram's are uncertain. The reader finds himself engaged in discussions

3. Laurence Sterne, *The Life and Opinions of Tristram Shandy, Gentleman*, ed. James A. Work, I.iv.8. Subsequent references will be to the Work edition and will be given in the text by volume, chapter, and page.
4. This point of view has been developed in detail by Harry Levin in *Contexts of Criticism*, pp. 79–96.

with Tristram, the ostensible author, over a host of issues including, at times, how the narrative itself should be managed. So successfully does Tristram draw us into his own effort to cope with the confusions of life with the Shandys and to understand the perplexities of a hobby-horsical world that our sense of his level of being is affected. From this direction, the appearance of the reader's perception of the hero's status is conditioned by a shift in his own position to the inside of the fiction. A corresponding ambivalence derives from the autobiographical format. Reflection on the actual experience of reading a conventional autobiography reveals the influence of the knowledge that it is not fiction; as Roman Ingarden says, it "changes the modality of our reading consciousness from a state of resistance and disbelief" in what is only fiction "into a state of feigned, or quasi-, belief, a state of spiritual consent and participation."[5] In Tristram's "autobiography," however, the process is complicated by the unusual intimacy of the autobiographical voice which is due to his lively sensitivity to his audience and to our participation in the narrative itself; but that intimacy is qualified by the "resistance" that comes from knowing that we are in fact reading fiction. Sterne only thinly disguises his own voice which at times speaks through Tristram's, though the voices are neither equivalent nor clearly discriminated. One senses that the living voice must often be speaking from his own experience since he could have such direct access to no consciousness but his own. The problems encountered in the process of writing, for example, are not fictional problems, one is convinced, even if they are the ostensible concerns of Tristram.

To increase the complexity of nearly indistinguishable fictional strata and to disarm complacent belief in the status of the hero as ideal, Sterne barely conceals within the book itself the fact that " 'Tis . . . a picture of myself,"[6] as he

---

5. *The Literary Work of Art,* trans. George G. Grabowicz, p. xxxvi.
6. *Letters of Laurence Sterne,* ed. Lewis P. Curtis, p. 87.

acknowledges in a letter to Garrick in 1760, just before the publication of the first two volumes of the novel. The resistance of disbelief—and suspended disbelief is disbelief still— is constantly being qualified by a consent elicited by means of the blurred line of demarcation between author and character. The external event of Sterne's publishing his own sermons under the title *The Sermons of Mr. Yorick,* after having included one of them in the first installment of his novel, contributes to the coalescence of the real world and the fictional. It is true that among the refinements that had not yet occurred in this seedtime of the novel as a form is the desire of the novelist to conceal himself "like the God of the creation . . . within or behind or beyond or above his handiwork, invisible, refined out of existence, indifferent, paring his fingernails."[7] But Sterne's presence is not due to any lack of technical refinement; it is a way of maintaining the authenticity of the autobiographical voice and, at the same time, the psychic distancing of the fictional character in a tension that holds the reader in a state of some uncertainty.[8] The critic would normally prefer to distinguish clearly between biographical and critical issues, leaving it to the biographer to estimate how the characters of Tristram and Yorick open out into the life of Sterne on the back side of the novel. As in Cervantes, however, the line between the inside and the outside of the fiction has been deliberately blurred so that one cannot settle into either comfortable disbelief or easy consent. In *Don Quixote,* to be sure, the ambivalence is part of the fiction; we do *really* know the status of the hero. In *Tristram Shandy* the reverse is the case; the ambivalence is indubitable. Not only do the identities of Sterne and Tristram tend to fuse; so do those of Sterne and Yorick, ground enough for suspecting concealed affinities between Tristram and Yorick. The effect is to tease the reader

7. James Joyce, *A Portrait of the Artist as a Young Man,* p. 215.
8. In order to maintain the same degree of distinction that is evident in the novel, I shall refer to Tristram as author throughout this study.

with an uncertainty that makes an issue both of the ontological question, which is the central thematic concern of the book, and of the problem of interpretation which is influenced as much by the position of the reader as by the thing to be understood.

Hermeneutics and Hobby-Horses

It will eventually be argued in this discussion that Tristram's whole enterprise is a hermeneutics, a process of self-interpretation which is required by his awareness of being part of a family and of a tradition in which there has been serious misinterpretation. It is not surprising that the parson whose sermons interpret biblical texts by imaginatively filling out the human setting of those texts should raise the problem of a general hermeneutics in a work that professes to give an account of the mind. Nothing is more obvious to the most casual reader of the novel than the fact that in Shandy Hall every mode of experience down to the simplest sense perception—of the crevice in the parlor wall, say—offers a problem of interpretation. Historically, hermeneutics may still have been an ancillary discipline of rules for interpreting biblical and legal texts, but in Sterne's novel it undergoes an intuitive expansion of application that was not to reach its full theoretical development until the twentieth century.[9]

9. The modern development of hermeneutics begins with Friedrich Schleiermacher who undertakes to interpret texts, specifically scripture, by means of understanding the individual personalities of the writers (*Hermeneutik,* trans. Heinz Kimmerle). Wilhelm Dilthey deepens the study of the writer by claiming that the individual can be understood only from the broad perspective of historical lived experience. Heidegger, in turn, overcomes the romantic illusion that reader and text, subject and object, interpenetrate in the interpretive encounter and avoids Dilthey's relativism of historical perspectives with its underlying psychological notion of lived experience by expanding the hermeneutic question to the nature of interpretation itself as the primary activity of man (*Dasein*), the being who

A reasonable starting place is with the narrower question of interpreting the novel, and Tristram does not leave us without advice on that point:

> Writing, when properly managed, (as you may be sure I think mine is) is but a different name for conversation: As no one, who knows what he is about in good company, would venture to talk all;——so no author, who understands the just boundaries of decorum and good breeding, would presume to think all: The truest respect which you can pay to the reader's understanding, is to halve this matter amicably, and leave him something to imagine, in his turn, as well as yourself. [II.ii.108–09]

"Conversation" in Tristram's remark is more than metaphoric: it is an effort to preserve the original spontaneity of spoken language and to overcome the inherent recalcitrance of the written word in catching the movement of thinking. The intention acknowledged in this passage is to write in a way that will keep the reader's imagination "as busy as my own"; but that indication of how the writing is to be carried forward also implies how reading is done when it is rightly done, implicitly, a prescription about how the text is to be interpreted. In *Truth and Method,* Hans-Georg Gadamer makes extensive use of the analogy of conversation as a means of describing the event of interpretation which underlies even the most sophisticated epistemological methods. Tristram's similar concern with the event of understanding the spoken word is also concentrated in that term *conversation* which is the foundation of his reflections, and it invites one to consider what exactly constitutes authentic conversation and

---

seeks to interpret his own experience. Heidegger's own development of the question moves from interpreting the interpreting being in *Being and Time* to attempting to understand the hermeneutical experience in *Unterwegs zur Sprache,* the essence of which he locates in language and the role of Hermes, the bringer of tidings and the god of boundaries.

authentic interpretation. Three features in Gadamer's discussion (pp. 330 ff., 344 ff.) are especially revealing, though the analysis may appear to make illicitly free use of a casual analogy in the passage quoted above from the novel. I believe, however, that the point of view will be amply justified in the course of the ensuing discussion when interpretation is viewed ontologically, that is, as a way of being instead of merely a way to knowledge.

The first requirement for conversation is that the conversants engage in a give and take in which each tries to enter into what the other says rather than talking at cross-purposes. Such an openness to the other is the posture of one who, unlike the Shandys, is willing to risk the security of one's prior grasp of reality by listening to what another says. Authentic conversation presupposes such an attitude of true enquiry and such a will to understand. Since the implication of that openness for the reader is a requirement for considerably more than mere aesthetic appreciation of the form and technique of his book, it will be well to ask what exactly Tristram requires in this respect, what quality of openness he expects in the exchange with his text. The question is important enough to him that he teases and taunts the reader throughout the novel for inattention, misreading, and misinterpretation. Most conspicuous, however, is the vivid example of how Yorick's sermon on a good conscience, the most important self-contained text within the book because of its normative function, is abused by inattention to its inner significance on the part of the company assembled at its reading in the parlor. It attacks conscience as undependable, inconsistent, and deceptive, thereby accounting for its own poor reception as due to human resources for subverting it. The reading completed, Walter expresses an attitude of abstract aesthetic appreciation: "Thou hast read the sermon extremely well, *Trim,* quoth my father. . . . I like the sermon well . . . 'tis dramatic,——and there is something in that way of writing, when skilfully managed, which catches the attention" (II.xvii.140–41). The character in the novel most guilty of the self-deceptions which the sermon anatomizes listens only to the aesthetic surface, one might say "listens away from" the moral and religious meaning that informs the words and that he is called upon to appropriate. Thus well before Kant's *Critique of Judgment* completes the subjectivization of aesthetics, Sterne criticizes that aesthetic consciousness which ignores the existential roots in the context of the world from which and about which a text speaks and makes it accessible to an audience. Language for him is still preeminently a signifying milieu which demands that one understand what is said. Walter's response demonstrates how those connections between a text and its world may be dissolved by the preference for the pure immediacy of surface attractiveness, stripping it of its power to speak, judging it in abstraction from the context to which it belongs, and neutralizing its claim to truth.

How fully Sterne is in agreement with his conservative Augustan forebears, for whom art and nature were complementary and nature the framework and norm within which art functioned, may also be inferred from the passage. Aesthetic consciousness was destined to dissolve that old sovereignty of nature and to detach art from reality. In *Either/Or* Kierkegaard makes a moral analysis of the aesthetic as a way of life that demonstrates how it abstracts its object of interest from all ties with the life to which it belongs and attempts to hold it in the simultaneity of purely immediate experience. To do so is for the ego to assume a universal and sovereign authority over everything in a manner comparable to the spirit of technology. Inherent in that spirit is the impulse to dissolve the unity of being and to make the ego the measure of all things, treating the world as a collection of tools or, in the case of the aesthete, pleasures to be manipulated for the immediate gratification of the ego.[10] The subjective con-

10. See pp. 184–92 below where this dimension of Walter's character as rhetor is explored.

sequence which interests Kierkegaard is that the need for continuity and unity in life itself is frustrated by that self-destructive demand for immediacy. Tristram plainly discourages our dwelling on the aesthetic appearances of his work by encouraging us to see the significance of the work in its relation to reality and to grasp what it attempts to say. His criterion of conversation, in contrast to autonomous aesthetic consciousness, demands that one become engaged with the extra-aesthetic content of his work, with the book's context of meaningfulness. Gadamer's description of the way in which a common world of reference underlies the comprehension of a text summarizes the point clearly:

> Inasmuch as we encounter the work of art in the world and a world in the individual work of art, this does not remain a strange universe into which we are magically transported for a time. Rather, we learn to understand ourselves in it, and that means that we preserve the discontinuity of the experience in the continuity of our existence. Therefore it is necessary to adopt an attitude to the beautiful and to art that does not lay claim to immediacy, but corresponds to the historical reality of man. The appeal to immediacy, to the genius of the moment, to the significance of the 'experience', cannot withstand the claim of human existence to continuity and unity of self-understanding. The experience of art must not be side-tracked into the uncommittedness of aesthetic awareness. . . . Art is knowledge and the experience of the work of art is a sharing of this knowledge. [Gadamer, pp. 86–87]

However, openness even to the world that speaks through the work does not exhaust the implications of Tristram's example of interpretation as conversation.

The second characteristic of conversation that is pertinent to Tristram's statement is a "fusion of horizons" that occurs when there is a meeting of minds. One who suspends his own point of view in order to understand the perspective of another, as when the physician interviews his patient or the attorney his client, is not conversing in the true sense of the term: no *conversation* can occur because the *with* is suspended and there can be no exchange of views and mutual expansion of the understanding of both parties. Likewise, in interpreting the text, if a reader tries to suspend his own point of view and to cultivate a detached appreciation of the perspective Tristram adopts toward his life, he thereby ignores the historical dimension of his own being and fails in his task, for all understanding is interpretation and requires assimilation of the new materials to the old structures of its preunderstanding. The aim is "not to get inside another person and relive his experiences"; reproduction, were it possible, would not be interpretation.[11] Detaching himself from his own orientation, attempting to suspend his own historical conditioning insures a reader's failure as conversationalist, for Tristram has laid down the prior condition that his reader engage in an exchange that presupposes the integrity of each person's horizon. And he never forgets that the reader is maintaining his own horizon as demonstrated by frequent interrogation about what he thinks, how he feels, how he is responding. Never in the annals of fiction is the awareness of the integrity of the reader more explicit and sensitive than here.

The third feature of conversation according to Gadamer's analysis is that when it is real it is an activity that guides the conversants rather than being guided by them. Its extraordinary value in this regard is that it leads one into new territory, revealing the unthought and even uncovering what heretofore lay concealed in one's own thinking. Thus when Tristram comments on his "most religious" manner of proceeding, writing "the first sentence——and trusting to Almighty God

---

11. Gadamer, p. 345. This reconstruction of others' experience was the goal of the early hermeneutics of Schleiermacher.

for the second (VIII.ii.540), he is not being facetious; he is admitting that he is surrendering himself to the conversation rather than approaching his task with a preconceived method. His ideal requires that both he and his reader abandon themselves and their methods of procedure to the free play of the event in which new meanings unpredictably occur. This question of method is exceedingly important, for choosing a rational method establishes a ratio between reader and text. Questions imply answers and methods filter from experience what the methods have prejudged as important. The general problem of interpretation is not a matter of settling on a procedure for finding what one seeks as in those enquiries where the goal is established in advance; it is a more primitive experience and a more extensive concept than the scientific one of method. Whereas the question of method properly belongs to the domain of objective knowledge, the general problem of understanding is concerned with a mode of being rather than a mode of knowing. In fact, understanding is coextensive with "the total human experience of the world."[12] However, the example of conversation—and hence the denial of method—would appear to be limited by the stasis of Tristram's side of the exchange. How can the relationship be a dialogue when the printed word is a unilateral speaking, a kind of denial of reciprocity? The answer is that the text speaks in the reading and, by Tristram's having anticipated and in large measure controlled our responses, we participate, even more than in reading most books, in the advent of meaning that is not only a common ground of understanding, but also a literal fusing of horizons.[13] This is the real meaning of

12. Schleiermacher, p. xi.

13. The phenomenological metaphor of horizon brings into view the whole spatial, temporal, and cultural context of meaningfulness of an object or phenomenon, the encircling sphere that constitutes the setting within which an object reveals itself as what it is. Thus Heidegger introduces the thesis of *Being and Time* with the statement, "Our provisional

Tristram's confidence that our association with him in the reading will lead gradually from acquaintance to the kind of unique understanding and affection that exists between friends (I.vi.10–11).

According to contemporary hermeneutic theory a linguistic event does not consist merely of univocal statements about particular things or events; it puts into words in a less intense way than does poetry the manner in which one comports oneself toward the whole of being. In authentic conversation, then, one listens not only to what is said but to the unsaid, the horizon of meaningfulness, that wells up within it. In the complicated act of reading this means that while holding on to one's own relation with being, one must catch, beyond the literal references of words spoken, another manner of comportment within the whole of things which is part of the meaning of what is said. It is in this sense that language is inherently speculative. In Gadamer's words, "the finite possibilities of the word are oriented towards the sense intended, as towards the infinite" (p. 426). Accordingly, it will be part of the purpose of this critical study to attempt to retrieve in all its original vitality the problem that occupies Tristram's attention. He insists that we respond to the question with which he is engaged and that we think it through with him. Our thinking is not a reiteration of his, but a reworking which is completely unlike abstract aesthetic appreciation. To retrieve Sterne's problem may even involve a certain violence in wresting the book free from the pattern of references that customarily surround it, and it is in this sense that the present study is speculative: to retrieve the problem of being that lies at the heart of the work and to explore new ways in which the

---

aim is the Interpretation of *time* as the possible horizon for any understanding whatsoever of Being" (trans. John Macquarrie and Edward Robinson, p. 21). Later Heidegger gives up the concept of horizon as belonging to metaphysics and its concern with objects (*Siendes*) and their representation rather than with being (*Sein*).

meaning of the text deploys itself in the cultural horizon of the twentieth century. The tension between Tristram's thinking and our own parallels the dialectical relation between his thinking and the family tradition from which he springs and which occupies most of his reflections. The close relation between understanding an "other"—person, event, text, or tradition—and understanding oneself, Tristram's ultimate aim in his book and ours in the reading, occupies Paul Ricoeur in his essay "Existence and Hermeneutics." He remarks that "all interpretation is to conquer a remoteness, a distance between the past cultural epoch to which the text belongs and the interpreter himself. . . . It is thus the growth of his own understanding of himself that he [the exegete] pursues through his understanding of the other. Every hermeneutics is thus, explicitly or implicitly, self-understanding by means of understanding others" (pp. 16–17).

Tristram's enquiry is stimulated and shaped by a need to understand himself through discovering his relations to a tradition. He does not look back for positive historical fact, doubting, questioning the integrity of his tradition, for the old dichotomy between reality and appearance, events-in-themselves and events-as-they-appear, has been obviated by the ontological character of the events of understanding. His, like other histories, is no more discovered than invented. As readers often observe, there is no way that he could have a visually accurate picture of Trim's oratorical posture as he reads the sermon in the parlor or know his exact tone of voice as he discourses on death to the servants in the kitchen. He could not have positive knowledge of a thousand other details, many of which occurred before he was even born. What is important is why this lack of verification is at the least irrelevant, and perhaps even an advantage. Tristram's procedure leaves little doubt that his imaginative grasp of his heritage has, from the point of view of historical objectivism, altered the "facts"; but the ultimate result is a kind of preservation of the truth that he *is,* as a participant in that tradition, rather than positive knowledge of alien events with which he has no living tie. To the scientific mind such an apparently careless disregard for verification must remain fallacious until it recognizes that the empirical principle itself derives, laden with prejudgments, from just such a primitive and precritical engagement with the historical world. In an entirely different sense, Tristram is highly critical, not factually but morally. His reflections are critical of the aberrations in the life of Shandy Hall, and he comes gradually to a superior understanding which in effect is a purifying of the tradition as represented in a comically debased form by Walter, Toby, and Elizabeth Shandy. The form of that purification is the retrieval of a much older and wiser stratum of his tradition represented by Yorick. His problem is not one of historical knowledge; it is interpretive and, hence, necessarily historical in a more radical sense. While it may be assumed, then, that Tristram has not deliberately misrepresented his family history, on the ground that misrepresentation would hinder rather than serve his purposes, the issue of historical accuracy simply does not fall within the purview of his project. His concern is with the primitive events of understanding as a mode of being. Our own act of participation in his book, which on his model requires that we let the text become contemporaneous and address us in our present world, will, however, raise the issue of validity in an urgent form.

The implications of Tristram's analogy interpreted in this way are extensive for criticism and need to be made explicit since they demand an approach to the text substantially different from critical methods based on the model of scientific knowledge which assumes a false objectification. In fact, the implications weigh heavily against all procedures which stress either side of the subject-object schema that underlies most modern literary theory. On the one hand there is the realist assumption that a text is an objective thing-in-itself to be manipulated according to specified methods by an unconditioned reader, and, on the other, the idealist assumption that the reader projects his own meaning into the text, using it to launch into his own orbit. Both ignore the fact that the event of understanding is anterior to this epistemological model of a subject confronting an alien object and calls for a critique of positivity. That model is not simply given in primary experience as is so often assumed; it is an abstraction, derived from concrete experience, for the purpose of dealing with a world of objects. As such it is specifically unsuited to literary criticism. More appropriate for critical purposes is the analogy of human relationships such as Tristram's conversation. Gadamer uses the term *I-Thou* to distinguish three different qualities of relationships which parallel ways of addressing a text and offer distinct critical alternatives.

The first is an "I," a subject, confronting a "Thou" who is not a thou at all but an it, an object with which the subject has nothing in common; the resulting relationship of "objectivity" consists in subsuming the object under various universal concepts by specific methods of procedure. Thus one may find that a person exemplifies one or another trait of "human nature," to use an eighteenth-century category, or, as in twentieth-century social science, he may predict how the person would behave under some specified circumstances. In such a "scientific" procedure everything about the person that does not exemplify some universal concept is submerged, including the uniqueness that is the person himself. The objective habit of mind approaches all reality with what Victor Shklovský calls an "'algebraic' method of thought" which facilitates one's dealing with a world of objects with great economy though the price of that abstract economy is the gradual evacuation of reality which, one might argue, it is a function of art to rehabilitate.[14] An objectivist posture toward a text

14. "Art as Technique," in *Russian Formalist Criticism: Four Essays,* trans. Lee T. Lemon and Marian J. Reis, p. 11.

strips it of its power to make a personal claim on the reader and effectively silences it. In the domain of natural science it is as true as in the study of literature that the event of understanding cannot itself be understood by constructing and retrospectively imposing such a pattern on the event of interpretation. Subjects and objects are possible only because of the rich texture of relationships that obtain in the world prior to reflection. A realist criticism that attempts to study the text objectively, as if it were an autonomous entity, is uninterested in the concealed processes by means of which the object is accessible and in the subjective conditions that influence the way it presents itself to consciousness. "To speak of the being of a thing as it 'actually is' is to indulge in metaphysical speculation: as it is for whom? There is no human perspective from which one can say what a being 'actually is.' "[15]

Underlying the objectivist position is a legitimate concern with the question of verification and an apprehension of the critical anarchy, not to say generally shabby thinking, that would be fostered by an unrestrained impressionism. Hermeneutical theorists, especially Gadamer, though the criticism applies better to Heidegger, have been blamed for an indifference to the possibility of valid interpretation.[16] All critics are

15. Richard Palmer, *Hermeneutics: Interpretation Theory in Schleiermacher, Dilthey, Heidegger, and Gadamer,* p. 229.

16. Emilio Betti in *Die Hermeneutik als allgemeine Methodik der Geisteswissenschaften* and E. D. Hirsch in *Validity in Interpretation* both argue this point against Gadamer. Hirsch is concerned with limiting hermeneutics to a philological method of establishing the "verbal meaning" of a text as opposed to its "significance" for the reader. But Gadamer is interested in a different question, and one that apparently does not interest Hirsch since he excludes it from hermeneutics, namely, the distinguishing features of all events of understanding. Based on Gadamer's response to Betti in Supplement I of *Truth and Method* where he insists, "I am *not proposing a method,* but I am describing *what is the case*" and thus going "beyond the concept of method ... to envisage ... what always happens" (Gadamer's italics, pp. 465–66), one suspects that his intention is to dissolve the question of validity in instances of premethodical understanding by confining it to its proper scientific sphere.

convinced, of course, that there is a discernible difference between getting a point of interpretation right and getting it wrong, but that does not imply that only one way of interpreting a text is admissible. What needs to be examined carefully is the notion of objectively valid results. Just as the object "as it really is" is as problematic in physics as in historical criticism, so is the notion of objective validity. In the introduction to the *Cartesian Meditations,* Edmund Husserl observes that the phrase "objectively valid results . . . signifies nothing but results that have been refined by mutual criticism and that now withstand every criticism" (p. 5). Not even the positive sciences "attain actualization of a system of absolute truths"; they must settle for "an infinite horizon of approximations" (p. 12). As Aron Gurwitsch puts it, objectivity is "identifiableness, i.e. the possibility of reverting again and again to what, through the present experienced act, is offered to consciousness."[17] Hence, that claim may be said to have objective, empirical validity which withstands public criticism. In discussing the historian's effort to achieve objectivity, Ricoeur says that the meaning of such objectivity is an educated subjectivity, that is, "not just *any* subjectivity," not "a subjectivity adrift," but one shaped by history whose predispositions derive from the tradition of which it is part and "are dimensions of historical objectivity itself."[18]

The task of criticism is not to dissect a rationally structured object with the intellectual scalpel from a position of detached contemplation. There are dimensions of the critical enterprise that can be and should be reduced to method, regions that require empirical research and formal analysis; but those regions of enquiry presuppose a more primitive *living* relationship with the text which makes rational analysis worth the trouble

17. "On the Intentionality of Consciousness," in *Philosophical Essays in Memory of Edmund Husserl,* ed. Marvin Farber, p. 83.
18. "Objectivity and Subjectivity in History," in *History and Truth,* trans. Charles A. Kelbley, pp. 30–31.

and establishes the directions of interest which it will take. A pertinent example for the study of *Tristram Shandy* is the case of the historical text. Approached as an objective entity the historical text can be nothing more than an object of antiquarian interest which has lost the power to speak. Antiquarianism which attempts to reconstruct some original meaning or the response of the original audience fails utterly to understand the historical nature of either the text or the interpreter and thus misses the work entirely. As R. G. Collingwood correctly observes, the historian "is a part of the process he is studying, has his own place in that process, and can see it only from the point of view which at this present moment he occupies within it."[19] The proper aim is not the futile effort to restore the irretrievable life of the past or to return to some original meaning; it is to establish that reciprocity between historian and text that was described above as a fusion of horizons. When judiciously practiced, historicism escapes its absurdly deterministic implications by searching for formative influences rather than "causes" in the strict sense. Its excesses are frequent enough, however, to justify the observation that whatever antecedents might be recoverable, a writer is a self, a transcendence, that does not respond to ideas in books as billiard ball responds to cue. [20] In his relatedness to himself there is an open space of reflection that breaks the deterministic friction of causality, setting him at a distance from the self that is acted upon by causes and motives. The motives for thought and the influences giving it shape are as likely to be "a good dinner" or "a bad wife"[21] as the reading of Montaigne; but, in any case, there is an agency guiding from the front as causes push from behind.

The idealist who stresses the opposite pole of the subject-

19. *The Idea of History*, p. 248.

20. See the discussion of the epistemology of sophism in chapter 4 below.

21. Duke Maskell, "Locke and Sterne, or Can Philosophy Influence Literature?" *Essays in Criticism* 23 (1973), 25.

object relation in criticism chooses a relation to the text that corresponds to Gadamer's second "I-Thou" model in which the thou is a reflection of the I. In personal relationships the thou is thereby allowed a uniqueness of its own, but at the same time that uniqueness is subordinated to projective patterns of explanation by which one establishes supremacy over the other. There is reciprocity in this relationship, but it does not allow the other to speak for himself. As a model of interpretation it has one advantage over the objectivist position in that it closes the distance between reader and text and allows the intimacy of encounter that is the beginning of meaning. But the advantage is offset by the absence of any principle restraining the imposition of wanton subjective patterns that distort the objective outlines of the text. The threat posed by this subject-centered impressionism is qualified by one fact that is not always recognized: the projecting of patterns of meaning is not the completely private gesture of a *solus ipse* isolated within the walls of its own subjectivity. The fabric of prejudgments that are thus imposed on the text are part of the historical sedimentation of the tradition in which one lives with others and with the text itself. The issue is simply the difference between what Ricoeur calls a "bad" or uncultivated subjectivity and a "good" or educated one.[22]

Criticism based on the subject pole of the subject-object schema contains a practical truth which has often been overlooked to the detriment of literary studies. Classroom experience richly demonstrates the impossibility of engaging readers in abstract analysis of such features of a work as form until imaginative reading or imaginative teaching has enabled the text to establish its authority over the prestructured consciousness of the reader by means of the dialectic of participation. Once that interaction has taken place, analysis has its *raison d'etre,* namely, the extension of the understanding and the

22. "Objectivity and Subjectivity'in History," p. 30.

power of the work. To proceed in the opposite direction is to encourage the common, naive misunderstanding of criticism as stifling the life of the text. When all the formal problems have been explained, the life of the author written, the books in his library cataloged, sources and influences traced, and archetypes explicated, the central challenge of the text and the reason it is read will still be untouched unless the reader's separation from the work has been overcome by a bridging of the gulf that divides his values, experiences, and preconceptions from the horizon of the work. What is needed is close attention to the actual patterns of understanding in concrete experience which can show the way that interpretation occurs, as distinguished from the calculation of abstract methods with their lumber of philosophical presuppositions.

The third "I-Thou" relation illuminates the hermeneutic experience in precisely the way that is needed; the thou, whether person or text, is allowed to reveal itself in its own integrity in the manner of authentic conversation. It assumes neither a commitment to an underlying philosophical system nor a presuppositionless starting point; it leaves the act of interpretation in its inherent setting, what Heidegger has taught us to recognize as "the hermeneutical circle," and thereby makes full allowance for the historical and finite character of both reader and text. By means of the sedimentation of experience in his tradition, his standpoint in history, and his language, he brings a rich texture of prejudices to his reading which are the subjective conditions out of which his kinship with the text grows and which are to some extent objectively present in the work itself. Increase in understanding causes revisions and corrections in those prejudices, but without them there could be no understanding, the text would not even be identifiable as a work of art. It should also be observed that the understanding of the necessary role of bias encourages such corrections, whereas objectivism conceals them from itself by assuming the possibility of an ideal or at least a partial objectivity. This structure of preunderstanding completes the circle of believing in order to understand and understanding in order to believe. Such a basis of criticism combines the ideals of truth to the objective outlines of the work with authentic response on the part of the historically situated reader whose horizon of interests makes his kinship with the text possible. *Tristram Shandy,* for example, attracts our attention first because it says things that seem true and important in the context of modern life and of our own thinking. At the same time that we attend to the author's intent in what the novel says, insofar as that is knowable to him or to us, we also understand it in ways he could not have foreseen, in the light of modern ideas and historical events of which he could have no knowledge. When Melvyn New remarks that the "meaningful context" of the novel "is not the novels of Proust and Beckett, but rather the Augustan view of man," he corrects a frequent error in historical understanding, but he also uses the term "meaningful" in a highly uncritical way that excludes the necessary contemporaneity of all understanding.[23] It is important to note that this dialectic is not a mere theoretical compromise between realism and idealism. That would combine the philosophical disadvantages of each rather than going behind both to their origin in the "life-world" and thereby escaping the disadvantages of each.[24] It is a description of the process of interpretation, what, for better or worse, happens in the event of understanding, combined with the thesis that although the inherent process may be elaborated by rational and methodical enquiries, the relationship is and must remain hierarchical. Systematic enquiry can bring speculative processes to clarity in retrospect, but it can

23. "Sterne and Henry Baker's *The Microscope Made Easy,*" *Studies in English Literature* 10 (1970), 597.

24. Husserl introduces the term *life-world* (*Lebenswelt*) to refer to the primordial world of immediate experience as opposed to the complexly conditioned, cultural world given by science.

only make explicit what is already implicit in the exchange in which one has been caught up and transformed. It cannot control without destroying that relationship: "The question is," as Humpty Dumpty says, "which is to be master—that's all."

It has been remarked above that the act of reading is an effort to recover more than is actually said, more than the work considered as a series of discursive statements can say. A criticism that aspires to become engaged with the text in the manner of conversation may properly be called speculative. The shift in emphasis in the word *speculation* over the last two hundred years illustrates the problem well: the primary meaning of the term in Dr. Johnson's *Dictionary* is "contemplation" and only secondarily "conjecture," whereas the reverse is now the case, so influential has the ideal of exact knowledge become. But since literature belongs to the world in which we live rather than the world known to science, the old and venerable sense of the term may be employed to articulate that free play of mind which Tristram properly demands. To engage in such a venture is to accept the risk of doing criticism under the aspect of the hobby-horse. The restriction of the concept of validity to those derivative enquiries which admit of genuine scientific precision and objectivity frees the critical impulse to attend to all that happens in the interaction with a text but without thereby enabling it to claim immunity from rational examination and revision. It might be objected that such an unmethodical criticism, in seeking to stimulate imaginative explorations of new appropriations of meaning such as renew the vitality of a cultural tradition, also encourages idiosyncrasy and even nonsense. That is no doubt true, but little is risked. There has never been a noticeable shortage of nonsense in the world, whatever methods have been in the ascendency, and the fact has rendered a service to humanity in that it "opens the heart and lungs . . . and makes the wheel of life run long and chearfully round" (IV.xxxii.338). Besides, "so long as a man rides his HOBBY-HORSE peaceably and quietly along the King's highway, and neither compels you or me to get up behind him,——pray, Sir, what have either you or I to do with it?" (I.vii.13). What is compelling in criticism as in any other discipline, is the advent of understanding, the act of interpretation in which illumination occurs. The important difference is between the comic incrustation of Walter Shandy's rationalism (which entertains without convincing because it offers no direct enlightenment) and the experience of clarity in the understanding of our common mode of being which derives from Tristram's reflections, as they will be described below. Just as it is possible for conclusions to be valid which are of no interest to anyone, so it is possible, at the opposite extreme, for insights to be of the greatest moment to a whole culture and yet lie beyond the bounds of validity in any rigorous sense of the term. Something of the kind is evident in the cases of mystery and paradox. Or again, Heidegger's reflections on the poetry of Hölderlin and Rilke or his explorations of the etymologies of Heraclitean Greek are, on the one hand, a scandal to objective criticism and deserve severe examination for the liberties that they take with texts, and yet they may be seen, on the other hand, as of greater importance to the life of the culture in some cases than the texts that occasion them. It is surely an important dimension of the life of those German poems and those Greek fragments that they have fostered such radical thought and illumination. Moreover, it is a predictable consequence of critical finitude that among the hobby-horses of today is the orthodoxy of tomorrow and the dogma of the day after.

The historical discussion of the kinship between empiricism and phenomenology to which we turn next will serve to demonstrate how historical verification is related to the more primitive event of interpretation. The historical question arises because the event of meaning, the power of the novel to speak within the apparently alien context of modern thought, has already occurred. Though it would by no means be uninteresting or inconsequential, the failure to establish the historical thesis would not effectively contradict the general claim of this study that Sterne's novel is a phenomenological analysis of the structures and meaning of Tristram's being. Contradictions, after all, must be on the same level of meaning. The movement toward positive historical knowledge with its criterion of verification is a derivative and narrower program than the hermeneutical experience. In point of fact the historical issue here would more appropriately come at the end of the study were it not for the persistence of objectivist historicism in literary critical practice.

Empiricism and Phenomenology

The historical question has a history of its own. Sterne does not regard his predecessors—Rabelais, Montaigne, Cervantes, or Burton—as historically different from himself. Their thinking is not only contemporaneous with his own, as in all interpretive encounters, but to his mind it is contemporary as well, since historical differences are not observed. He is fully aware of altering the original meanings when he borrows from one or another of them as the issue of plagiarism shows; but that is a process of imaginative appropriation that raises no historical problems in his mind. The historical situation of the twentieth century is very different. Reading Rabelais under the influence of Locke may raise no theoretical problems for Sterne, but reading *Tristram Shandy* under the influence of Husserl is likely to be as suspect as driving under the influence of drink: it clouds the judgment and dulls the wit.

The historical component of the present thesis is important, though not of supreme importance even within a purely historical frame of reference since the process of reflexivity, which, it will be argued, characterizes Tristram's procedure, is always available and requires neither a knowledge of the prior history of thought for its execution nor even that there be philosophical precedent for the method. But since there is precedent, and very close to Sterne at that, the historical conditions that would help account for an incipient phenomenology among the more unexpected and unrecognized achievements of a young literary genre has special interest. From the perspective of the twentieth century one can see that not only were the components available, but the project had been announced without being carried out. A brief excursus into the historical antecedents of phenomenology will demonstrate the potential kinship of that gradually unfolding tradition and Sterne's novel. The parallels are in no sense obscure since the extent to which the later method is indebted to Cartesian procedure and the "intolerable absurdity" of "empirical psychologism," as Husserl calls it, is fully recognized in his own work.[25] Moreover, each of the five preliminary stages, so numbered for the purposes of this study only, will prove to be pertinent in one way or another to the subsequent examination of the novel.

In his various introductions to phenomenology, most notably in his last book, *The Crisis of European Sciences,* Husserl returns to his modern predecessors, Galileo, Descartes, Locke, Hume, and Kant, to examine each philosopher's emphasis or lack of emphasis on self-reflection, which he regards as the nexus of modern thought and takes as the theme of his own work. His survey begins (first) with Galileo's mathematization of nature. Husserl, himself mathematician turned philosopher, has genuine respect for this step in the development of objective science, of course, but he argues that the inner meaning of the method remained concealed: Galileo did not recognize that his "geometrical ideal constructions" were based on "the free, imaginative variations of this world," that

---

25. *The Crisis of European Sciences and Transcendental Phenomenology,* trans. David Carr, p. 84.

they grew out of particular motivations and produced something less than "self-sufficient, absolute truth which . . . could be applied without further ado" (*Crisis of European Sciences,* p. 49). In the medieval university the quadrivium, that set of studies which devised theoretical languages for the study of nature, was securely founded on the trivium which rooted language in the concrete life-world. Science, in short, remained the servant of concrete life. The new science, by contrast,

> encompasses everything which, for scientists and the educated generally, *represents* the life-world, *dresses it up* as 'objectively actual and true' nature. It is through the garb of ideas that we take for *true being* what is actually a *method*—a method which is designed for the purpose of progressively improving, *in infinitum,* through 'scientific' predictions, those rough predictions which are the only ones originally possible within the sphere of what is actually experienced and experienceable in the life-world. It is because of the disguise of ideas that the true meaning of the method, the formulae, the 'theories,' remained unintelligible and, in the naive formation of the method, was never understood. [*Crisis of European Sciences,* pp. 51–52]

Nature for Galileo is a system of purely physical bodies in motion, imperfectly available to sensation but completely accessible to quantitative measurement. The new mathematical science allows the quadrivium to supersede the trivium, a condition which by the twentieth century is widely taken to be part of the order of nature.

To the student of English literature these implications are most accessible in Swift who makes the same general point as Husserl, though without the accompanying appreciation for the achievements of the method. In the *Travels,* part III, reason has turned whore and the Laputans, one eye gazing into the heavens, the other scrutinizing the mind, entirely miss the realm in between occupied by human beings and the concerns of practical life. Reflection on ordinary experience of the kind we shall find in Sterne suggests that the self-awareness of the ego is not original; it is derived from experience in the life-world, not something on the ground of which the life-world comes to be or to be known. The Laputans have got the relation of the ego to the world backward. The original purpose of theoretical, mathematical science was to clarify the world of ordinary experience rather than to substitute another, abstract world of theory for it. The Laputans do not make their mathematics follow the shapes of things and serve the interests of life; instead they cut their clothes to theory rather than bodies and prepare their food on the principles of geometry rather than of cuisine. Worst of all is the fact that in freeing itself from the life-world and becoming theoretical, having developed the power to manipulate both an alienated, object nature and other men, science has become the tool, the whore, of passion. It ceases to be theoretical finally and becomes technology.

The second crucial stage in the historical development toward phenomenology—if the imposition of direction may be allowed—is the Cartesian *Meditations* and the intention to overcome prejudice by rigorous and systematic doubt. Following Galileo's inauguration of the new science, Descartes at once established a comprehensive objectivistic rationalism and founded it on an indubitable self-evidence, the "I am" which is beyond doubt and which was destined ultimately to destroy the rationalism it was introduced to secure. "Descartes, in his haste to ground objectivism and the exact sciences as affording metaphysical, absolute knowledge, does not set himself the task of systematically investigating the pure ego ... with regard to what acts, what capacities, belong to it and what it brings about, as intentional accomplishment, through these acts and capacities" (*Crisis of European Sciences,* p. 82). In Husserl's view Descartes failed to understand the "great discovery" and adulterated the revolutionary turn to subjectivity with psychology; the ego in Descartes is inconsistently discussed as objective psychology, as though it were another among the innumerable objects in the world, rather than that to which the world and all its objects owe their significance. Furthermore, it was not clear to Descartes that his effort to remove all prejudice was itself a prejudice, that his search for a presuppositionless, Archimedean starting point already concealed within itself a rich content of presuppositions that motivated his thinking and deployed his goal. It is nevertheless in the *Meditations* that Husserl discovers the initial impulse to ground rational science in the thinking subject.[26]

Stage three is the extension of the effort to establish a secure epistemological basis for objective knowledge in Locke's *Essay Concerning Human Understanding*. There is a substantial difference, of consequence to the present study, between what Locke proposes to do in the *Essay* and what he actually does. In the "Epistle to the Reader" he describes the origin of the inquiry:

> *Were it fit to trouble thee with the History of this Essay, I should tell thee that five or six Friends meeting at my Chamber, and discoursing on a Subject very remote from this, found themselves quickly at a stand, by the Difficulties that rose on every side. After we had awhile puzzled our selves, without coming any nearer a Resolution of those Doubts which perplexed us, it came into my*

26. Ironically, Husserl himself labors under the presupposition of a presuppositionless philosophy in *Cartesian Meditations* (1931), and even as late as *The Crisis of European Sciences,* unfinished at his death in 1938, he had still not freed himself from the fault he sees so clearly in Descartes. He takes subjectivity as foundational where the later phenomenologists like Heidegger, Gadamer, and Ricoeur overcome the difficulty by observing that subjectivity must be interrogated—"Wer ist Dasein?" (Heidegger, *Being and Time,* pp. 150–53)—to discover that far from constituting an indubitable premise, the self is directed by the world before it directs itself. Thus it happens that Husserl prepares the way for an ontology of the self without actually achieving it. Only by looking back at him through the work of another generation of phenomenologists can we see these implications.

*Thoughts, that we took a wrong course; and that, before
we set our selves upon Enquiries of that Nature, it was
necessary to examine our own Abilities, and see, what
Objects our Understandings were, or were not fitted to
deal with.*[27]

And so he proposes to investigate "the Ways, whereby our
Understandings come to attain those Notions of Things we
have" and to do so "in this Historical, plain Method." One is
now able to see among implications that Locke could not see
clearly that his plan brings him to the threshold of phenomenology. By beginning with an examination of "our own
Abilities," he asserts that the first step in philosophical enquiry is a critical examination of consciousness. The immediate difficulty, as he says in the "Introduction," is that since the
understanding "like the eye, whilst it makes us see and perceive all other things, takes no notice of itself," one is at pains
"to set it at a distance and make it its own object"—or, in
phenomenological terms, to suspend the ordinary focus of
consciousness and turn its gaze upon itself.[28] Having come
thus to the brink of phenomenological analysis, Locke fails to
pursue the implications of his metaphor of the eye, which must
seek its reflection in a mirror if it is to examine itself, and instead of working out a reflexive method, he falls back on the
naive naturalism of objective psychology. Once he has derived
ideas of reflection from sensation, he sees no need for further
exploration of "that notice which the Mind takes of its own
Operations, and the manner of them.[29] Perhaps because he,

27. *An Essay Concerning Human Understanding,* ed. Peter H. Nidditch,
p. 7. Subsequent references to the *Essay* (by volume, chapter, page) are to
this edition.

28. Richard Zaner points out these implications in his useful introductory study, *The Way of Phenomenology,* pp. 200–02.

29. II.i.4. *Reflection* as it is used in this study, though based on Locke's
"ideas of reflection," is a broader term: in addition to awareness of the
processes of consciousness, it includes the awareness of a thing as an intentional object of consciousness as opposed to the object *simpliciter.*

like Descartes, had lost touch with the classical notion that differing subjects require differing methods of enquiry, he applies to the mind the empirical method appropriate to the observation of data. The direction toward phenomenological reflection in Locke is no accidental moment in classical empiricism, however. It is an essential line of philosophical development from the revolution marked by the Cartesian *Meditations*. In fact, eighteenth-century thought remains poised before the question of the human capacity to know until Kant's "second Copernican revolution" plunges it into the transcendental analysis of the grounds of knowledge.

The fourth stage is Hume. Although Husserl's grounding of science requires the complete defeat of Humean scepticism, he admires both Hume's radical formulation of the problem of objectivity and his tendency toward a critical philosophy: all the problems of *The Treatise of Human Nature,* he says, "belong entirely to the area dominated by phenomenology."[30] Hume's title indicates an expansion of Locke's focus. Only book I is directly concerned with the "understanding"; books II and III go on to different issues related to the "passions" and moral and aesthetic "sentiments." The "Introduction" describes the central problem of philosophy not as taking "now and then a castle or village on the frontier" of knowledge, as the studies of logic, morals, and politics do, but "to march up directly to the capital or center of these sciences, to human nature itself" upon which alone "a complete system of sciences" can be founded and then only through "experience and observation." Though the two terms *experience* and *observation* conceal a lack of distinction in method between what is available reflexively and what empirically, it is clear that "the science of man is the only solid foundation for the other sciences" (Hume, I.5). However solid, that foundation remains opaque to the end, for knowledge of the world con-

---

30. *Phenomenology and the Crisis of Philosophy,* trans. Quentin Lauer, pp. 113–14.

sists finally in nothing more substantial than "natural belief" in the causal connectedness of the objective world, and such knowledge is the work of "nothing but" custom and habit as Hume indicates in the "Conclusion" of book I:

> When we trace up the human understanding to its first principles, we find it to lead us into such sentiments as seem to turn into ridicule all our past pains and industry, and to discourage us from future inquiries. . . . We would not willingly stop before we are acquainted with that energy in the cause by which it operates on its effect; that tie, which connects them together; and that efficacious quality on which the tie depends. This is our aim in all our studies and reflections: and how must we be disappointed when we learn that this connection, tie, or energy lies merely in ourselves, and is nothing but that determination of mind which is acquired by custom and causes us to make a transition from an object to its usual attendant, and from the impression of one to the lively idea of the other: Such a discovery not only cuts off all hope of ever attaining satisfaction, but even prevents our very wishes. [Hume, I.251–52]

Having traced the understanding up to its first principles, Hume comes squarely up against the structures of subjectivity; but notwithstanding the discussions of the passions and sentiments, he does not get beyond this point to what is needed, namely, an examination of this domain of belief and custom in human nature. In Hume's design for the *Treatise* and in the grounds of his scepticism, even more dramatically than in Locke's general project for the *Essay,* one is led toward, but not through, a critical explication of the structures of consciousness. It was on this exact point, Hume's emphasis on human nature as the ground of all science, that Husserl would establish his doctrine of the transcendental, constitutive consciousness.

In an appendix to the work Hume openly confesses his inability "to explain perfectly" his doctrine of belief as a mode of feeling, available to reflection but not understanding:

> If perceptions are distinct existences, they form a whole only by being connected together. But no connections among distinct existences are ever discoverable by human understanding. We only *feel* a connection or determination of the thought to pass from one object to another. It follows, therefore, that the thought alone feels personal identity, when reflecting on the train of past perceptions that compose a mind, the ideas of them are felt to be connected together, and naturally introduce each other. ... But all my hopes vanish when I come to explain the principles that unite our successive perceptions in our thought or consciousness. I cannot discover any theory which gives me satisfaction on this head. ... For my part, I must plead the privilege of a sceptic, and confess that this difficulty is too hard for my understanding. I pretend not, however, to pronounce it absolutely insuperable. Others, perhaps, or myself, upon more mature reflections, may discover some hypothesis that will reconcile those contradictions. [II.319]

Of at least equal importance for the establishment of the "science of man" is Hume's admission of failure to give an adequate account of personal identity: "Upon a more strict review of the section concerning *personal identity,* I find myself involved in such a labyrinth that, I must confess, I neither know how to correct my former opinions, nor how to render them consistent" (II.317). Thus he modestly admits that he has failed in taking the capital to which he laid siege, but he has located its exact position and, without quite recognizing it, suggested the method by which it may be taken.

Since the first edition of the *Critique of Pure Reason* does not even appear until more than a decade after Sterne's death, nothing need be said about the fifth stage in this historical sequence beyond the observation that the turn toward the subjective preconditions of knowledge, though it was continued and revised among the German idealists of the nineteenth century, was not significantly advanced beyond its final eighteenth-century form until the beginning of the twentieth century when Husserl devoted his life to the investigation. He claims that "the first to perceive" this "secret longing" of all modern thought "truly" was Kant, and "although he was not yet able to appropriate it," the "A" edition of the first critique "already moves strictly on phenomenological ground."[31] Husserl himself returns to the problem as it was formulated by the tradition extending from Galileo to Kant, the importance of which fact for the present purpose is the degree of readiness for the phenomenological departure that one may observe eighteenth-century empiricism to have reached. During the period 1739 to 1752 when Hume was doing his philosophical writing and rousing no one from the dogmatic slumbers for which Kant was later to give him credit, he had few readers and almost none of congenial mind, the *Treatise* having fallen "dead-born from the press," as he said; but during the same years and for somewhat longer, including the decade of *Tristram Shandy,* Locke's *Essay* was at the full meridian of its influence and provoked no more remarkable response than Sterne's unique novel.

As brief and superficial as it is, this summary will serve to indicate the historical nexus of the study to follow: in making Tristram Shandy write his "life and opinions" out of the contents of his own consciousness, Sterne radicalizes the turn toward transcendental subjectivity in a way that neither Locke, Hume, nor Kant fully achieved, thereby realizing, albeit in a tentative and philosophically unsystematic way, the intuition that was to wait for its full exposition until the laborious and often esoteric analyses of twentieth-century phenomenology. The character of Sterne's narrative strategy

31. *Ideas,* trans. W. R. Boyce Gibson, p. 166.

approximates the complex methodologies of Husserl and his successors and avoids the distractions that led both Locke and Hume away from systematic reflection upon and explication of consciousness. In one of the most-quoted passages of the novel, Tristram describes the dimension of the *Essay* that he intends to emulate:

> I will tell you in three words what the book is.——It is a history.——A History!——of who? what? where? when? Don't hurry yourself.——It is a history-book, Sir (which may possibly recommend it to the world) of what passes in a man's own mind; and if you will say so much of the book, and no more, believe me, you will cut no contemptible figure in a metaphysical circle. [II.ii.85]

Notwithstanding the close relationship between the novel and the *Essay*, critics have never agreed on whether the novel follows it more or less faithfully or pursues its logic in order to expose the absurd implications of its arguments. John Traugott's thesis that it is broadly satirical of Locke is convincing: "Wherever Locke's skepticism searches out a source of obscurity, Sterne settles, and develops the possibilities of that obscurity into a jibe at system makers or at length into a Toby or Walter. Indeed, he stops not there, but continues ... to reduce even Locke's rationalism to confusion."[32] Traugott goes on to identify Sterne's position as approximately that of Humean skepticism, thereby failing to detect the positive strategy by which the novel builds on Locke's vision of the *Essay* as a history or an account of the mind. Locke does not realize the full promise of his initial insight because he studies the mind as an empirical object, almost as, being a physician, he might study the human body, and thus he misses the richly

---

32. *Tristram Shandy's World: Sterne's Philosophical Rhetoric*, p. 25. The opposing view is argued by John Laird in *Philosophical Incursions into English Literature;* he claims that Sterne is uncritical in following Locke except in the passage on wit and judgment in the "Author's Preface."

complex processes of consciousness available to a reflexive method. He, like Descartes, assumes the world of object as already constituted for an unconditioned, totally neutral subjectivity, never asking how world comes to be for consciousness. Sterne, by contrast, carries out the analysis that Locke only suggests and that Husserl defines in the *Crisis of European Sciences* as "transcendental subjectivity reflecting apodictically upon itself and apodictically explicating itself—[this] is precisely transcendental philosophy" (p. 259). In writing his autobiography Tristram engages in the reflective explication of his own consciousness as rooted in a particular time and place, as conditioned by as odd a collection of progenitors and as complex a concatenation of "pitiful misadventures and cross accidents as ever small HERO sustained" (I.v.10). As the full significance of this argument unfolds, it will become evident that Sterne was not only one of the greatest of comic writers but a thinker of unusual originality who caught, however tentatively, a radical insight into the general nature of consciousness that is able to shake our own assumptions no less than those of his own day. Before beginning to advance the argument in detail, an introduction to the question of the relation of the novel as comic to the novel as philosophic will be useful.

Philosophy versus Comedy

In the past both critics and readers have tended to divide among those on the one side who see the work as *jeu d'esprit* —playful, superficial, irresponsible, uncontaminated by intellectual issues and consequences more serious than Tristram's laughing and leering his way through nine volumes of inconsequential jests—and those on the other who see it as concerned with a serious account of the mind after the manner of Lockean empiricism. The alternative between taking Sterne in high seriousness and as an impious jester obscures an important issue to which Richard Lanham has recently called attention.[33] In fact, the disjunction of philosophy versus comedy is illicit. The question of which way the novel is to be understood can be answered only by demonstrating that the question is itself misguided and that the obvious comedy of the book is by its nature philosophic. Intellectual analysis of the deepest kind is in no way precluded by the mood of the jester; in fact, the openness to creative reflection is enhanced, if not guaranteed, by the comic spirit. It will be sufficient at this stage to observe the complementary character of comedy and thought and to reserve discussion of the essential kinship of foundational thinking and play until after the exploration of Tristram's reflections on "the being question." (Cf. chapter 5 below.)

There is of course an historical issue here that has important consequences in the novel and that is concerned as well in our approach to the book as readers. So long as similitude was accepted as the basis of knowledge, as in the medieval and Renaissance worlds where truth and play enjoyed a hearty reciprocity, comedy in its autochthonous form could be included within its domain, for in its root form comedy consists of that play of fancy that brings into temporal proximity two or more discordant systems of meaning.[34] But once the grounds of thought shift to make the discriminating power of judgment the way to truth and resemblance the source of error, cheating fancy, if not entirely exiled, is relegated to the shadows on the boundary of the clear light of judgment. One of the decisive consequences of this shift for European culture

33. "For those who seek—or deny—in *Tristram Shandy* a high seriousness, presume the novel a *debate,* Sterne working us finally toward his persuasion. Practically no one has considered the novel as a *game* in Rapoport's sense of the word, a continuing contest with, by its nature, only intermediate results" (*"Tristram Shandy": The Games of Pleasure,* p. 45).

34. For an examination of comedy and the problem of creativity in general, see Arthur Koestler, *The Act of Creation.*

is that playfulness and mirth came to be regarded as inappropriate for important affairs. Thus Mr. Oliver Edwards, whom Johnson knew in his youth at Pembroke College, Oxford, observes, "You are a philosopher, Dr. Johnson. I have tried too in my time to be a philosopher; but, I don't know how, cheerfulness was always breaking in."[35] David Hartley likewise excludes gaiety when in the *Observations on Man* he says, "Persons who give themselves much to Mirth, Wit, and Humour must thereby greatly disqualify their Understandings for the Search after Truth" (I.440). And when *The Sermons of Mr. Yorick* appeared, an anonymous reviewer wrote:

> ... We think it becomes us to make some animadversions on the manner of their publication, which we consider as the greatest outrage against Sense and Decency, that has been offered since the first establishment of Christianity— an outrage which would scarce have been tolerated in the days of paganism.
>
> Had these Discourses been sent into the world, as the Sermons of a Mr. *Yorick*, pursuant to the *first* title-page, every serious and sober Reader must have been offended at the indecency of such an assumed character. For who is this *Yorick?* We have read of a *Yorick* likewise, in an obscene Romance.—But are the solemn dictates of religion fit to be conveyed from the mouths of Buffoons, and ludicrous Romancers? Would any man believe that a Preacher was in earnest, who should mount the pulpit in a *Harlequin's coat?*[36]

This note is sounded frequently in the seventeenth and eighteenth centuries and is the distinctive tone of Victorian criticism of Sterne.

The suspicion of analogy which informs the debates over

35. James Boswell, *Life of Johnson,* ed. R. W. Chapman and J. D. Fleeman, p. 957.

36. *Monthly Review,* May 1760, p. 422; quoted in David Thompson, *Wild Excursions: The Life and Fiction of Laurence Sterne,* p. 148.

wit and judgment is an issue in *Tristram Shandy* itself, where it has two important consequences, the first of which is a deformity of mind. Yorick's ancestor enjoyed that Renaissance climate which took endless delight in the harmony of truth and play. To conceive of a wise fool in no way strained one's credulity or offended one's sense of propriety in the sixteenth century. But the eighteenth-century Yorick, as messenger of divine truth, is expected to wrap himself in a becoming cloak of gravity. Not that he does so—

> For to speak the truth, *Yorick* had an invincible dislike and opposition in his nature to gravity;——not to gravity as such;——for where gravity was wanted, he would be the most grave or serious of mortal men for days and weeks together;——but he was an enemy to the affectation of it, and declared open war against it, only as it appeared a cloak for ignorance, or for folly. . . . In the naked temper which a merry heart discovered, he would say, There was no danger,——but to itself:——whereas the very essence of gravity was design, and consequently deceit;——'twas a taught trick to gain credit of the world for more sense and knowledge than a man was worth; and that, with all its pretensions,——it was no better, but often worse, than what a *French* wit had long ago defined it,——*viz. A mysterious carriage of the body to cover the defects of the mind;*——which definition of gravity, *Yorick,* with great imprudence, would say, deserved to be wrote in letters of gold. [I.xi.26]

What Yorick stresses is the motive behind gravity and its effect upon oneself, a theme fully explored in the disposition and understanding of Walter Shandy. Tristram's own contribution to the doctrine of the imagination in the "Author's Preface" likewise points to the deformity of mind that results from subordinating wit or judgment either to the other.[37]

---

37. He uses the term *wit* in approximately the sense it has for Locke, namely, the prompt perception of resemblances.

Wit and judgment "are the highest and most ornamental parts" of our "frames" even as the matching knobs are of the frame of his famous cane chair. The chair without either would be "as miserable a sight as a sow with one ear" (III.xx.201). Yet it sometimes happens "that for near half a century together" both wit and judgment "seem quite dried up" (III.xx.197).

A second consequence of the divorce of wit from judgment which is much less obvious may be mentioned in passing and reserved for later analysis. At the heart of the world of Shandy Hall is an epistemology that has built an uncritical self-importance into the structures of knowledge, that unwittingly promulgates a particular anthropology which precludes healthy creativity, and that makes of the world a thing to be exploited by the will to power. So serious are the consequences of that cultural mutation that brings about the separation of wit and judgment that it ultimately issues in a general intellectual and spiritual impotence central to the meaning of the life of Shandy Hall.

In reading the criticism one sometimes feels a surprising amount of residual suspicion of wit among readers who want to take Sterne's book as philosophical, and a certain distaste for judgment among those who want to see it as only "a sporting little filly-folly," a hobby-horse of frivolous intent. Thus when Tristram says he is writing his "life and opinions"—the former for our amusement, the latter for our instruction—we are in danger of taking one as of greater importance than the other. What should be obvious in light of the "Author's Preface" is that the power of the one *is* the power of the other, that either without the other would be deformity. James Work is one who is responsible for the view that the book lacks serious issues like "the momentous intellectual or moral or social abuses upon which a satirist cannot but be in deadly earnest. . . . He [Sterne] toys with his satire in a kindly, almost affectionate manner, and makes it less a stricture on anything external to himself than an unconscious revelation of the triviality of his own mind" (Introduction, p. lxv). Since the publication of Work's edition in 1940, however, there has nevertheless come to be wide agreement that Sterne's comedy aims at something more than the surface gaiety often assumed to be the limit of the comic mood and that Tristram may be quite serious in intending, for example, "that all good people, both male and female, . . . may be taught to think as well as read" (I.xx.57).

Having once realized that it is in the nature of play to exclude aims that extend beyond the game itself, it is sometimes tempting to exclude all so-called serious issues and limit the motives of the game to pure hedonism. In fact, it is the pleasure principle rather than seriousness that tends to subvert play. The impulse to pure hedonism in art as in any field of human interest seeks to reduce the world to a ratio of the self. For the hedonist as for the technologist the logical governing motto is "The world is my predicate!" for the pursuit of pleasure is as utilitarian in spirit as the world of useful work and thus violates the spirit of the game to the spell of which the player must surrender himself.[38]

As epigraph to volume I and an apparent gloss on the phrase "life and opinions" in the title, Tristram quotes Epictetus: "It is not actions, but opinions concerning actions, which disturb men." How closely the comic and philosophic themes in the book are related and how perverse their separation, may be estimated by considering the relation of this epigraph to the novel itself. Since events rather than the attitudes in which people choose to regard the events are ordinarily taken to be the causes of distress, the philosopher points out the greater importance of opinion as cause. Likewise, in Tristram's life it would appear to be a sequence of his unfortunate misadventures with clocks and forceps and window

38. On the nature of play, see Gadamer, pp. 97 ff.

weights that has made him "the continual sport" of fortune; but, in fact, it is opinions—Walter's, Dr. Slop's, Uncle Toby's —that are the true causes of all his adversities. Now in reading his life we tend to find both opinions and actions amusing. By insisting that the opinions, the causes of disturbance, are for our instruction, the life, or action, for our amusement, the two poles—instruction and amusement; at a deeper level, mind and body—coalesce and the identity of comedy and philosophic reflection is established. The epigraph to volume III plays on the same theme. From John of Salisbury—"I do not fear the opinions of the ignorant crowd; nevertheless I pray that they spare my little work, in which it has been my purpose to pass from the gay to the serious and from the serious again to the gay." Sterne has changed the end of the passage from the original, ". . . in which it has ever been my purpose to pass from jests to worthy seriousness," a change that seems to stress the perpetual mixing of serious and comic.

A common and correct objection to taking the work as "seriously" philosophical is Tristram's blatant contempt of systematic reasoning that reduces the richness of experience to systems of thought. Of Walter he observes, "like all systematick reasoners, he would move both heaven and earth, and twist and torture every thing in nature to support his hypothesis. In a word, I repeat it over again;——he was serious" (I.xix.53). In the sense that the modern world understands the term, Tristram is no philosopher; but in the ancient and venerable sense of a person who tries to confront his own life and the general life of mankind directly and with understanding, he is philosophic. The difference in the two senses of "philosophy" is decisive, for Tristram's thinking is always directed against the kind of rationality that conceals one's relation to being and which is constructed out of an arrogant self-consciousness. What he exemplifies is an act of clarification of his own being in the course of which a rich mine of philosophical insights is revealed, not in spite of, but in large measure owing to the comedy. The lack of earnestness and insecurity contribute directly to making the work courageous and unstinting in its examination of all assumptions, systems, and doctrines that fall within its range. The willingness to forsake caution, to follow intuition through all its devious paths, to court even the most radical scepticism, is essential to the character of the work as play. Tristram's hostility to systematic views of the world contributes greater philosophical suggestiveness to the novel than is generally available even to the most vigorous of rationally self-enclosed and logically disciplined enquiry.

The principle of free imaginative variation leaves him free to beat over the fields of memory and of possibility in pursuit of every conceivable notion that might offer clarification of his own being, unhampered by the taboos against contradiction, unimpeded by the dogmas of reason, undistracted by the demand for verification. The kinship in spirit between Tristram's enterprise and the spirit of phenomenology is clear even in this preliminary point. In *Ideas* Husserl remarks on what he calls "free-fantasy variation": There are reasons why, in phenomenology as in all eidetic sciences, representations, or to speak more accurately, *free fancies,* assume *a privileged position over against perceptions.* . . . If anyone loves a paradox, he can really say, and say with strict truth if he will allow for the ambiguity, that the *element* which *makes up the life of phenomenology as of all eidetic science* is '*fiction,*' that fiction is the source whence the knowledge of 'eternal truths' draws its sustenance" (pp. 182, 184). There is nothing surprising, of course, in an imaginative writer's loyalty to the fancy, notwithstanding a certain spiritual east wind of earnestness in the modern zeitgeist; but it is an unusual note in a modern philosopher. It is in just the sense that Husserl mentions that comedy is an advantage to Tristram's reflections. He is engaged in a game of exploring his own consciousness for no utilitarian motives, thereby illuminating numerous themes—psychological, social, historical, and philosophical—that are constituents of the patterns of consciousness in Shandy Hall and in a mid-eighteenth-century mind that is steeped in Christian and Lockean lore and the tradition of learned wit.

In the effort to satisfy Tristram's interpretive criterion of authentic conversation with his text, we must not only seek to retrieve the intellectual issues of his reflections but to share in the mood that is part of the undifferentiated background of consciousness from which they arise. In short, we must give way to the comic spirit of the game as well as to its aims and its rules.

The Itinerary of Issues

Having specified the general critical orientation that Tristram invites, the historical nexus between empirical and phenomenology, and, in a tentative way, the relation between comedy and thought, we will take a brief inventory of the issues that will ultimately bring us around again to the question of comedy not as a merely contingent feature of the work but as an essential function of the being whose way of be-ing[39] is understanding. The general thesis of the study is that the novel is an incipient phenomenology the ultimate aim of which is an ontological analysis of the meaning of Tristram's being.

Chapter 2 is situated well within the boundaries of current critical understanding in its claim that the unifying principle of the novel is Tristram's own consciousness; but it seeks to

---

39. This awkward circumlocution of the present progressive tense will occasionally be used to stress a temporal act extended through time like Hamlet's "to be." In claiming that Tristram's act of being is an act of interpretation the argument will follow in a somewhat superficial way Heidegger's *Dasein*-analysis as the grounding of ontology and phenomenology in the hermeneutics of consciousness.

bring greater clarity and precision to that thesis in order to follow up its radical consequences more consistently than has been done heretofore. The specific argument of chapter 2 will be (1) that Tristram discovers the clue to the structure of consciousness as a unitary system with a permeating teleology in the hobby-horses of other members of his family, (the principle of intentionality that Husserl, following Brentano, would later rejuvenate from medieval thought); and (2) that he discovers his relation to tradition, later to be analyzed under the category of temporality, in the social nature of the self. It will become evident that the community of Shandy Hall exists *in* him and that only through it, onotologically as well as genetically, does he come to be as a self.

The third chapter will extend the reflections upon the self by arguing four propositions: (1) that time for Tristram is, in St. Augustine's words, "an extension ... of the mind itself" and that his conceptual horizon is itself temporal; (2) that within the temporal horizon he assigns priority to the mode of the future which conditions his understanding of present events and patterns of memory from the past; (3) that the analytic of Tristram's finitude reveals its meaning as a promise which opens up his access to meaning in the world; and (4) that the horizon of his own death, the possibility of ceasing to be, gives special value and direction to his being.

Chapter 4 raises the question of language as a region of the general ontological problematic rather than as the merely ontic issue it is usually taken for. (1) Though Tristram has inherited an empirical approach to language from Locke, his reflexive method opens the enquiry to the position of language in the play of his being. (2) He extends the Lockean criticism of language to the point of completely disrupting signification, with the positive consequence that he discovers that the tendency of words to loose their assigned meaning is also their power to speak into being the world that is the locus of human being. (3) Notwithstanding the manipulative egotism of Walter's rhetoric, Tristram discovers the necessary mutuality of rhetoric and dialectic, which is essential to language understood as act rather than thing and which he uses to interpret his own being simultaneously to himself and to his audience.

The final chapter argues (1) that Tristram's inner-reflection is also the self-examination of the European mind upon the spiritual conditions of its own existence; (2) that the strategy of the narrative associates the problem of artistic creativity in Tristram with sexual impotence which comes to an appropriate climax in the examination of Toby's love affair with the widow Wadman; (3) that the novel offers hope that psychic reintegration can occur by means of (4) the example of Yorick and the power of play; and (5) that the form of the novel is an exact image of the finite temporal structure of Tristram's being which is simultaneously whole and unfinished.

2

The Structure of Consciousness and the Unity of the Self

In the critical work that has been devoted to *Tristram Shandy* in recent years, it has been generally acknowledged that the focus of the novel and the point of departure for criticism is Tristram's own consciousness. Implicitly the criticism has sought to detect the organizing principles of the mind that provide the unity of the work. Thus William Holtz summarizes what numerous commentaries assume: "If *Tristram Shandy* can be said to have an action, it must be the continued unsuccessful struggle of its hero to shape the flux of his mind into a coherent narrative, a struggle that reveals the inadequacy of narrative, and of temporal analysis generally, as a means of telling the reader what is in his mind."[1]

There is obviously nothing new in the notion that a single consciousness occupies the center of interest in the novel; it is the character of that consciousness and of the ultimate aims and achievements of the fiction that have yet to be adequately described. Holtz correctly points out that the effect of the book is to reveal "the unity of an intensely imagined personality possessing the same wholeness among its

1. *Image and Immorality: A Study of "Tristram Shandy,"* p. 100. Also see B. H. Lehman, "Of Time, Personality, and the Author: A Study of *Tristram Shandy,"* *Studies in the Comic, University of California Studies in English* 8, no. 2 (1941), pp. 233–50.

disparate elements as does a human identity that compre-
hends the totality of its experience at every moment of its
life." However, this does not isolate the underlying principles by which Tristram is enabled to discover and to reveal
himself. By reducing his character to a mere integration of
perceptions as in Coleridge's "primary imagination" and
James's "specious present," Holtz makes of him nothing more
than "a kind of subtle rhetoric . . . the undeniable and immediate sense of a unified identity extending through diverse
perceptions. For the events of the literary portrait . . . make
sense only if the reader conceives of them as belonging to the
same person."[2] If so, then Hume must be right; identity is
an inference based on natural belief, and the whole achievement of the fiction is a rhetorical trick to convince us of the
integrity of the character the truth of whose being is inaccessible. Helen Moglen comes much nearer the mark in observing that the project of the novel is Tristram's looking
"into himself in order to find a principle of unity that will
give order to the constantly changing self and meaning to the
external world that cannot be objectively known."[3] The un-
justified subjectivism of the comment aside, Moglen states the
essential problem that criticism must now investigate. And
yet, given the failure of classical empiricism to account for
personal identity by means of memory, it is small help to say
that Tristram's effort is "to reach self-definition through the
analysis of memory" in which case he would discover not "a

2. Holtz, p. 136. The presupposition that the novel remains in the arena
of empiricism accounts for John Stedmond's hesitancy to attribute a convincing coherence to the portrait of Tristram: "Sterne, also in his way very
conscious of the implication of Locke's theories, could hardly write the
'life and opinions' of a nonexistent personality. . . . He must give *some*
coherence, *some* significance, to that flux in order to construct a literary
portrait" (*The Comic Art of Laurence Sterne*, p. 24).

3. Helen Moglen, *The Philosophical Irony of Laurence Sterne* (Gainesville, 1975), p. 155.

principle of unity" at all but the faculty by which he retains his past and through whose weakness, as empirically observed, he is constantly losing it. Memory, with its highly selective patterns of retention and omission, is part of what needs accounting for rather than a solution. Just how remote memory is from the principle that is wanted may be indicated by recalling that most of the events in the novel are not Tristram's memories at all but only what he receives from an oral tradition. Moglen's analysis does not explain Tristram's process of self-discovery (which is presumably futile anyway since for Sterne, as for Joyce, she says, "there can be no self-discovery. There is only the endless repetition of the quest," p. 158).

The crucial starting point is the "flux of the mind" but it is in need of more radical examination than it has received. The aim is not the mere cataloging "of what passes in a man's own mind" as a means of bringing us into intimate acquaintance with the protagonist, but a genuine process of self-discovery. The crucial distinction to be insisted upon initially is between Tristram's reflections as a straightforward psychological record of his mental experience, hence not literally reflections at all, and his reflections as an ontological enquiry into the character of his psychic experience and what that enquiry reveals about the structure and meaning of his being.

The most striking feature of Tristram's procedure in the light of Sterne's kinship with Locke is his radical departure from the actual method of the *Essay*. Locke seeks the genesis of subjective life in the elements of sensory experience imprinted on a passive psyche. The mind serves as a repository of "ideas of sensation" which it actively combines into "ideas of reflection," but all states of consciousness are reducible to antecedent relations with the physical world. The external world aside, the mind is composed of atomistic elements like the local pieces of a mosaic or like marbles in a bag that co-exist without cohering. This dimension of the Lockean mind is vividly revealed by an elegaic passage in book II of the

Essay: "Thus the Ideas, as well as Children, of our Youth, often die before us: And our Minds represent to us those Tombs, to which we are approaching; where though the Brass and Marble remain, yet the Inscriptions are effaced by time, and the Imagery moulders away" (II.x.5). The issue of personal identity is a major problem under this conception of consciousness as a unidimensional sequence of mental events, and it, rather than the epistemological question, is the major focus of attention in the reflections of Sterne's small hero. In contrast with Locke's elemental psychology Tristram makes the whole of consciousness primary and keeps himself before us as agent—sifting, reflecting, deciphering, appropriating his heritage, his intentions, and even, occasionally, his activities in the present. Where Locke neglects to account for the existence of reflection, beyond deriving its contents from sensation, Tristram shows relatively little interest in the empirical thesis. His emphasis instead is on the interpretive influence or the subjective preconditions of sensation.

Association as the organizing principle of mental events undergoes considerable refinement between Locke, who attributes only mental aberrations to associational patterns (whereas ideas have natural connections), and Hume, who finds in the patterns of association revelations of the patterns of thought and belief by means of which we deal with reality but no natural connections among ideas themselves. A variety of claims has been made about the role of association in the novel: MacLean makes Sterne the leading exponent of the doctrine in English literature; Watkins says it is the organizational principle of the novel; Putney, that the mazes of Tristram's digressions derive from Locke's account of association. Traugott sees that associationism could not be a structural principle for the novel, but he argues that it functions "as a dialectical drama which defines motives." Cash suggests that Sterne's psychology is not associational at all but of the older "instinct" variety, a view that would seem to be supported by Tristram's occasional reference to the notion of the ruling passion.[4] Traugott is certainly right in holding that a series of ideas, contiguous but with no intrinsic coherence, would not make a novel. Furthermore, if Tristram's mental process were simply associational, his mind would move among data which coexist in mutual irrelevance and indifference, a misunderstanding of the sequences in the book that no experienced reader is guilty of. What appear to be incessant variations of unidimensional psychic events in Tristram's mind are in fact guided by a deeper principle of psychic organization that makes "associationism" a misnomer. Cash's mention of "instinct psychology" is useful because it suggests some *telos* permeating the stream of reflections that is only apparently random. The thesis in this chapter is that the novel offers a detailed recording of a stratified consciousness whose transcendental unity and continuity reveal and are revealed by the principle of intentionality.

Two conceptions of the self prevail in eighteenth-century thought: the Cartesian *cogito,* with its exclusion of all but thinking for which the term *subject* is more appropriate than *self,* and the empirical self, which is more "object" than self. The distinction and its consequences are difficult to trace in fiction. At one extreme in a first person narrative of the kind where experience is immediately present to the reader, as in Richardson's epistolary novels, character is revealed primarily as subject though an object of the readers' contemplation. In Fielding's third person narratives, characters, exclusive of

4. Kenneth MacLean, *John Locke and English Literature of the Eighteenth Century,* p. 132; W. B. C. Watkins, *Perilous Balance: The Tragic Genius of Swift, Johnson, and Sterne,* p. 140; Rufus D. S. Putney, "Laurence Sterne: Apostle of Laughter," in *The Age of Johnson: Essays Presented to Chauncey Brewster Tinker,* p. 163; Traugott, p. 49; Arthur Hill Cash, *Sterne's Comedy of Moral Sentiments: The Ethical Dimension of the Journey,* p. 37.

the narrator, are revealed primarily as objects in the world. The distinction between these two abstractions is easily obliterated in fiction: Moll Flanders's memories of her former self, engaged in past experiences, may be recalled as belonging to her subsisting self or to a former self which is objectified. The difference in Defoe's narratives is indistinguishable. There is reason to maintain the distinction for a moment, however, in order to stress (1) the difference between Tristram and the other characters in his book and (2) the transformation in Tristram's own case of subject into self."[5] The difference in status of Tristram and his family is not consistently acknowledged, and that frequently results in his own character's being treated as coordinate with the others and the role of the family in his own life obscured. In fact, they are objects of his contemplations, and he is considerably more than the locus of the contemplating.

Neither the empirical access to character as object nor the psychological revelation of character as subject adequately explains the phenomenon of the self as it is explored in the central consciousness of Sterne's novel. In writing his "life and opinions"—the former, as he says, for "the amusement of the world"; the latter "for its instruction"—Tristram adopts a peculiar method for revealing himself that may be clarified by comparing it with that by which another well known character in eighteenth-century fiction, Clarissa Harlowe, is presented. Among the novelists of the age Richardson

---

5. The term *self* is highly ambiguous in ordinary usage and will seem so here. It is chosen nevertheless as a means of avoiding technical jargon and begins in this passage as a way of distinguishing between the unconditioned Cartesian thinking thing (subject) and the global being of the protagonist which Sterne presents as situated in concrete relations with a world, in a tradition, with other people, in relation to himself as a transcendence, and open toward possibilities in the future. Thus the term *self* will gradually take on the significance of the Heideggerean *Dasein* as the discussion proceeds.

has no equal in exploring the psychological dimensions of character. His viewpoint, like Locke's, is that of naturalistic psychology, in which acts of consciousness are approached as events in the ordinary world like other events, subject to the same causal processes and realistic analyses as fit the physical sciences. As astonishing as his achievements are, his view is always naive in an important sense: his characters reveal their deepest interests, but those interests are limited to their engagement in worldly affairs. The measure of Richardson's concern to reveal the depths of character may be clearly observed in the neglected opening third of the novel where Clarissa searches for a way to maintain that spiritual integrity which Puritanism had extended to women. Her cautious deliberations on an appropriate course of action in the world are meticulously chronicled as she balances the demands of filial duty against those of personal integrity. However, all these reflections are concerned with the world. Her contemplations, however searching, are limited to the realm of prereflective dealing with the world. And the same may be said of the deepest probings of her mind. She gives Anna Howe an account of the dream that follows her promise to elope with Lovelace—she dreams that Lovelace stabs her with a dagger and tumbles her into a grave among decaying corpses, a remarkable foreshadowing of her rape at Mrs. Sinclair's disreputable establishment and of her own eventual death. All this notwithstanding, she is yet totally enmeshed in the complicated fabric of her own experience, and we, as a result, are often perplexed by the problem of what exactly she knows about herself and when she comes to know it. She never detaches herself from the stream of experience or suspends her engagement with events to reflect on her own awareness. Hence the theme of what or who exactly she is never arises, for no amount of cataloguing the moments of her existence can lead to a clarifying of the meaning of her being.

Sterne does not treat Tristram's consciousness as a mere

entity existing alongside of, or in the same realm as external things. He is not engaged as an actor in a course of action in the world; he is reflecting upon his own mode of being, exploring the ordinarily unspoken grounds of consciousness. By beginning *ab ovo* if not *tabula rasa,* he attempts to exhume stratum after stratum of the very field in which his life experiences take place, moving backward, at first, toward his earliest formative influences. His reflection searches into the "upon which" of his being. He begins his book with the notion that but for the accident at his conception he might have been less prone to misfortune: "I am verily persuaded I should have made a quite different figure in the world, from that, in which the reader is likely to see me" (I.i.4). Clearly he has set out to find an explanation for his oddity. Walter and Toby agree that his peculiarity is traceable to his conception, and in the second chapter Tristram agrees that "a foundation had been laid for a thousand weaknesses both of body and mind." In chapter 4 the cause is traced back another step to Mrs. Shandy's associational thinking which had somehow got the winding of the clock confused with other domestic duties habitually attended to on the first Sunday night of the month, and the confusion happens at the precise moment of Tristram's conception. Even later the malaise is expanded to include the whole family extending back for several generations. The genetic strategy quickly becomes problematic because, first, there is no absolute starting point and, second, the unitary consciousness which it seeks to investigate is in a position of priority to the enquiry itself, and everything must be understood before anything can be told. His procedure nevertheless is to exclude from his reflections the kind of events that concern one in ordinary living, except of course for his writing, which is both action and reflection and hence part of the flow of experience. Borrowing from Husserl, let us call Clarissa's posture toward the world the "natural attitude" and Tristram's, the "critical attitude." Tristram's method is remarkably similar to the kind of analysis through which, Husserl says, "the foundations of a general phenomenology are laid." "The study of the stream of consciousness takes place, on its own side, through various acts of reflexion of peculiar structure, which themselves, again, belong to the stream of experience" (*Ideas*, p. 200). Phenomenology is interested in various perspectives that one can take in making observations, especially by suspending ordinary attitudes toward the world, and it is just such a suspension of the ordinary concerns of his life that enables Tristram to focus upon the structures of consciousness both his own and those of others. Whereas in Richardson we are invited to turn the analytical gaze upon the psychical states of characters, in Sterne we observe an activity of descriptive exhumation of layer after layer of the central consciousness. It is not only in Richardson that the novel owes more to the Puritan habit of moral self-scrutiny or introspection than to the Cartesian *cogito,* but Tristram's exacting self-analysis does not set out to discover the self in the psychological dimension of anguish and inner contortions that many of his contemporaries and not a few of his descendants have chosen. So little is our attention focused upon his mind itself that some critics have found, mistakenly but understandably, that his mind is "lost in the flux of thought" and that the novel "seems to abolish the ego altogether."[6] If Tristram's history were psychological (as it is usually taken to be) rather than ontological (as claimed here, since he is engaged in the amorphous activity of recording what passes in his mind rather than in a delimited course of action in the world like most fictional characters), there would be no intrinsic principle by which either to include or exclude any mental event whatever. There would be no ground for saying that the events so much as derive from one another or even that they belong

6. Putney, p. 163; Lanham, p. 156.

to a consecutive process. In the latter case, the ontological, the opposite is true: a simplicity and a constancy pervades all and unites all, providing a structured consciousness that admits some and excludes other possible psychic events. The implications for the ultimate patterns of meaning and therefore the structure of the novel itself are substantial.

The two different general kinds of analysis of consciousness, the psychological and the philosophic, are distinguishable even within the novel. First, Tristram has at least empirical access to the minds of other members of the Shandy community. In fact, he is not a positionless observer of the family since he is deeply involved in their history, and hence his access is more than "empirical" in the strict sense. Though they are revealed primarily as objects in the world rather than from the first person perspective of Richardson, they are the occasions for the protagonist's observations of how other minds work. His presentation of the thought processes of uncle Toby, for example, is an instance of existential analysis, concerned with the ways in which Toby's consciousness works in his engagement with the world. Second, Tristram's most direct access to consciousness, and the one without which he could not understand the behavior of others, consists in reflection upon his own mental processes, which provides a radical deepening of what he observes in others and leads finally to an ontological analysis not merely of the processes of his own thought but of the meaning of his being.

The Structure of Consciousness as Intending

Tristram's account of his own life and opinions is oddly concerned throughout most of the book with events that he is not directly concerned in and with people whose chief actions, as often as not, occur before he is born. Furthermore, his focus upon them is not a straightforward narrative account of the kind we might expect. In chapter 23 of the first volume he regrets that Momus' glass had not been fixed in the human breast so that one might have stood on a chair and looked in—

> view'd the soul stark naked;——observ'd all her motions,
> ——her machinations;——traced all her maggots from
> their first engendering to their crawling forth;——
> watched her loose in her frisks, her gambols, her capricios;
> and after some notice of her more solemn deportment,
> consequent upon such frisks, *etc.*——then taken your
> pen and ink and set down nothing but what you had seen,
> and could have sworn to:——But this is an advantage
> not to be had by the biographer in this planet. . . . Our
> minds shine not through the body, but are wrapt up here
> in a dark covering of uncrystalized flesh and blood; so
> that if we would come to the specifick characters of them,
> we must go some other way to work.
>
> Many, in good truth, are the ways which human wit
> has been forced to take to do this thing with exactness.
> [I.xxiii.74–75]

As Tristram considers the problem of presenting character "with exactness," he mentions several ways that have been established by others: there is Virgil's reliance upon "wind instruments" or rumor "in the affair of Dido and Æneas"; there are the Italians who detect the character in the voice, with great exactness in the case of the castrati; there are those who "draw a man's character" from his "evacuations," presumably his works which "smell too strong of the lamp"; others, "the Pentagraphic Brethern of the brush," prefer to rely upon one's full-length appearance which can be "hard upon the character of the man who sits"; and a last group who "will make a drawing of you in the *Camera*" or closet which may chance to catch "some of your most ridiculous attitudes," Richardson, perhaps, for example. Having rejected all these ways, Tristram reveals that he has found a new way to draw a person's character.

He catches uncle Toby, striking his social pipe against "the left nail of his thumb," preliminary to some account of the noise overheard in Mrs. Shandy's chamber. After six weeks of steady writing Tristram is about to get himself born above stairs, when he interrupts Toby's gesture by saying, "But to enter rightly into my uncle *Toby's* sentiments upon this matter, you must be made to enter first a little into his character, the out-lines of which I shall just give you" (I.xxi.63). There follows a well-known sequence of digressions "some millions of miles into the very heart of the planetary system," a fascinating metaphor for Toby's mind, before he settles on the expedient of drawing Toby from his hobby-horse by means of which he will give his intellectual, though not his moral character (II.xii.114). Having decided that we will only understand the account of that noise above stairs by first thoroughly understanding uncle Toby himself, Tristram provides the history of Toby's wound at Namur, the science of fortifications, and so on through thirty-six pages of digressions during which Toby stands, pipe in hand, waiting to finish his account of matters obstetrical above stairs. At last Tristram returns to Toby's opening expression: "I think, replied he, ——it would not be amiss, brother, if we rung the bell" (II. vi.99).

We must ask why Tristram rejects straightforward characterization, what he hopes to gain by these digressions beyond mere whimsicality. In fact he implies two claims in this sequence: first, we can only understand Toby's sentence after understanding Toby himself; we must know everything before we can understand anything, by implication a statement of the hermeneutical circle in which understanding moves from whole to part to whole again. The meaning of that "I think" in Toby's sentence might have been the abstract identification of thinking with being in the Cartesian *cogito,* but Tristram's interruption acknowledges the need to question the being of this "I" and to understand its thinking in the light of its living in the world. And so he explicates the "I" in terms of its concrete existence and then returns us to the original "I think" with the new light that renders Toby's anticlimactic remark transparent. The context of King William's wars, a wound upon the groin, modest ignorance of the right and wrong ends of a woman, and discomfiture at the slightest mention of aunt Dinah's escapades with the coachman, all account for Toby's evasion of what in fact is happening upstairs. Tristram's view, like the field theory of the Gestalt psychologist, emphasizes the necessity of considering parts only in interdependence within the wholes which they form. He thereby rejects the analysis of isolated units either of consciousness or of behavior, though both are within the bounds of his concern.

The second claim implicit in this example is that a person is best understood by examining the intentional focus of his consciousness, "that remarkable property of consciousness to be a consciousness *of*," to move "out from itself toward something else."[7] There is no reason to deny the apparent strategy whereby ideas seem to flow in nearly arbitrary sequence. The observation of a temporal sequence of mental acts associated, as Aristotle says, by similarity, contrast, or contiguity (for which last Hume substitutes causality), is true to experience; but there is reason to recognize the precise relationship that acts of consciousness bear to what confronts consciousness in the novel. The result of discovering such deeper relationships in the associational patterns is that the experience presented reveals itself as richer. Tristram shows by implication that experience, even sense experience, is much broader, more articulate and complicated than empiricism can know. In empirical theory from Locke through Hume consciousness is presented as a linear succession of events whose single dimension is a linear temporality. Thus Hume says that "the true idea of the human mind, is to consider it as a system of dif-

---

7. Paul Ricoeur, *Husserl: An Analysis of His Phenomenology*, trans. Edward G. Ballard and Lester E. Embree, p. 6.

ferent perceptions or different existences, which . . . mutually produce, destroy, influence, and modify each other. . . . One thought chases another, and draws after it a third, by which it is expelled in its turn" *(Treatise,* I.247). This is what one observes on the surface of Toby's mind. Tristram's whole strategy of digression, by contrast, is to uncover the total connected process of consciousness that is "activated" by that sound above stairs. The terms *theme* and *thematic field* help bring to light the implicit features and constituent elements of Toby's state of consciousness which constitute the background of the given meaning.[8] There is a difference between the noise above stairs as an auditory datum and the sound as Toby thematizes or focuses upon it. In like manner there is a difference between Toby's statement as an objective historical event and that event as it is drawn within the intentional arc of Tristram's mind. Though there is an "external horizon" to Toby's perceptive act and its thematic field—the house he is in, the imminence of childbirth, and so on—Tristram is not calling attention to the objective background but to Toby's "internal horizon," the penumbra of factors not actually given in the experience but that influence his hearing and the meaning which he experiences it as having. One must bear in mind, of course, that digressions which contribute directly to delineating the thematic field of Toby's consciousness simultaneously and indirectly contribute to filling in the corresponding field of Tristram's own consciousness. For Tristram's aim is a complete analysis of a single subject, and, even when he confines his attention to others, there is a subtle search underway to find the internal meaning, to cut to the core of his own single case. Thus his search proceeds without his ever reducing his own life to the abstraction of patterns of behavior under observation.

8. These terms are borrowed from Aron Gurwitsch, *The Field of Consciousness.*

For Hume the coherence of mental states, lacking observable ties, is finally reduced to "belief"; in the characterization of Toby, however, Tristram is in effect using a distinction that Husserl was to make the center of his analysis of the intentionality of consciousness, namely, the *noesis-noema* doctrine (*Ideas*, pp. 235–59). Consciousness is a correlation between the perceived thing as it is given and the perceiving act by which I comport myself toward the given. Thus the desk at which I write is in my library, the library in my house, the house in the city, and so on in ever-expanding concentric zones of meaning which define the context of my perception. The same desk might be perceived by an aborigine, but the intentional act would be radically different because he would not bring the same contextual zones to bear upon the perception. The distinction enables Tristram to see how it happens that Toby selects one use of the word *seige,* for example, as being important and addresses his attention to that, while Walter selects another and understanding is confounded.

Such analytical disclosure of the richness of a unified mental state is like the plurality of musical notes that constitutes the texture of a chord. But it remains to bring to full clarity what is meant by saying that the structural principle that organizes consciousness into a field in Tristram's reflections is intentionality. In discussing that "infinity of oddities" in his father which made it "baffle all calculations" to predict "by which handle he would take a thing," Tristram arrives at an approximate statement of the thesis of intentionality:

> The truth was, his road lay so very far on one side, from that wherein most men travelled,——that every object before him presented a face and section of itself to his eye, altogether different from the plan and elevation of it seen by the rest of mankind.——In other words, 'twas a different object,——and in course was differently considered:
> This is the true reason, that my dear *Jenny* and I, as

well as all the world besides us, have such eternal squab-
bles about nothing.——She looks at her outside,——I,
at her in——. How is it possible we should agree about
her value? [V.xxiv.382]

It is thus not Walter and the other hobby-horsical Shandys
alone, in Tristram's view, whose world is in part—but only
in part—a projection of their own intentional acts. He has
taken a clue from the others that helps him understand
himself.

It should be observed in passing that early in the book
Tristram comes close to using the word *world* in the phenomenological sense of *"Lebenswelt."* The midwife's reputation
is good, Tristram says, "in the world;——by which word
world, need I in this place inform your worship, that I would
be understood to mean no more of it, than a small circle
described upon the circle of the great world, of four *English*
miles diameter, or thereabouts, of which the cottage where
the good old woman lived, is supposed to be the centre"
(I.vii.11). The metaphor applies primarily to the physical
horizon in this passage, but he returns to it in a later chapter
and expands the meaning: "her fame had spread itself to the
very outedge and circumference of that circle of importance,
of which kind every soul living, whether he has a shirt to his
back or no,——has one surrounding him;——which said
circle, by the way, whenever 'tis said that such a one is of great
weight and importance in the *world,*——I desire may be en-
larged or contracted in your worship's fancy, in a compound-
ratio of the station, profession, knowledge, abilities, height
and depth (measuring both ways) of the personage brought
before you" (I.xiii.35). Thus by *world* he suggests the
phenomenological usage, namely, the horizon of one's consciousness of which one is necessarily the center, organized
according to the selective and directional thrust of one's interest. Both the terms *world* and *horizon,* with its suggestion of
a moving frontier, implicitly deny the thesis of objectivism.

Another example will sharpen the point. When Tristram is finally born and Trim chances to step into the parlor, Walter asks who is in the kitchen. "Dr. Slop," answers Trim, "busy, an' please your honour . . . in making a bridge." Toby's immediate response to the word *bridge* is " 'Tis very obliging in him . . . pray give my humble service to Dr. *Slop, Trim,* and tell him I thank him heartily" (III.xxiii.206), for Toby's hobby-horse has run away with him again, and he has taken the wrong bridge. He has been reminded of his own Dutch drawbridge which was "broke down, and some how or other crush'd all to pieces" during an affectionate encounter between Trim and the widow Wadman's maid Bridget one "moon-shiny night" in "the year 18." In point of fact, the bridge Dr. Slop is busily at work upon in the kitchen is a whalebone and cotton bridge for Tristram's nose, unhappily mutilated in being drawn headfirst into "this scurvy and disasterous world" with the aid of Dr. Slop's recent contribution to obstetrical science, the forceps.

If we are to win Sterne's insight here, we must acknowledge that he has grasped something radical about the general nature of consciousness, that what occupies a person focally is never merely a contingent occurrence, an atomic piece of stone in a mosaic of mental patterns where each element is indifferent to the nature of its neighbors. In place of the psychological atomism of the empiricists, Sterne represents mind as a clear and unitary system in which each element is colored and enriched by the texture of its milieu. The unity itself is a function of the permeating teleology, comic in Toby's case because the rigidity of his inner horizon excludes large dimensions of the outer horizon that should also be attended to. But the directional force of hobby-horsical thinking, its power to point toward or intend its object, reveals the intentional structure of thought, and the directedness of the beam of thought toward a particular matter includes the apprehension of the matter as valued in some way. Tristram's analysis of the marginal zones of consciousness, especially where a single phenomenon is intended by different characters in disparate ways, makes the point clear. When Obadiah carries the news of brother Bobby's death into the kitchen, the variety of ways in which the information is received brings to light idiosyncratic backgrounds of interpretation. Mrs. Shandy's maid Susannah responds to the news by a vision of "a green sattin night-gown" which she will inherit when Mrs. Shandy goes into mourning. The "fat Foolish scullion" who suffers from the dropsy can think only of her own death; Obadiah himself, of the labor of "stubbing the ox-moor," a project set aside in order to finance Bobby's ill-fated grand tour. These various ways of responding to the news distinguish the information as it falls within the intentional arcs of different characters from the information as given or, to be very precise, as intended by the community composed of Tristram and his readers, a vivid example of the grounding of objectivity in the space of intersubjectivity. This most radical discovery in Tristram's existential analysis of the manner of being of other members of the Shandy household has brought to light the effect of the human situation upon which even the simplest perception is interpreted as significant.

Since that hobby-horsical thinking is generally represented, if not as a mental disorder, then at least as a source of error, one may ask how such mental events can be taken as evidence of a radical departure in our understanding of normal conscious acts. The answer is that Sterne, like Freud later, isolates general features of conscious life by observing closely what is pathological. It is not the intentional focus of the hobby-horsical mind *per se* that is abnormal and the object of satire; it is the self-centered inattention to zones of meaning beyond the inner horizon, to things perceivable but not perceived, as one might say, that makes fools of the Shandys.

There is a point of strategy to mark as we turn from Tristram's analysis of other minds to his revelation of him-

self. Faced with the alternative of presenting either the concrete processes of Tristram's existence or his reflections upon
that being—his life *or* his opinions—Sterne realized that an
exclusive choice of either would exact a high price. Ernst
Cassirer explains the dilemma: "The truth of life seems to be
given only in its pure *immediacy,* to be enclosed in it—but
any attempt to understand and apprehend life seems to en-
danger, if not to negate, this immediacy."[9] If, on the contrary, one begins with the "concept of being, the dualism of
thought and being becomes more and more pronounced as
we advance in our investigations," and we run the risk of
losing the "truth of life." Eighteenth-century novelists had
tried several solutions to this problem of which one of the
happier is Fielding's narrator. Sterne needed a different solution, however, and the subtilty of the one he worked out is a
deft stroke of genius which perhaps owes something, though
not all, to Montaigne for whom the process of revising his
essays is a representation of living itself. The process is radically historical, a living process of vision and revision from
no point of which a final view of the life is possible.

It has already been suggested that Tristram's way of presenting his life bears comparing with Husserl's central
methodological procedure, the phenomenological reduction
which consists in exclusion of existential concerns antecedent
to reflection. Admitting in advance the risk one runs in projecting random philosophical patterns upon literature in a
merely fanciful way, a kind of literary criticism *as if,* I accept
the risk in suggesting that Sterne has shrewdly detected the
root issue that would later mark the parting of ways between
transcendental and existential phenomenology. When Heidegger makes this shift, the major emphasis is his rejection
of Husserl's reduction with its explicit distrust of the natural
attitude and its consequent abstraction from the perspective

9. *The Philosophy of Symbolic Forms,* I, 111.

of ordinary life. Where Husserl had substituted a different state of consciousness in the place of the natural attitude and made that new reflective attitude a model for the whole of experience, Heidegger himself insists on the primitive presence of the world in a kind of prephilosophic realism as an essential feature of subjectivity. Human existence is fused with a characteristic and indispensable environment without which no description of that being is possible; it is always and everywhere being-in-the-world.

Tristram's reflections open to him the dimension of the formal structures of consciousness from which constriction of his interest to immediate experience would exclude him: but reflection alone would provide little insight into the actual content of his experience. Sterne's strategy is to focus directly upon Tristram's contemplations upon his total being while preserving the immediate sense of the processes of construction by which he comes to be. He does so by focusing those contemplations in turn upon the life of Shandy Hall and upon Tristram in his study trying to record his reflections. First, in describing in vivid concreteness the social environment of his family he does not simply make empirical observations on the workings of those minds as though he were an absolutely unconditioned spectator; he presents a community, albeit somewhat deformed, to which he is bound both generatively and socially, one that exists in him and without which he would not be. When therefore he studies the structures of consciousness in his kinsman, Toby, by reflecting upon Toby's actual existential engagements (and broken engagements) with the world, he simultaneously maintains the truth of life as it is revealed to him in observation and explores his own characteristic environment. Without understanding that environment he can never understand himself. Second, when Tristram shows himself to us directly, not as engaged in growing up in Shandy Hall, but as sitting in his study, occupied with reflecting upon his own being and, as an extension of that project, writing his book, he thereby removes the wedge of abstraction that ordinarily separates thought from the immediacy of life. This is a fictional development of a point which Husserl later insists upon, namely, that in the reflective act the thinker, while procedurally disengaged from the ordinary sequence of worldly concerns, nevertheless goes on living so that the reflecting itself is, in a sense, a part of his existential engagement. As we observe Tristram bringing what he had formerly taken for granted to clarity through reflection now upon his family, now upon himself, we become aware of the whole range of his connectedness with others, ultimately even with human history, and of the intentional orientation that casts the content of his life into a unified configuration.

In Tristram's revelation of himself we find confirmation of the claim that he views consciousness as an intentional structure. Uncle Toby's "I think" turned out to be no absolute Cartesian gaze before which events pass, but a unity of the flux of consciousness from within the flux itself, and a unity that is open so long as he lives, to perpetual revision. The unity of another consciousness is always hypothetical and its behavior unpredictable. When, for example, Walter learns of the damage to Tristram's nose at birth, he goes upstairs and falls across his bed in a posture of extreme grief; but when, after having chosen the name Trismegistus as the single name in Christiandom that can counteract the evil effect of a crushed nose, a combination of unhappy accidents —Walter's difficulty in getting his pants buttoned and the leaky vessel of Susannah's memory—result in Tristram's being given the name of all others the worst for the purpose, Walter unpredictably "walked composedly out with it to the fish-pond." Tristram comments that "unless he has a great insight into human nature" the reader is apt to expect a predictable response. He knows better: "But mark, madam, we live amongst riddles and mysteries—the most obvious things, which come in our way, have dark sides, which the quickest sight cannot penetrate into; and even the clearest and most exalted understandings amongst us find ourselves puzzled and at a loss in almost every cranny of nature's works" (IV.xvii.292–93).

Tristram's project of writing his life is the focus of his own consciousness and the clue to the intentional principle that permeates his mind, albeit a complexly intentive mind. He can only make inferences about others but when he reveals his own consciousness, he shares with us his immediate access to his mental acts and ultimately to the unity of his own transcendence. The evidence of the intentional organization of his consciousness lies in his peculiar strategy in telling his story. He may play with the notion of writing his life as an action or as a discursive sequence that proceeds straightforward like a line, but in fact he has thought on consciousness deeply enough to realize that if we wish to speak of it as moving at all, then it does so by doubling back upon itself, by leaping beyond all bounds of logical progression, by deepening itself in multitudinous and labyrinthine ways as it assimilates disparate materials to itself.

Just as he found it necessary to present the whole of Toby's consciousness in order to make us understand a single sentence, so he must present the whole of his own, by means of a digressive method that sketches in the field in which the themes of consciousness stand forth:

> Could a historiographer drive on his history, as a muleteer drives on his mule,——straight forward . . . without ever once turning his head aside either to the right hand or to the left,——he might venture to foretell you to an hour when he should get to his journey's end;——but the thing is, morally speaking, impossible: For, if he is a man of the least spirit, he will have fifty deviations from a straight line to make with this or that party as he goes along, which he can no ways avoid. He will have views

and prospects to himself perpetually solliciting his eye, which he can no more help standing still to look at than he can fly. [I.xiv.36–37]

Hence Tristram resolves "not to be in a hurry," so that he can fill in the field in which the subject thematically focused on is surrounded by interconnected and interpenetrating structures. He even warns us against a "vicious taste . . . of reading straight forwards," and Madame Reader is chastised for being "in quest for adventures" instead of concentrating on the meaning of what is being said along the way. If we give him the attention he demands, it will become possible to see his project as the unifying principle of both his life and his book. The apparent associationism on the narrative surface of his book has in fact been grounded in the principle of intentionality, or, to put it another way, association occurs within the scope of the intentional focus of consciousness and hence ceases to be associationism at all in any strict sense. The themes he develops, the sequences of reflections he engages in, however remote from his stated purpose they may appear to be, Walter's dissertation on time and eternity, or uncle Toby's love affair with the widow Wadman, or Elizabeth Shandy's apparent intellectual vacuity—all are clues to what and who he is. As he writes his book, he at once lives and interrogates that life to discover its basis and ultimately its meaning. It is that project and problem that casts the particular shadows of memory that fall across the pages of his work.

When his reflections wander in an apparently loose, associational manner, we must seek the unity that informs those reflections, how they form systems of relevance to the self in the subjective context to which they contribute. To the reader Tristram is the theme; and the events, experiences, ideas, and persons he speaks of contribute to the thematic field in the light of which he stands out. Having recognized that the patterns of Tristram's memory are not arbitrary, we ask why he remembers what he remembers of Yorick, say. To turn his attention to Yorick's reflections on gravity is implicitly to admit the value of those reflections to himself because the intentional act of his consciousness includes the apprehension of the object contemplated as it is valued. The real bearing of Tristram's remarks on Yorick tells us little about Yorick as he may have been himself; it tells us much about Tristram. He is not led to the passage about Yorick's "invincible dislike and opposition" to gravity merely by a surface sequence which moves from his conception, to the midwife, to Yorick's lending her his horse, to Yorick's character itself. There is a deep structure in Tristram's procedure which establishes Yorick in volume I as the moral center of the novel and a decisive force upon Tristram's life. The combination of court jester and country parson may be inconvenient in an Anglican divine, but both sides of that character are reflected in Tristram's dual intention to amuse and to instruct. Likewise Yorick's death with its echoes of skulls and infinite jest and his facing it in a "cervantick" spirit are at once Tristram's first experience at facing the possibility of ceasing to be, a theme of major proportions in the book, and a revelation of Yorick as a constituent theme of his own self-analysis. Thus, Tristram goes beneath the empiricists' assumption of memory as the locus of identity to discover the intentional structures underlying memory itself. Susannah makes the need evident: with a memory like hers one might just go out altogether, "bang" like a candle, as Alice says. And so with every reflection in the book, Tristram's aim is to understand and to convey the unity that he is. He does not try to observe or define that unity directly by a pseudoempirical description of his own behavior or by making of himself both subject and object in introspective observation.

The distinction between Husserl's distrust of the perspective of ordinary life and Heidegger's insistence on the primitive unity of human being with its environment as being-in-the-world, mentioned above, prepares us to understand the self that Tristram succeeds in evoking: it is in no sense an object, a thing that he comes across in his dealings with the world. Other characters stand out as empirical objects with a density or opacity like substantial things that one can get hold of. But not Tristram. Or rarely.[10] In a sense, he is the least real of all the Shandys, for he is a dynamic, structured event, a happening, which cannot be appropriately conceived in substantive terms. For him to give an external picture of his own character would be like Max Planck's analogy of a runner who overtakes himself, the impossibility of which he points out when he is fretting about how fast he would have to write to keep up with his living: he laments, "write as I will, and rush as I may into the middle of things, as *Horace* advises,——I shall never overtake myself" (IV.xiii.286). He is not an ego at the center of the world, not a subjectivity (*subjectum*), an essence underlying his experience. He is an opening in being or, in Merleau-Ponty's phrase, a "window" on his world, both a transparency and a focal point, just as each of us experiences himself to be. We simply observe thinking going on, language being spoken, a project in process, and we have a sense of the unity of his unfinished being. To Tristram himself, he is a question for which there is answering but no answer.

If we ask, then, what Tristram finds himself to be, we must answer that he is the complex reflexivity that we observe being called forth by the tension between his project[11] and the re-

10. This seems to be what Lanham has in mind when, without distinguishing between Tristram's level of being and that of the family, he comments on the paradox of "a collection of discrete, forever colliding selves, but no dependable sense of *self*, all acting and no action" (pp. 157–58).

11. The term *project* as it will be used here is intended to signify not only an ontic plan of action, as in Tristram's plan for writing his book, but also the ontological process of actuating some of his possibilities for being.

sistance to its fulfillment that is offered by his context. His being comes to clarity in the fact of reflecting upon his own existence, and that being, like Heidegger's *Dasein,* stands out as a relation to itself, a being beyond itself that demonstrates its transcendence, a dimension not available in the "characters" of the book who must be represented "externally" as objects of Tristram's contemplations. The point is made explicitly in Tristram's telling the story of himself telling his own story like mirrors reflecting each other *ad infinitum*. This is a concrete demonstration of Kierkegaard's syntactic gymnastics on the subject: "The self is a relation which relates itself to its own self, or it is that in the relation [which accounts for it] that the relation relates itself to its own self; the self is not the relation but [consists in the fact] that the relation relates itself to its own self."[12] Or as Henry James expresses a similar complexity in *What Maisie Knew,* "There was an extraordinary mute passage between her vision of this vision of his, his vision of her vision, and her vision of his vision of her vision" (p. 182). Tristram's self is precisely that act of relating to himself that arises in his reflections upon his life and opinions, in the opening toward his own possibilities for being.

The term *transcendence* for this peculiar way of being which is a relatedness to itself is a more radical term than *consciousness* as it has been used in this chapter. In reflecting on consciousness, Tristram has found the structural pattern of intentionality which explains the subjective context of the experience of things and helps provide the inner coherence of the sequence of mental events; but the term "consciousness" limits the enquiry therefore to subjectivity as it is opposed to a correlative world of meanings and thus remains

12. Sören Kierkegaard, *Fear and Trembling and The Sickness Unto Death,* trans. Walter Lowrie, p. 146. This passage is admittedly problematic: Kierkegaard may be simply indulging in ironical polemics, and yet it successfully illustrates the character of Tristram's transcendence.

within the bounds of idealism. To be sure, Tristram's project is idealist in orientation since his interpretations are made from the viewpoint of the subjective thinker; but he goes beyond the subject-object model when he seeks to account for the structure of that subjectivity and its primitive orientation toward the world. In transcendence the subject-object polarity is suspended in favor of the more radical event of the presubjective self that is the origin of consciousness and its intentional focus. For Kant *transcendental* refers to the functional possibilities and limitations that underlie all knowledge; and his program is to chart the range of possible knowledge and its necessary structure in the operational synthesis of sense intuition and thought. Transcendence in the sense that Tristram discovers it is broader in that he is interested in the transcendental ground of his being and not simply in the preconditions of his knowing. In this respect his purpose is more like Heidegger's than Kant's, but examination of the temporal character of that relation to himself that arises in his reflections must be deferred until we have observed his primitive engagement with other selves. It should be evident in advance that such a deepening of Tristram's account of his being will constitute a refutation of idealism, for it will not be true as in Locke "that men know, not reality, but their own experience only and that the 'reality' of identity is transferred from the fixed ego or soul to the separate and shifting ideas which make up the content of the consciousness."[13]

Tristram's transcendental reflections constitute the project of writing his life, the most general possibility that he has embraced, and by the nature of that enterprise it includes the summons to self-knowledge. Since we know Tristram

---

13. Stedmond, pp. 23–24. Cf. Ernest Tuveson, "Locke and 'the Dissolution of the Ego,'" *Modern Philology* 52 (1955), 159–74; and *The Imagination as a Means of Grace,* pp. 25–41.

quite as fully as he can know himself, we observe how that self arises to self-consciousness in response to the tensions of its context. His reflexivity is called forth by the resistance offered by his context to his plan of action in the world. Just as a building has its being in the tension between the principles of stress and counterstress, or a play in its action and counteraction, so, having set himself an objective, Tristram meets obstacles and discovers his domain in the tension between aim and obstacle. Quite literally as a character in a fiction, he comes to be in the act of presenting his life, for the writing is his act of being. Just as Toby was best characterized intellectually by means of the intentional focus according to which he organizes his world and lives in it, his hobby-horse in short, so Tristram reveals that dimension of himself in the same manner. He responds to a life filled with misfortunes and cross-purposes, to the frustrations of fickle language, to writing a life that will not stand still for him to catch up, or to escaping that *"son of a whore"* Death by scampering away to Vesuvius, to Joppa, and "to the world's end, where, if he follows me, I pray God he may break his neck" (VII.i.480). In short, it is his assault upon the restraints of his own finitude, his occupying a certain position *vis-à-vis* his world that brings him into the light of actuality as a self. This self, furthermore, is an ecstatic unity, a tension between two poles, a person who is and a person who was, might have been, or may be. As Henry Johnstone says in his splendid book *The Problem of the Self*, "to be a man is to be the unity of what is and what might have been" (p. 68). The contradictory posture of the self, the unity of the Tristram who is and the Tristram who might have been but for the winding of clocks, the weak memories of chambermaids, and the military uses of window weights, reveals in concrete form what is meant by the unity of transcendence that permeates the flux of consciousness and is constituted by the flux. Johnstone concludes that "the self arises in the very act of contemplating one's existence, since the act of contemplation can be carried out only from a vantage point beyond existence" (p. 74). The most decisive vantage point beyond Tristram's existence is his openness to possibility in the future, for the unity of the self that he presents is sustained by the contingency of change and ultimately by the possibility of death.

If Tristram's purpose is to uncover the structures of his own being, then we can understand why he excludes from concern the entire range of ordinary daily activities, for they tend to obscure the ontological question. He is not interested in the evolving self such as we find in *Clarissa* or even in Montaigne's *Essays*. If he gave a merely existential analysis of himself, a kind of diachronic, horizontal presentation of the ways of his being, the events of his life as he passes through moments of time, we would see the process of becoming. But that focus upon the ways of his being would tend to obscure the very problem he wishes to get at. Consequently, he chooses a vertical or synchronic presentation whereby he uncovers stratum after stratum of his own consciousness in order to find out what kind of "thing" he is. The process of reflection reveals that he is the kind of thing that can reflect upon itself, that is, a transcendence, a "who," not a "what." As he makes himself the theme of his own intentional field and interrogates the being that he is, the meaning that arises in this intentional realm is the meaning of his own being, a response to the very ancient and very modern question implied in the act of self-interrogation, "Who am I?"

"Being-with" and Tristram's Two Communities

In Sermon VII, "A Vindication of Human Nature," Yorick takes as his text Romans 14:7, "For none of us liveth to himself," and he interprets it in the following manner:

> No one . . . who lives in society, can be said to live to himself,—he lives to his GOD,—to his king, and his country. —He lives to his family, to his friends, to all under his trust, and in a word, he lives to the whole race of man-

kind; whatsoever has the character of man, and wears the same image of GOD that he does, is truly his brother, and has a just claim to his kindness.[14]

The fresh statement of the old doctrine of the communion of saints would appear to contrast with the experience of *Tristram Shandy,* which is usually understood to exemplify the thesis of individualism in one of the most extreme forms to be found in eighteenth-century fiction. In this section we shall see that the reverse is the case, that Tristram could even have been attempting to test or to "naturalize" the traditional doctrine within the setting of Shandy Hall. The result is that, through his examination of his family and their relation to the structure of his own being, he reaches an understanding of "intersubjectivity" or the social character of the self that contrasts markedly with the individualism presumed to be normative in the work. The question also has a secondary importance in this discussion because chapter 1 above has placed the novel in the tradition of subjectivity extending from Descartes to Husserl which tends either to assign to the public, social world a position derivative from an autonomous subjectivity—an extreme instance is Berkeley—or to attribute the status of the subject to a more primitive social realm—as in Hegel. Tristram's reflections endorse neither of these extremes.

One frequently hears the view expressed that in this novel "everyone is subjectively alone," that intellectual estrangement is the normal condition of being represented in it, that no one is able "to convince anyone else of anything,"[15] that the life of the mind and the use of language are futile. The view is true enough of the Shandys: their world is tending toward isolation and even solipsism as demonstrated by events

14. Laurence Sterne, *The Sermons of Mr. Yorick,* ed. Wilbur L. Cross, I, 116.

15. Earl R. Wasserman, *The Subtler Language,* p. 171; Lanham, p. 46.

outside the immediate family, between Toby and Mrs. Wadman, for example, or among the participants in "the Visitation Dinner" at York. But such critical observations fail to distinguish between what is true for the Shandys, who are all dead now, and what is true for Tristram and his work as a whole. He and the family are not coordinate entities, and the habit of treating them as if they were demonstrates that the thesis of reflection has not been taken seriously and pursued with consistency. Of course the tendency in eighteenth-century culture was toward the "vigorous impotence" of "the Shaftesburian solitary," as Wasserman demonstrates, but Sterne is an uncommon man who includes within himself the new sensibilities in uneasy juxtaposition with an intelligence cultivated, however haphazardly, in the traditions that distinguish the more confident and conservative voices of the period. His central character takes the condition of the family and the age as a starting point and tries, I think successfully, to understand its causes, its implications, and, to a considerable extent, its solution. The point of departure is the family because they *are* Tristram in the important sense demonstrated by the fact that his analysis does not begin with a pure ego, as in the idealism of Husserl, but with his concrete involvement as a historical being among other beings in the world.

The prominent theme of the relation between the individual and the social group in eighteenth-century fiction, then, gets its most thorough examination in Sterne's novel where the theme of intersubjectivity or of one's "being-with" others is shown to be not merely adventitious but essential to the constitution of Tristram as a self. I will argue here that the self that Tristram is comes to be for itself, first, by adopting the perspectives of a second community, the audience to which the book is addressed, thereby taking up a critical view of the Shandys and necessarily therefore of himself.

The Shandys

There is an interesting paradox in the fact that the members of the Shandy household, for whom intellectual isolation and nearly private universes of discourse have replaced community, are held together in that solitude only by the tenuous bonds of sentiment and spatial proximity in the parlor, while Tristram, who writes from the solitude of his own reflections, finds himself essentially rooted in a community composed of those very isolated, and now departed, souls. This circumstance provides a vivid sense of the self as coming to be in the context of community even though it is one where the spiritual aristocrats live in conditions of reality, as Paul Tillich says of our own world, unprotected by any system of communal myth.

Since the social life of Shandy Hall occupies stage center for much of the book in which Tristram's main subject is himself, we may assume that for Tristram to present himself accurately, he feels the need to present that community to which he is bound both generatively and socially. His reflections reveal an awareness that this community of minds exists *in* him and that it is only through this connectedness with his original community that he is as a self. Intersubjectivity is not therefore merely tangential to the theme of the self; its importance is equivalent to the position of the Shandy family in the book: Tristram's story must be the story of life in Shandy Hall. Although his genetic approach to the self leads him to focus on its social origins, a view that hardly prevails in eighteenth-century thought, his theory by no means goes unchallenged, for Walter, having thought the problem through with customary self-serving acumen, has a position of his own on the subject.

The two Shandys, father and son, manifest the classic opposition of social and individualistic theories of the self. As George Herbert Mead describes them, "the first type assumes a social process or social order as the logical and biological precondition of the appearance of the selves of the individual organisms involved in that process or belonging to that order. The other type, on the contrary, assumes individual selves as the presuppositions, logically and biologically, of the social process or order within which they interact."[16] Tristram reveals his own existence and experience, his "life and opinions," as being originally in part and parcel the organized social environment of Shandy Hall, omitting which he could neither understand himself nor make himself understood. Walter, by contrast, seems to conceive of the self, albeit the epistemological self, as an absolutely unconditioned spectator with no point of view whose social relations might be, and in eighteenth-century theories usually are, contractual ties with other totally autonomous subjects. Discussion of the first of the two communities of the novel will concentrate on this conflict, beginning with Walter's individualism.

The essence of Walter's position may be stressed and its far-reaching consequences suggested by reference to that archetypal *solus ipse* in eighteenth-century fiction, Robinson Crusoe.[17] As the epitome of individualism, Crusoe is Puritan, capitalist, self-sufficient, practical, an incorrigible bourgeois who even addresses God with the most self-centered and utilitarian of motives. His social needs do not extend beyond the obvious requirement for goods and services, and hence he feels no need whatever for personal relationships, not even to cheer his own solitude. Nature on his island, consequently, consists in a radical debasement of the ancient order (*taxis*) and the beauty of that order (*cosmos*) into mere objects, things on hand to be used for his own purposes. It is both a

16. *Mind, Self and Society,* p. 222.

17. For the parallel with Crusoe, stressing characteristics of class consciousness in Toby more than Walter, see Howard Anderson, "A Version of Pastoral: Class and Society in *Tristram Shandy,*" *Studies in English Literature* 7 (1967), 509–29.

fascinating and a prophetic aspect of the position of the ego in Defoe's tales that it should result in a decline in the presence of things and a gradual evacuation of phenomenal reality. The value of everything in Crusoe's universe consists in the ratio it bears to the self, and hence what does not appear as useful in achieving his own goals, in fulfilling his own will, simply is not seen. When one tries to imagine the landscapes and seascapes of that island which would have been available to a person who was open to wonder, the absence of those phenomena in the story brings strikingly to mind the price the ego pays for the arrogance of relegating the real to the instrumental interests of the self. Rather than dwelling in the presence of what is worthy of contemplation and understanding, Crusoe abstracts the useful from the real and thereby misses the profound and mysterious relatedness with the world that is his birthright. The consequent exploitation of the island, of Friday, and, most important, of himself as tool of the will to power is a forecast of the spirit of technology. Though Defoe's story is about the acquisitive self in solitary pursuit of things, a self that nevertheless imports communally produced tools and materials into its lonely domain (not to mention a language by the sole means of which it has access to the reality it seeks to exploit) before closing the door on society, Crusoe's position nonetheless parallels that of the typical thinker in the modern world. If Crusoe were less interested in goods and more interested in the pursuit of truth, as Walter Shandy presumably is, he would seem to be ideally situated from the point of view of the rationalist prejudice against prejudice, optimally situated for judging facts and arriving at truth—if, that is, truth be mistaken for a function of the ego.

Walter Shandy does not appear to be the extreme individualist that Crusoe is, and he clearly is not simply *homo oeconomicus*. His individualism is almost subtle by comparison though all the more telling for being traced in its effects rather than articulated in principle. In fact, Walter repeatedly demonstrates his sense of kinship, in sentiment at least, with Toby; he stresses the kinship of a son to his father, though not to his mother; he is vividly aware of the hereditary impotence that has marred the fortunes of his family; in the opening pages of the Tristrapaedia he even gives an account of the genesis of civil government out of the family—one man, one woman, and one bull. But the very point of all these examples is the poor repair of the human relationships in the novel and that provides the occasion of Tristram's reflections on the subject. Although Walter does not defend the social contract theory as both rationalists and empiricists of his day tend to (his primary concern after all is not social theory), from Tristram's perspective he does exemplify the assumption of the primacy of the ego in another domain: all his intellectual theories go awry and entangle him in a net of self-deception precisely because of his uncritical egoism. Whereas Tristram is engaged in an effort to understand the self, Walter exemplifies instead a way of thinking that debases the mind in the service of the limited ends of the ego (on Walter's egoism, see chapter 5 below).

Tristram's social view of the self saves him from such epistemological errors by providing him with an awareness of the forces that condition all his enquiries. The comparison with his father is somewhat asymmetrical in that his reflections are not primarily epistemological; his emphasis is upon the genesis, structure, and meaning of the self, and hence his reflections show us the social order that exists in him though its members are now dead. He understands himself as dependent upon community not only for his geniture but for satisfying the universal human need to be perpetually sustained by being-with others. It is thus not only consciousness that is intentional in structure; his very being is intentional in this social directedness. He implies a conception of man according to which his being is essentially *with* others from the beginning and can neither be thought nor described except in terms of that *with*. He is not *in* a community as wine is *in* a bottle, never simply in juxtaposition with others; there is a profound, ontological intimacy in the relationship that precludes his being solitary, enclosed within himself, even as he sits alone in his library writing his book.

Contrary to the common assumption about the egoism of the child, as though it had an innate understanding of itself as ego, self-awareness arises out of a background of indeterminacy in the encounter with the other, especially with other persons. Tristram's early experience is not recounted—in a sense he has none—but the sedimentation from his dawning self-awareness is available to reflection. Mead, who has analyzed this subject most clearly, explains the process whereby the child assimilates the various social attitudes in his environment by adopting the roles of the people around him in the format of play. Thus he may imaginatively assume the role of teacher and speak to himself, then shift to the role of student and respond in a way that calls in turn for a response in the first character. Tristram would in the normal course of things have played out the roles of the older Shandys. But consistent with his reflective stance, which, unlike most fictions, does not seek to objectify the self for scrutiny, in his book he practices an admirable economy by not showing himself as a child actually assuming the roles available to him and encountering in the others a limiting concept of the self. Instead as he recreates the dialogue of persons situated in the parlor, for example, he thereby duplicates the child's game, playing out the roles of each character in writing his book. This strategy amplifies an earlier observation that Tristram shares a living relationship with his tradition rather than one of objective knowledge of facts. His approach to his genetic community is so intimate in fact that the distinction between himself and the others fades: they are not the absolute others of objective history; they are part of himself. He at once shows how fully he has assimilated them, how fully he belongs to that community, how totally he bears it within him, and he does so with the additional depths of consciousness and revised perspectives that subsequent life and especially reading have provided. That Tristram intends us to understand his presentation of the Shandys in this way is supported by his presenting them in reflection as though events that happened in his infancy and even before his birth were contemporaneous with his writing. There is a sense in which that is literally true: as influences upon him, as determining possibilities for his own being, as subjects for his interpretation, they are concurrent.

His imaginative ability to play the role of the other is also his ability to understand the other, "to call out" in himself "a set of definite responses which belong to the others of the group,"[18] and, more important, it is the ground of his own self-consciousness. Self-consciousness comes about by getting outside the self, and that is what happens when Tristram imaginatively adopts—we usually say understands—the attitudes of the elder Shandys toward him. In fact, his sense of his own life as a pitiful affair and of himself as being the "continual sport of what the world calls fortune" is an adoption of his father's view of him in the Lamentation:

> Unhappy *Tristram!* child of wrath! child of decrepitude! interruption! mistake! and discontent! What one misfortune or disaster in the book of embryotic evils, that could unmechanize thy frame, or entangle thy filaments! which has not fallen upon thy head, or ever thou comest into the world——what evils in thy passage into it!—— What evils since!——produced into being, in the decline of thy father's days——when the powers of his imagination and of his body were waxing feeble——when radical heat and radical moisture, the elements which should

18. Mead, p. 163.

have temper'd thine, were drying up; and nothing left
to found thy stamina in, but negations. [IV.xix.296]

Here is the genesis of Tristram's whole project, the clarification of a being so improvidently thrown into the world. Here
too are the categories of thought that he has inherited. Only
by overcoming this vocabulary of mechanical physiology will
he be enabled to arrive at an understanding of himself that
differs from Walter's.

In addition, Tristram's early social context is explicated
in order to show the derivation of the whole range of social
meanings that constitute his own horizon of interests. By
adopting Walter's point of view he acquires his father's
phenomenal world without accepting that view as normative;
by adopting Toby's point of view he acquires an alternative
version of the world. In this flexibility he is most like Corporal
Trim who is able to understand all the other characters and
is yet said to be *"Non Hobby-Horsical per se."* The inability
of the hobby-horsical characters to assume points of view
other than their own is a deliberate, pathological constriction
of the imagination that, as Tristram shows, results from a de-
ficiency in self-knowledge. The role that is most important
for Tristram and that has never been fully integrated into
our understanding of the novel is Yorick's: the ability to
adopt Yorick's perspective and thereby understand it, is the
major intellectual catalyst in the novel. Walter omits religion
entirely from the curriculum of the Tristrapaedia just as he
omits comedy from his life though serving, all the same, as
a superb comic character. Thus in the juxtaposed roles of
Walter and Yorick, Tristram is thrust into the intellectual
controversy that divides the incoherent modern theorizing
of his father from the ancient wisdom of the jester-parson;
from this arises the necessity for the enquiry into his own
being. Presenting directly the characters who are his early
roles makes explicit the social context of and the values im-

plicit in the structures of his thinking, and the multiple relations concealed in the processes of his consciousness stand forth for our contemplation.

Not only does the social context explain Tristram's self-awareness, the issues that occupy his thinking and the communal character of comprehending, but his method reveals this intrinsically social self as therefore a full-blooded Shandy and to the manor born in that most eminently social relation, language. If the conceptual space opened up by the Shandy community delimits the interests that are available to him, it is no less true that the language he learns provides his original tools for working with those interests. One of the greatest barriers to describing clearly the exact lines of agreement and disagreement between Tristram and Walter has been the fact that they speak the same language. The son is quite as addicted to images of mechanism, for example, as the father. It would appear therefore that he is equally guilty of judging wholes by parts, the essence of the mechanical conception. The fact is, however, that his strategy in presenting his "life and opinions" has not been adequately understood because he tries to present the whole *Gestalt* of his consciousness by means of a kind of archaeology of the self. The digressions in which he characterized uncle Toby demonstrated his conviction that even a single word, the analysis of which must always include the notion of someone speaking to someone about something, can be understood only in the light of the global structure of wholes: in Toby's case, the full context of his military interests and his sexual inhibitions. Walter's language and his thought are dominated by the view classically expressed in the third part of Newton's *Principia* called "Rules for Reasoning in Natural Philosophy," where the inductive rule is explicitly formulated as judging the whole on the basis of the parts available to experience. Tristram's conceptual habits, his vocabulary notwithstanding, more clearly correspond to Leibniz's organic view: "the concept of the *whole* has gained a different and deeper significance. For the universal whole which is to be grasped can no longer be reduced to a mere sum of its parts. The new whole is organic, not mechanical; its nature ... is presupposed by its parts and constitutes the condition of the possibility of their nature and being."[19]

Thus Tristram's account of the workings of his family is cast in the language of mechanism, "a simple machine" consisting of a few "wheels ... set in motion by so many different springs ... it had all the honor and advantages of a complex one" (V.vi.358). Likewise, his theory of laughter is a mechanical account of the effect of his book on the readers: it is to cause "a more convulsive elevation and depression of the diaphragm ... to drive the *gall* and other *bitter juices*... down into their duodenums" (IV.xxi.301–02); and yet it is Yorick's remarks on gravity, already glanced at, that provide the deeper theory of comedy dramatized in turn by the spirit of liberation implicit in Tristram's own hearty laughter, which has the effect of relaxing in himself those rigid structures of egotistic thought that confine his father. In short, the language in which he expresses his view reveals his rootedness in the linguistic and conceptual community of Shandy Hall, while he arrives in understanding at a view much more cogent and subtle. Thus it is that when in volume VII he spends a day in *Lyons* where he proposes to see the "great clock of *Lippius* of *Basil*," he confesses,

> Now, of all things in the world, I understand the least of mechanism——I have neither genius, or taste, or fancy ——and I have a brain so entirely unapt for every thing of that kind, that I solemnly declare I was never yet able to comprehend the principles of motion of a squirrel cage, or a common knife-grinder's wheel. [VII.xxx.519]

The chapter then closes with his thinking of "the Tomb of the two lovers" and crossing the room of the inn in long

19. Ernst Cassirer, *The Philosophy of the Enlightenment,* p. 31.

strides, which strides, "as no principle of clock-work is con-cern'd in it," he will explain in the next chapter. On the surface the whole sequence of "pitiful misadventures and cross accidents" that have made up Tristram's life is reduced to Mrs. Shandy's wayward association of the clock with the act of procreation; understood in the light of Tristram's reflec-tions, his fate is bound up with the spiritual conditions of his world, and he simply shares, as we all do, in that fate. Once more, what appears to be contradiction in fact shows that Tristram has moved beyond the Shandy community while yet remaining grounded in it. Later we shall consider in some detail the relation between word and world as Tris-tram understands it, and the reason why language acquired in such a family of "originals" necessarily leaves an indelible mark upon his world forever after. For the present it is suffi-cient to remark that having a language presupposes being in touch with other persons who respond to words in ways that strike one as akin to one's own responses. Tristram's reflec-tions on the social self make it clear that Walter's presupposi-tion of an essentially isolated subject, an alien among other isolated substances, is logically incoherent, for such a subject would have no language, would be no self, and hence no subject at all. The things Tristram thinks about, the ques-tions he asks, the issues he tries to resolve arise in the cross-currents of that original community as does the language in which he lives, moves, and has his being. His consciousness is clearly not a solitary enterprise even in the solitude of re-flection; it is irrevocably "with" others in an act of partici-pation. Nor is his relatedness to others an external, contingent attachment; it is a genuine mutuality, an ontological depen-dency of the self upon being-with others in his communal heritage. Thus he contradicts the alienation that marks the life of the family. So intimate and essential are social ties that part of the evil future that he foresees for his world includes the tendency to alter surnames "owing to the pride, or to the shame of the respective proprietors." The current tendency toward obliterating relationships "will one day so blend and confound us all together, that no one shall be able to stand up and say, 'That his own great grand father was the man who did either this or that' " (I.xi.24). The context of these remarks, furthermore, evokes a sense of their normative function, the discussion of Yorick's nine-hundred-year-old name.

The Audience

Our examination of the first of the two communities in the novel has shown the social process whereby self-consciousness is constituted and has demonstrated that Tristram is no solipsistic product of isolation. But his audience, which might be called the fourth wall of that playroom of a library, is as important to his project of self-explication as are the Shandys and must be brought right into the game itself. In this respect as in others, the novel is decidedly a child of its own age rather than of the age of the absurd, however numerous the points of kinship between the two. Its modern counterparts tend to ignore the social dimension without which the self is totally inexplicable. Tristram's relationship to his audience denies what Nietzsche's subtitle to *Zarathustra* affirms, namely, that it is *Ein Buch für alle und keinen,* a book for everyone and no one.

Tristram is a convivial person whose spirit of jovial companionship, evoked in the company of his reader, is one of the characteristic features of his book. Or, to mention another example, in volume VII where he tours the Continent, he deliberately excludes every subject that conventionally occupies the English tourist, concentrating instead and almost indiscriminately on the people of France with whom he chances to meet. The second community, established almost immediately and gradually delineated as we read, is much more abstract than the first, but it also represents a more nearly universal community. To account for himself *as* a Shandy is, on the whole, a much simpler program than accounting for himself *to* all the world besides.

One of Tristram's major concerns is the chasm that separates one person's mind from another's and the power of language to close that chasm. One might even say that the demise of the Shandy family, himself excepted, has left the social Tristram alone in his study and that his writing is an effort to establish by the power of language another community, though that would be a relatively uninteresting psychological guess only. His repeatedly introducing "our Worships" into the novel is another instance of comic devices with unplumbed depths. Having recognized the intersubjective character of language, he adds to that a recognition that is immediately available to reflection, though concealed from empirical observation of language, namely, that in talk one comes to know his own mind and that in talk (or writing), even in solitude, one imagines an audience. This recognition suggests that Tristram's public rhetoric has another side which we may characterize as reflexive and that the two sides are mutually dependent.

On the public side he brings his audience into imaginative presence within the bounds of the fiction and then watches our responses just as though we were really face to face, for he understands that when a person speaks he does not seek merely to embody in language some preconceived idea without reference to someone who hears. Examples of Tristram's direct glances at his readers are numerous and usually brief. One of the earliest and most revealing instances of direct address used to help establish the rapport, the tolerance even, that his peculiar method will require if he is to bring about in us and in himself an understanding of the significance of his life is in the first volume:

I have undertaken, you see, to write not only my life,

but my opinions also; hoping and expecting that your knowledge of my character, and of what kind of a mortal I am, by the one, would give you a better relish for the other: As you proceed further with me, the slight acquaintance which is now beginning betwixt us, will grow into familiarity; and that, unless one of us is at fault, will terminate in friendship.———*O diem praeclarum!*——— then nothing which has touched me will be thought trifling in its nature, or tedious in its telling. Therefore, my dear friend and companion, if you should think me somewhat sparing of my narrative on my first setting out, ———bear with me,———and let me go on, and tell my story my own way:———or if I should seem now and then to trifle upon the road,———or should sometimes put on a fool's cap with a bell to it, for a moment or two as we pass along,———don't fly off,———but rather courteously give me credit for a little more wisdom than appears upon my outside;———and as we jogg on, either laugh with me, at me, or in short, do anything,———only keep your temper. [I.vi.10–11]

Throughout his long, playful tale of domestic misadventures, of names and noses and forceps and window weights, of the intellectual limitations one suffers under in such a family of originals, of the unruly nature of words and the incapacity of spatial form to carry the full meaning of temporal experience, he keeps an eye on our responses to assure that his rhetoric is succeeding. Thus he chastises "Madam reader" for "a vicious taste . . . of reading straight forwards, more in quest of the adventures," than of the knowledge that such a book "would infallibly impart" (I.xx.56); or, when he needs to clear the stage of Toby's ordnance, "I Beg the reader will assist me . . . " (VI.xxix.455); or again he pleads, "Therefore, my dear friend . . . only keep your temper" (I.vi.11). In numerous other instances he betrays an intense consciousness of how his audience is responding to the narrative, how our heads feel after so much reading, how much our healths are improved by so much laughing, and how much wiser we are with so much thinking.

An understanding of the language act as rooted in a speaking community recognizes that interpretation requires a transforming of what is heard by adapting it to the prior mental structures of the reader. Unlike what happens when a computer is fed information, when reading proceeds like conversation both content and the reader are changed much as the two sides of a metaphor alter one another. Tristram's rhetoric makes a good-humored but aggressive attack on unconsciousness in his reader and seeks to change "unawareness, naive acceptance, shortsightedness, complacency, blind confidence, unquestioning conformity to habits of thought and action,"[20] as well as the habit of reading straightforward out of curiosity, into a thinking acceptance-transformation of what he says. In order to judge his success he must observe, not the form of his sentences, as though the meaning were contained in the form of the utterance and there were some kind of ideal embodiment of an idea in words, but the effects of his words, gestures, and even his silence upon us. His language act is hence not only social in origin: his writing is an essentially social act that makes his audience imaginatively present and responsive to every word. The value of this fact to his interpretive process is that in the effort to achieve a clear, hence valid, interpretation of his life, he must place it in the largest possible frame of reference. His project therefore requires the most diverse audience he can get or what was referred to above as a universal community of discourse. William Bowman Piper points out the diversity of his audience: it includes people of various ages and conditions, of both sexes, and of widely different interests.[21] The resulting

20. Johnstone, p. 125.
21. *Laurence Sterne*, pp. 21–25. Arthur Sherbo in *Studies in Eighteenth-Century English Novel*, pp. 35–57, makes a distinction between readers "inside" and readers "outside" the novel, the former serving to entangle

variety of responses has the advantage that he desires.

On the other and more obscure side, Tristram's rhetoric is reflexive, that is, addressed to himself. His ability as *rhetor* to understand the readers' hermeneutic situation is matched by his understanding of his own, and the clarity he gains occurs in the encounter as required by his example of conversation. Mead observes that "a person who is saying something is saying to himself what he says to others; otherwise he does not know what he is talking about" (p. 147). If Tristram may be presumed to understand what he says, it follows that he does so, altering it and being altered by it in turn. This phenomenon of understanding oneself by listening to what one says presupposes the transcendence of temporal consciousness. The possibility of juxtaposing different perspectives is implicit in the notion of transcendence: he is a self with a past and a self with a future. He encounters both that past and that future in the present and in fact derives his conception of past and future from the awareness that he is a being endowed with such rich possibilities as being related to itself through having been in the past and, as Heidegger says, meeting itself coming back from its future. It is within this complex texture of self-relatedness that the phenomenon of understanding oneself through speaking may be explained. His consciousness is ecstatic; it is outside of or beyond itself in the exchange with the reader, and only from that point beyond itself can new understanding arise. Mead's somewhat simpler distinction between two aspects of the self is helpful in explaining this important reflexive dimension of rhetoric: first there is the "me," the "organized sets of attitudes" which I bring with me from the past, the "me" that is given and

---

the latter in the processes of the work, but the function of the ontological ambivalence of both reader and writer, designed to blur the line between fiction and reality, would seem to insure that each "outside" reader also becomes an "inside" reader.

that occupies a position of actuality. Then there is the "I," open toward possibilities, responsive to the given situation, perpetually threatening the established actuality of the "me" with further development or revision. Thus, it is as though an earlier consciousness (the "me") interrogated a later one (the "I") about the acceptance of a given datum. Such a reflexive rhetoric puts distance between the datum and consciousness. Just as in the social origin of the self Tristram came to understand himself from a position beyond himself, namely, in the attitude of others, so he understands what he says from the position of the other. He speaks with the spontaneity of the "I"—not even the speaker himself can predict in advance what the "I" will say—and interprets what he says from the perspective of the established "me"; and since the subject spoken of is himself, the transformation of what is said results in an advance or revision of his understanding of himself. Early in "The Story of LeFever" he pulls himself up with the remark, "But this is neither here nor there——why do I mention it?——Ask my pen,——it governs me,——I govern not it" (VI.vi.416). The remark contains as much truth as roguishness, for there is a perfectly accurate sense in which he may be said not to understand what he says until after he has said it.

The essential point that must be stressed is that the two sides of Tristram's rhetoric, the public and the reflexive, though analytically distinguishable, are necessarily one. Since his subject is himself, the language in which he interprets himself to his audience is necessarily reflexive: he not only knows what he is talking about, but he is a member of the audience whose interpretive responses are an essential part of the speaking. The fact that the audience is a fabrication of his imagination at the time of writing in no way qualifies the radical understanding of the essentially social character of the language act nor of how exquisitely it is fitted to the social character of the self. It is in the dynamic relationship of these two communities, the Shandys and the audience, upon each other and upon himself that brings to light not only the social ground of the self but the perpetual process of revision opened up by living thus the examined life. The manner in which the juxtaposition of the two communities is carried out, Tristram and the Shandys submitted to the scrutiny of the audience, the Shandys and the audience to the scrutiny of Tristram, is a complex strategy which shows how profoundly the theme of intersubjectivity is studied in the novel and with what remarkable insights that study has been rewarded. If Tristram's rhetoric is genuinely reflexive, his view of himself actually in process of revision, then the position from beyond his given self that he adopts for that revision is one that he shares with and that is even made possible by his audience. His clarification of himself necessarily involves an exposition of the Shandys, for genetically he is what they are. As he watches our responses to them, moreover, he implicitly tests them and comes to understand them, and himself, from a more general human perspective, though never, being finite, from an absolutely universal one. In short, it is the intersubjective ties of Tristram with the Shandys and of Tristram with his audience that is the essence of the dialectic out of which new understanding arises for him in the act of writing his book.

Let us acknowledge the superb stroke of craftsmanship in Sterne's presenting the two communities simultaneously. Fiction usually reveals character through diachronic or horizontal presentation of the character's engagement with his world, a sequence of events in a life that passes through moments of time. Tristram's story is not concerned with the process of becoming *per se;* that would obscure the central problem Sterne wishes to explore. Instead the strategy is a synchronic or vertical presentation of the structures of Tristram's being exemplified in the juxtaposition of the two communities with which Tristram's being is bound up, however remote from each other they may be on a linear time scale, one deceased, one as yet unformed as he writes. His whole synchrony, his simultaneous being-with both communities, is present to his reflection throughout, the whole work thereby focused upon the question of the origin, structure, and, ultimately, the meaning of his being.

Sterne's reinterpretation of the relation between the individual and the social group is an important consequence of the reflexive strategy of the novel. "The classical problem was a question of passing from consciousness of self to consciousness of others," or it was "a question of constructing a representative self from others."[22] The solution that Tristram appears to favor is neither and both: he clearly derives his being from his genetic community, but he also constitutes himself by making those meanings that are derived from social relationships his own by means of an act of appropriation which makes that derived existence decisively his own. A full examination of that step in his process of retrieving himself must wait for further exploration until the problem of freedom arises later (see chapter 5 below). The understanding of the relation between Tristram's being and other selves may be summarized in the words of Merleau-Ponty: "Thus, the self and others are not two substances that are distinct from one another. Other people are what deliver me from my own *ambivalence:* we are both, he and I, two variables of the same system. By a mechanism of *pro*jection, I attribute to him qualities which in reality are my own, and inversely by *intro*jection I consider qualities which are his as my own" (p. 67). This observation explains why the act of interpretation, Tristram's of his family and thereby his being, ours of his life and his opinions, is always either implicitly or explicitly an act of self-interpretation in that fusion of horizons of which Gadamer speaks.

22. Maurice Merleau-Ponty, *Consciousness and Language Acquisition,* trans. Hugh J. Silverman, p. 37.

It should be obvious from the preceding discussion of the self that for Sterne the identity of the self is much richer and more complex than it is for Locke and those modern thinkers whose names are most frequently invoked in discussions of the novel: for the latter group (Locke, James, Bergson) to grasp the self in its totality means to see it as a past that is constitutive of its present, but Tristram's reflections provide a principle by which the structure of that past, its interpretation, and the patterns of its retention can be understood, namely, the prospect of a future possibility, a project (or projects) underway. Hence he does not recount his own past experiences but explores the dynamics of his genetic community and its constituent members. The actual dynamics of the transcendence by means of which that subjectivity with its intentional focus is constituted is the subject to which we will turn next.

3

Time, Death, and Finitude

Let us begin with St. Augustine: "it appeared to me that time is nothing but extension, but I do not know of what. It is amazing if it is not of the mind itself" (*Confessions*, p. 358). Thus in the eleventh book of *The Confessions* and a century and a half after Plotinus's *Third Ennead* had made time the life of the soul, Augustine raises the question of time in as profound a form as appears in Western thought: "What, then, is time? If no one asks me, I know; but if I want to explain it to a questioner, I do not know. Yet, I say with confidence that I know that, if nothing passed away, there would be no past time, and if nothing were coming there would be no future time" (p. 224). Augustine and everyone else who has thought seriously on the subject may have been perplexed by time, but Walter Shandy, lacking Augustine's penchant for reflective interpretation, encounters no such obstruction.

It has been just "two hours, and ten minutes" since Obadiah returned to Shandy Hall with Dr. Slop, the man-midwife, after their impromptu "Rencounter" at "an acute angle of the garden wall" which left Dr. Slop "with the broadest part of him sunk about twelve inches deep in the mire." Of the time passed Walter says,

> I know not how it happens, brother *Toby*,——but to my imagination it seems almost an age. . . . Though my father said *"he knew not how it happen'd,"*——yet he knew very well, how it happen'd;——and at the instant he

spoke it, was pre-determined in his mind, to give my uncle *Toby* a clear account of the matter by a metaphyscal dissertation upon the subject of *duration and its simple modes.* [III.xviii.188]

Then follows what Tristram calls a "discourse upon time and eternity . . . devoutly to be wished for," in fact a paraphrase from the second book of Locke's *Essay:*

> . . . *if you will turn your eyes inwards upon your mind . . . and observe attentively, you will perceive, brother, that whilst you and I are talking together, and thinking and smoking our pipes: or whilst we receive successively ideas in our minds, we know that we do exist, and so we estimate the existence, or the continuation of the existence of ourselves, or anything else commensurate to the succession of any ideas in our minds, the duration of ourselves, or any such other thing co existing with our thinking.* [III.xviii.190]

Walter goes on to regret the use of isochronous, external motions, like those of a clock as the measure of time, a regret for which he has grounds other than its threat to replace the "regular succession of ideas" as the primary experience of time.

The issue as Walter, paraphrasing Locke, presents it is whether time is as Aristotle had said, simply the "number of motion in respect of 'before' and 'after,'" in fact an ignoring of temporality in favor of the more important phenomenon of motion in space or whether it is grounded, as Locke says, in the experience of succession among mental events, an unsuccessful approach to the phenomenological description of the temporal character of all experience. In fact whether it is conceived as an objective entity independent of human existence or as a subjective way of grasping change, in either case time is reduced to a succession of discrete present moments along a linear scale. This traditional conception, which is still generally assumed in literary discussion, is useful in providing an

objective reference for dating events even as Tristram carefully works out the objective time of events in their serial
order for his book, choosing then to scramble them in a way
that may appear the most capricious. Arthur Lovejoy describes
the ordinary view in a way that suggests its limitations: "Time
as ordinarily conceived is sundered into separate moments
which are perpetually passing away. The past is forever dead
and gone, the future is non-existent and uncertain, and the
present seems, *at most, a bare knife-edge of existence* separating these two unrealities."[1] It is perhaps true to say of every
great work of fiction that in it the past is never dead, often, as
Faulkner says, "it isn't even past,"—an observation that indicates how far Walter's theory is from the truth as it is available
to reflection. And of Sterne's ability to reveal the secrets of
time in his fiction Henri Fluchère says, "La digression est plus
qu'une exultante affirmation de liberté, elle devient le docil
instrument de capture d'un réel malévole et fuyant, elle explore des domaines secrets de l'espace et du temps, de la connaissance et du mystére."[2]

Tristram's Temporalism

The Shandys do not change. Even in the protagonist there
is no development in the usual sense—either moral, intellectual, or circumstantial—in the course of nine volumes; and it
has therefore been argued that where there is no becoming,
there is no "being time" as opposed to public or calendar
time.[3] The observation about the characters is correct, of
course, but from what has already been said it should now be
clear that a sequence of events or a process of growth would be
extraneous to the ontological character of the work. The

1. *The Reason, the Understanding and Time*, p. 75.
2. *Laurence Sterne, de l'homme à l'oeuvre*, p. 248.
3. Traugott, p. 39.

analysis is of a being whose existence is process, but the method is the reflexive explication of the synchronic structures of that being. It would appear to be strange, then, that the question of time should arise at all. And yet the subject comes up repeatedly, for in Tristram's effort at self-interpretation, he collides against a temporal phenomenon that cannot be explained by Aristotle's reduction of time to a tool for measuring being nor by Locke's making the origin of time the psychological experience of sequence. What we shall be examining is only secondarily those passages in which the problematic of time is explicitly raised. The primary concern is with Tristram's general posture throughout the novel. It is in the effort to reveal the full panorama of his conscious field just as it is present to him (simultaneously, that is) and in his inability to do so with the single blinding flash of a syllable, that consciousness is revealed as a simultaneity of past, present, and future and not as a series of one thing after another like words on a string.

In one of the best-known passages concerned with the theme Tristram remarks that although it has been "about an hour and a half's tolerable good reading" since Obadiah was sent for Dr. Slop, a "hypercritic" who measures fictional time objectively by the pendulum will object that it has in fact been "no more than two minutes, thirteen seconds, and three fifths." Tristram, however, rejects all but "the true scholastic pendulum," the "succession of our ideas" from which derives "the idea of duration and of its simple modes." Using Locke's own language he thereby grounds temporal verisimilitude upon subjective time:

> I would, therefore, desire [the critic] to consider that it is but poor eight miles from *Shandy-Hall* to Dr. *Slop,* the man midwife's house;——and that whilst *Obadiah* has been going those said miles and back, I have brought my uncle *Toby* from *Namur,* quite across all *Flanders,* into *England:*——That I have had him ill upon my hands

near four years;——and have since travelled him and Corporal *Trim*, in a chariot and four, a journey of near two hundred miles down into *Yorkshire*;——all which put together, must have prepared the reader's imagination for the entrance of Dr. *Slop* upon the stage. [II.viii. 103–04]

In this passage Tristram is clearly in agreement with Walter's "metaphysical dissertation" already examined. There is one important difference, however: where Walter is offering an explanation of time itself, Tristram is only giving an account of the reader's sense of the passage of narrative time. This point must be stressed because I wish to argue that the implication of Tristram's reflections is that time, instead of being grounded upon the "succession of our ideas," is itself the ground of our idea of succession, that time is a function of the self understood as transcendence. Tristram traces our idea of the duration of Obadiah's journey to the psychical fact of the succession and duration of our ideas in reading his narrative. But the succession of ideas is not the same as the idea of succession; nor is the duration of an idea the same as the idea of duration. Walter and Locke overlook the distinction, but Tristram's interest in time passes over the mere succession of sensations to focus instead upon the conscious recognition of sequence itself which is grounded upon the immanent experience of temporality.

Having recognized a fictional time in the novel, it is only necessary to say of it what has been widely recognized, that Tristram suggests the absurd consequences of realism by claiming that he must provide an hour's reading for each lived hour of his life.[4] The consequent dilemma is well known:

4. Ian Watt, *The Rise of the Novel: Studies in Defoe, Richardson, and Fielding*, p. 292. The term *specious present* is sometimes used for this idea, but it is ambiguous. Sometimes it refers to the recent past retained in the present, but in William James's usage it looks forward as well as behind: "In short, the practically cognized present is no knife-edge, but a saddle-

I am this month one whole year older than I was this time twelve-month; and having got, as you perceive, almost into the middle of my fourth volume———and no farther than to my first day's life———'tis demonstrative that I have three hundred and sixty-four days more life to write just now, than when I first set out; so that instead of advancing, as a common writer, in my work with what I have been doing at it———on the contrary, I am just thrown so many volumes back.... At this rate I should just live 364 times faster than I should write———It must follow, an' please your worships, that the more I write, the more I shall have to write———and consequently, the more your worships read, the more your worships will have to read. [IV.xiii.285–86]

We need only pause to wonder that this passage has so often been taken as a serious statement of an impossible objective which dooms Tristram's enterprise to failure. How can he possibly be serious in saying that we shall have an hour of reading for each hour of living when he makes no effort anywhere in his book to give us anything of the actual texture of his daily life?—I except volume VII for now as a special case. In claiming that fiction must convey the texture of the public scale of time measured in hours and days, implicitly therefore that objective time is primary, this passage is not even as sophisticated as that of Walter for whom public time is at least

---

back, with a certain breadth of its own on which we sit perched, and from which we look in two directions into time. The unit of composition of our perception of time is a *duration,* with a bow and a stern, as it were—a rearward- and a forward-looking end. It is only as parts of this *duration-block* that the relation of *succession* of one end to the other is perceived. We do not first feel one end and then feel the other after it, and from the perception of the succession infer an interval of time between, but we seem to feel the interval of time as a whole, with its two ends embedded in it. The experience is from the outset a synthetic datum, not a simple one; and to sensible perception its elements are inseparable, although attention looking back may easily decompose the experience, and distinguish its beginning from its end" (*The Principles of Psychology,* I, 609–10).

a derived form. The consequence of Walter's view, and of Tristram's, unless we acknowledge that he deepens Locke's understanding, would be that realism of presentation must consist in simply conveying the sequence of the protagonist's subjective experience. But Tristram does much more.

Just as the surface texture of mental events in the characters may be understood as having a surface resemblance to a Humean doctrine of associationism, while actually being grounded in a purposive focus expressed in the principle of intentionality, so the surface of its temporal texture would appear to be a shallow Lockean subjectivism. In fact, Tristram's moments of subjective experience are founded upon an experiential orientation of consciousness which simultaneously includes within its scope the three modes of time, present-past-future.

Walter's subjective view can say about the present moment only that it is before him, of the past that it is gone, and of the future that it is "not yet." Of the relations that obtain among the triune modes of time therefore he can say nothing. In fact he cannot even account for our recognizing the moment as present since his theory allows for no temporal depth to the apprehension, depth of the kind that would distinguish this moment as other than the moment just past. Nor does the invocation of memory help since that locates the function by which the past becomes significant, but without explaining how the past is related to consciousness in the present. It is only by virtue of the time-forming activity of consciousness that one conceives of a continuity of present moments or even of any particular moment whatever. Only by reference to the temporality of consciousness would we know, for example, if the sequence of present moments began somehow to run backward. Awareness of a present is possible because of a subjective temporal context analyzed by Husserl in what he refers to as "retentions" and "protentions."[5] The present is not a

5. *The Phenomenology of Internal Time-Consciousness,* trans. James S. Churchill, section 2.

simple moment; it is highly complex in that it contains elements of both the immediate past and the immediate future. If we listen to uncle Toby's whistling his *argumentum fistulatorium* in the form of "Lillibulero," it is obvious that with each passing tone the context of each subsequent tone in the melody is enriched by our retention of what has preceded, especially by the essential retention of the key that governs the tune. Equally obvious is the way the melody points forward to (or protends) its completion, the resolution of its progression, the achievement of its final wholeness. A given tone is no more an isolated phenomenon for us than an idea in Tristram's mind is an atom of mental experience unrelated to its neighbors. There is more than just analogy in the parallel with music: the temporal processes of the book are those of consciousness and those of music.[6] The two temporal arts derive their power from their close kinship with the most intimate function of consciousness, though language also adds the significative function. Joan Stambaugh has pointed out that in musical time, past, present, and future are simultaneous:

> Musical time does not have an objective, abstract, "non-musical" future and past as its orientation. It sets up, so to speak, its own future and past, and it does this *constantly in the process of its own motion.* . . . This is the very essence of musical motion: the constant creation of a future and a past in the actual present moment, in *each* present moment. Even this moment is not present in the strict sense; it is not there in front of the listener in the manner of an object. The moment of musical time is not present, it is at best present*ing,* creating the temporal tension of what has gone before and what is to come, the tension of the whole in the moment.[7]

6. Cf. William Freedman, *"Tristram Shandy:* The Art of Literary Counterpoint," *Modern Language Quarterly* 32 (1971), 268–80. Freedman points out the unusual emphasis on music in the novel and argues that the novel is structurally similar to music.

7. "Music as a Temporal Form," *Journal of Philosophy* 61 (1964), 276; quoted in Freedman, p. 273.

Likewise, in Tristram's revelation of the primitive form of time the experience of the present is possible in the context of a past retained and a future expected, and the sequential scale of present moments, as Walter conceives of it, is derived from the temporality of consciousness itself which simultaneously includes within its glance all three modes of time.

However, it is one thing to argue that this way of accounting for inner-time consciousness is valid; quite another to claim that Tristram's own view of time is phenomenological. In the light of what has already been established about the character of Tristram's enterprise, we need not expect him to argue for or against any intellectual position or proposition. As he seeks an understanding of the foundations of his own being, he often speaks satirically of views that he may be presumed not to share (to my mind Walter's understanding of time is one), but a danger implicit in using the satiric tone as evidence is that as critics we are tempted to regard as satiric whatever in the book does not support our own conclusions. I prefer therefore to go another way around.

Two points must be established: first, that the conceptual horizon as represented in the novel is itself temporal; and second, that the mode of future is prior to the modes of past and present in that temporal glance.

We have discussed Tristram's explication of Toby's consciousness by observing the relation of focal theme to its marginal thematic field. We now add the observation that the field of consciousness is itself temporal. Thus when Tristram explains his father's extravagant affliction upon learning of the mutilation of Tristram's nose at birth, he leaves Walter lying in an attitude of despair across the bed while he writes a "chapter of noses" for the purpose of explaining what the present moment cannot give us, the interpretive synthesis of the three modes of time that constitutes Walter's simultaneous understanding of the misfortune. The effect of that "uninterrupted sequence of six or seven short noses" upon the family is a past context which contributes materially to Walter's anguish; but it also has a future dimension, for he wants a son who can remove the stigma of impotence from the House of Shandy, a malaise that we recognize as more than sexual, a general spiritual impotence which makes oiling the squeaking hinge on the parlor door quite as impossible as begetting healthy sons. The dimension of the future, of frustrated expectations and dashed hopes, has its part in the synthesis that is Walter's response to the unhappy event.

All of Walter's theoretical projects exemplify the temporal structure of his conceptual horizon, but to external observation such as Tristram makes of Walter, the phenomenon of anticipation is so commonplace as to be hardly worth mentioning except as it emphasizes the role of end-directedness which turns otherwise random events into an organized project, an acting *toward* or *for* rather than the more commonly assumed causality of acting *because* of, of being pushed from behind. Confirming evidence that the historical shape of Tristram's phenomenal world derives from the temporality of his own being must come from his reflections upon himself, but it is important to observe that he explains the behavior of other characters by specifically exploring the temporal dimensions of their interpretations of events and that the exploration reveals more than just the cumulative effect of a past. The use of Bergson's "durée" and James's "specious present" in the criticism has pointed to a certain temporal density in Tristram's experience with special emphasis on how the past is brought forward, somewhat like a snowball, into the constitution of the present. The view helps show "that the total past of any individual is implicit in any given moment,"[8] but this essentially geometrical notion that reduces time to a process of becoming is not part of Sterne's novel and, therefore, does not explain the radical temporalism of the book. Heidegger's analysis of temporality as the meaning of care

8. Holtz, p. 104.

provides the conceptual tools that bring to clarity this still obscure theme of the novel.[9] Tristram's general stance in the entire novel is to hold in the field of his mind the full range of his being, his past experience, his present activity of writing, and his future possibilities. Nor is this merely a strategy of his art. It is the essential condition of self-consciousness, for that consciousness consists in a relatedness of the self to itself from points beyond itself, a synthesis of the self that is as having

9. *Being and Time*, pp. 349–82. Heidegger's explanation of the term *care* (*Sorge*) as it refers to the meaning of human being is explicitly onto-logical and may not be reduced to contingent (ontic) psychological states such as worry and grief: "the Being of Dasein means ahead-of-itself-Being-already-in-(the-world) as Being-alongside (entities encountered within-the-world)" (ibid., p. 237). The definition implies that as *under-standing*, human being *is* its possibilities (ahead-of-itself); as *state-of-mind*, it *is* thrown or situated in a word that imposes actual limits upon it; and as *falleness* it *is* occupied with everyday affairs. These three "existentials," furthermore, correspond to the modes of future, past, and present respec-tively. Heidegger illustrates his view by citing one of the fables of Hyginus which I quote for the grace and clarity it brings to this important but enigmatical analysis: "Once when 'Care' was crossing a river, she saw some clay; she thoughtfully took up a piece and began to shape it. While she was meditating on what she had made, Jupiter came by. 'Care' asked him to give it spirit, and this he gladly granted. But when she wanted her name to be bestowed upon it, he forbade this, and demanded that it be given his name instead. While 'Care' and Jupiter were disputing, Earth arose and desired that her own name be conferred on the creature, since she had furnished it with part of her body. They asked Saturn to be their arbiter, and he made the following decision, which seemed a just one: 'Since you, Jupiter, have given its spirit, you shall receive that spirit at its death; and since you, Earth, have given its body, you shall receive its body. But since "Care" first shaped this creature, she shall possess it as long as it lives. And because there is now a dispute among you as to its name, let it be called "*homo*," for it is made out of *humus* (earth)' " (ibid., p. 242). It is also of historical interest to note that in the so-called Kant Books (*Kant and the Problem of Metaphysics* and *What is a Thing?*) Heidegger traces his analysis of time to the "A" edition of *The Critique of Pure Reason* though it is a largely original effort to retrieve Kant's perspective on the problem, not an interpretation of what the critique says.

been (that is, a retention of the self as past), the self that is now, and the self that is as future possibility (that is, a protention of a future self that is possible). This temporal density of self-consciousness in the present moment is the ground which Locke did not discover of the experience of sequence, the necessary point of reference from which one can be aware that one thing follows another or, for that matter, even be aware of anything at all. Time thus is the structure of Tristram's being, the transcendence on the ground of which consciousness or subjectivity is possible.

The second claim, that Tristram reveals the future as the primary or foundational mode in the temporal structure of the conscious act or that he lives in terms of the future, is explained by a principle apparently first introduced into the discussion of time by Heidegger. Examples of Tristram's recognition of the priority of the possible over the actual in conceptual experience may begin with recalling the kitchen scene when the servants hear of Bobby's death. To each it is the opening of a future possibility—Susannah of inheriting the green gown; Obadiah, of clearing the ox-moor—that decisively conditions their understanding of the news. The deeper significance of anticipation is revealed when Tristram's gaze is turned on himself. In that interior, reflexive perspective, conventional ways of treating time give way to radical exploration that is not even approached by the ordinary distinction between clock time and psychological time, for in Tristram himself we have direct access to temporality as the meaning of being human and, within the temporal mode of human being, to the priority of the future.

As he confronts his project, the understanding and articulation of his own present being, he sees his being simultaneously reaching toward its origin in the past, which is only approximately his conception and birth, and toward his destiny in the future, which is certainly his death. These temporal modes are not parts of a thing called time which he passes through; they are not even merely the structures of his understanding or, as Kant says, the form of inner sense; they are the structures of his own temporal existing. Thus he does not seek to reveal what is most important about himself by offering a sequence of present moments of experience. As he confronts himself, he projects a time field in which his experiences of the other (people, objects, events) take place and are organized "in respect of 'before' and 'after.' " Furthermore, it is in this temporally conditioned encounter with the other that he becomes aware of his own transcendence; or, to put it another way, it is the experience of the other in the temporal field of his consciousness that enables him to recognize himself experiencing. Among the three tenses of his being it is the future or his openness to possibility that shapes both the past and the present dimensions of himself and his experience. The most decisive of the anticipations to which his being is open is death, but the most important intermediate possibility is writing or completing his book. It is the choice to be in this way, to write his life, that supplies the principle of relevance or defines the field in which the highly selective function of memory will dredge up his past. The present activity of writing does not shape the past of which he is aware; indeed, the present moment, whenever it comes into view at all, as when he is frustrated by the number of things he must say all at once, takes its own meaning from within the field defined by his intentional orientation toward a future goal. It is in this sense that the future may be said to be prior to the past as the past is to the present, the key interpretive concept in the structure of consciousness.

A particular event in the text that reveals this strange futurism in his point of view occurs in volume III where Tristram is baffled by the need to arrange the contents of his simultaneous temporal field along the unidimensional scale of sequential narrative time:

> My mother, you must know,———but I have fifty things
> more necessary to let you know first,———I have a hundred

difficulties which I have promised to clear up, and a thousand distresses and domestic misadventures crouding in upon me thick and three-fold, one upon the neck of another,——a cow broke in (tomorrow morning) to my uncle *Toby's* fortifications, and eat up two ratios and a half of dried grass. . . . ——*Trim* insists upon being tried by a court-martial,——the cow to be shot,——*Slop* to be *crucifix'd,*——myself to be *tristram'd,* and at my very baptism made a martyr of;——poor unhappy devils that we all are!——I want swaddling,——but there is no time to be lost in exclamations.——I have left my father lying across his bed, and my uncle *Toby* in his old fringed chair, sitting beside him, and promised I would go back to them in half an hour, and five and thirty minutes are laps'd already.——Of all the perplexities a mortal author was ever seen in,——this certainly is the greatest,——for I have *Hafen Slawkenbergius's* folio, Sir, to finish——a dialogue between my father and my uncle *Toby,* upon the solution of *Prignitz, Scroderus, Ambrose Paraeus, Ponocrates,* and *Grangousier* to relate,——a tale out of *Slawkenbergius* to translate, and all this in five minutes less, than no time at all;——such a head!——would to heaven! my enemies only saw the inside of it! [III. xxxviii.235]

This passage is usually understood as a comment on both human limitations and the formal limitations of the novel,[10] and that is correct so far as it goes. But the passage is cast in the language of possibility, futurity, and Tristram's own finitude which reveals much more than such general limitations. The sense of what is to be done arouses this legion of memories, bringing them into presence where he encounters his essential inability to present them all in less than no public time. In a sense this emphasis upon the future is a reversal of

10. New, "Laurence Sterne and Henry Baker's *The Microscope Made Easy,*" pp. 596–97. New correctly observes that the theme of time has importance beyond its function in ordering the narrative events.

time, a kind of blueprint in the present, for Tristram sees the history of his own mind and the history of his family in the light of his potential for achieving his aim, in the light of a goal that provides the unifying principle of his selfhood.

The correlative question of craftsmanship and of formal restraints is derivative from this temporalism. The simultaneity of various things to be done might be compared to a later technical solution: Huxley's shifts in narration back and forth between different but related events in *Point Counterpoint* create the illusion of simultaneity that cannot actually be expressed in a row of words. When Tristram is ready to write his preface, he disposes of all his characters in a brief synchronistic account that stresses the simultaneity of actions under way:

> As for my uncle *Toby*, his smoak-jack had not made a dozen revolutions, before he fell asleep also.——Peace be with them both.——Dr. *Slop* is engaged with the midwife, and my mother above stairs.——*Trim* is busy in turning an old pair of jack-boots into a couple of mortars to be employed in the siege of *Messina* next summer,—— and is this instant boring the touch holes with the point of a hot poker.——All my heroes are off my hands;—— 'tis the first time I have had a moment to spare,——and I'll make use of it, and write my preface. [III.xx.192]

Just as various lines of action proceed at the same time, so Tristram holds them in mind at the same time. The technical limitation is not, as it is usually assumed, a limitation of language or of narrative. He has succeeded in representing the dense texturing of the present moment of awareness, the contents of which are arranged into earlier than, later than, and simultaneous with. The restriction resides in the way one acquires the particular constituents of that field. He cannot convey a variety of experiences in a moment any more than he acquired them in a moment, but once we have read the book, the word "Tristram" alone can "say" or call into presence not only the whole field of his mind but the whole world of the novel. But before we can pursue the question of the word, other issues associated with temporality require attention.

The foregoing analysis of the temporal structure of transcendence extends the earlier understanding of the self as a subjectivity, reaching out toward an object world, to a more primitive level at which the self is a temporal project already immersed in presubjective relationships with a preobjective world. There is not sufficient evidence to argue finally that Tristram actually understands human temporality to be the basis of objective standard time. His interest after all is not in time *per se* or in any other philosophic thesis. But when he reflects upon his own being and its temporality, that future-past-present synthesis of its gaze stands out, and when he is engaged in recording his reflections, his temporal being and the public scale of time tend to conflict, with the effect of recalling to his awareness his own essential finitude. We are now prepared to understand why the coherent objective time scheme of the book remains submerged in an apparent chaos of temporal sequences. If we assume a linear structure of time, then Tristram will be observed to perform acrobatic leaps from fifty years after his death to the reign of Harry VIII to "five minutes less than no time at all." But if we see that an objective historical scale is an abstraction from, a kind of public grid we put over this primordial time-forming activity of consciousness, then we will understand that he gives us a just representation of his future-past-present being *as it appears* to reflection.

This account of the theme of time differs substantially from the view that has prevailed in the recent critical discussions of the novel in two major respects. First and as has already been shown, it argues that neither time nor any other major thematic concern in the book is merely a theme among themes, as appropriate, but no more appropriate, than any other that happens to occupy Tristram's attention. Instead time is a regional enquiry dictated by the central ontological character of the novel. This means among other things that Tristram is not at liberty to adopt just any conceptual description of time that he might find comically, satirically, or otherwise intellectually useful. He comes to the subject because his own being, and hence his project, is necessarily involved in the issue, and in his treatment of it he is guided by the nature of that involvement rather than by either a logic of concepts or by whim. The second way in which this manner of treating the problem differs from current views is in claiming that instead of being in retreat from his own temporality, and ultimately from the possibility of death, he embraces it.

Spatial Form and Temporal Being

Before turning to the large issue of Tristram's finitude and the theme of death, there is a question of form that is inseparable from this general discussion of time, namely, so-called spatial form. When Joseph Frank developed the theory from Lessing's fairly conventional eighteenth-century distinction between the art of painting with its "form and color in space" and the art of poetry with its "articulated sounds in time," he was seeking to account only for modern departures in narrative structure.[11] He does not mention *Tristram Shandy* specifically, but in recent years the theory has been extended to Sterne's novel, notably by William Holtz's *Image and Immortality* (see pp. 90–106).

In the *Laocoön* Lessing says that painting must present "subjects of which the wholes or parts exist in juxtaposition; while consecutive symbols can only express subjects of which the wholes or parts are themselves consecutive."[12] The theory of spatial form claims that the tendency of literature that aims

---

11. "Spatial Form in Modern Literature," *The Sewanee Review* 53 (Spring, Summer, Autumn 1945), p. 223.

12. Quoted in Frank, p. 223.

at simultaneous apprehension of fields of meaning is to use the inevitable sequential character of language to create spatial forms that are apprehended in an instant of time. Frank quotes Pound's definition of "image" as "that which presents an intellectual and emotional complex in an instant of time,"[13] a presumed endorsement of spatiality as more nearly approximating the character of apprehension than temporality, though Pound explicitly says that the presentation that he has in mind gives "a sense of sudden liberation; that sense of freedom from time limits and space limits."[14] In point of fact Frank's use of the term *spatial form* is highly misleading in that the structures he has in mind are no more spatial than is linear narrative. Whenever we describe time, we do so in metaphors of space; thus we think of narrative as a unidimensional, linear movement in a spatial field whereas *spatial form* is a metaphor of an organization in a two-dimensional field. Though the metaphor is unfortunate in some of its consequences, the emphasis upon synchronic patterns of meaning is highly useful.

The discussion of time has pointed out how every moment contains within its own character residues of past moments and anticipations of future moments without which the present moment would not be distinguishable at all. But the need to know all of a discourse before fully understanding the parts, the need for global presentation, to use a three-dimensional metaphor, encourages the development of forms that give the illusion at least of simultaneous apprehension. The term "simultaneous" remains, of course, a temporal frame that places an event in the time of human experience, not a qualifier that removes it to an inconceivable realm of timelessness.

13. Quoted from "A Few Don'ts by an Imagiste," *Poetry* 1 (March 1913), 200–01.

14. Walter Sutton makes this point in "The Literary Image and the Reader," *Journal of Aesthetics and Art Criticism* 16, no. 1 (1957–58), 113.

It is important for the sake of clarity to insist that there is nothing inherently spatial about simultaneous apprehension: simultaneity is as temporal as twenty years, only shorter. Moreover, it is an exaggerated characterization of the temporal aspect of the happening of a picture to a temporal being whose eye must move around the canvas, studying, gathering, responding, in briefer time perhaps, but not in principle different from reading a text, for a proper understanding of any work of literature requires that one finish it and hold it present in mind as a totality. Pound, by contrast, speaks of an experience that is truly simultaneous like the sudden burst of insight.

The theory of spatial form is a response to the need for a more nearly adequate model of time, one that will supersede the linear sequences of now-moments, each without synchronic depth. Modern literature has succeeded in bringing the temporal sequences of language more in line with the natural sequences of mental experience; but it has not denied its basic temporalism. Thus Proust juxtaposes two "snapshots" of a character at two different periods of his life in order to dramatize the significance of time itself. These moments of Proust's "pure time," in Frank's view, "are not time at all—it is perception in a moment of time, that is to say, space" (p. 239). But Proust's "pure time" is primordial time, the very heart of the matter, not space. The unity of past and present, instead of obliterating history, is its necessary prior condition in the sense that the pervasive temporality of consciousness by which events are arranged into before and after is the essential form in which all representations, as of objects in space, become available.

One of the reasons for confusion is that the conceptions of space and time that dominate the discussion of spatial form are Newtonian, that is, space and time as containers in which things and events occur. Instead, modern discussion must respond to the new formulation of the issue implicit in the

Copernican Revolution of Kant's first critique and its exploration of the logical structure of all human knowledge. The Transcendental Aesthetic opens with an examination of space and time as the "two pure [that is, devoid of content] forms [that is, ways of receiving] of sensible intuition."[15] In saying that pictures are best suited to imitations of objects, Lessing had anticipated Kant's view that space belongs to the domain of objects, but for Kant this is true in a radically subjective way, namely, it is the form of "outer sense" or the logically prior condition for the apprehension of any sensible thing. Time is the form of "inner sense" and, as the Analytic shows, is not simply coordinate with, but is more pervasive than space inasmuch as time is the principle of internal order which in governing all human experience includes the experience of external objects that must fall within its domain in order to appear at all. Thus everything spatial is necessarily also temporal. As has already been observed, time is not a thing that a character or an event can be *in;* it is "the capacity of the subject to have internally coherent experience ... the universal element in all experience,"[16] and this not only in the Kantian sense of grounding all cognition but in the ontological sense of the rudimentary structure of the being of man. (To be precise we would need to say that events occur temporally, take time, have duration or belong to history, rather than that they are *in* time.) Were it not for this important principle of the priority of the temporal over the spatial, it would follow that either space and time would be entirely separate dimensions of experience requiring a third term to unify them in experience or temporality would have to be grounded in the category of space, both unlikely alternatives for reasons that need not delay us here.

15. Immanuel Kant, *The Critique of Pure Reason,* trans. Norman Kemp Smith, p. 67.
16. Charles M. Sherover, *Heidegger, Kant and Time*, pp. 54–55.

Holtz has opened the issue of spatial form in *Tristram Shandy* in a provocative way by analyzing Sterne's handling of the chronological narrative that was a staple of fictive technique and by discussing Sterne's relation to eighteenth-century pictorialism in general. Whereas the novel had been limited to demands of ordinary chronology, or in the mischievous phrase, one damn thing after another, Sterne recognized "the inadequacy of chronological narrative as a record of inner experience." The term *spatial form,* Holtz points out, is a metaphor for "a unity or gestalt . . . perceived among elements temporally presented but not necessarily related by . . . narrative principles." The point is not a specifically "pictorial or even spatial quality" but "the implied stasis of the artifact as 'wholly known' " (p. 103). The central problem in Tristram's book is to establish his own identity as enduring through the flux of temporal experience (Holtz, p. 138).

If one keeps in mind that Holtz's use of the word *time* refers exclusively to conventional, linear time, his discussion is illuminating. The distinction that Lessing clarifies between words and pictures for actions and things, respectively (which permeates eighteenth-century literature, motivating poets to create illusions of pictorial presentation of the external world of things in sequences of words and tempting painters to create illusions of action in the static dimensions of canvas) is brought to a new degree of complexity in Sterne's novel. As he inherited it, the form presented life in a temporal sequence of acts dominated by chronology, but the narrative of action leaves out most of the complexities that Tristram's life must reveal. In place of external action, it is concerned with "the movement of the human mind" (Holtz, p. 100), but not simply with inner sequences, for "its ultimate goal" is to make us "share Tristram's own awareness of himself as the complex result of a history still totally present in his mind" (p. 105). Thus the tension between the rival needs for diachronic structure to present the subjective process for experience and synchronic structure to reveal the enduring identity or integrity of the protagonist as a person—metaphorically the journey and the picture—come into irreconcilable conflict. Sterne therefore subverts the normal linear structure which among his predecessors was "a capitulation to time" by shattering the time scheme of the novel and substituting "a nontemporal principle of order" (Holtz, pp. 99, 101).

By bringing to light this underlying conflict in the novel, Holtz enables us to advance the boundaries of our understanding a bit farther provided we do not limit ourselves to the conception of time as a linear scale. In truth, to claim that Tristram rejects a temporal scheme and yet to acknowledge that "spatial form" is only metaphoric is to leave us with a nontemporal, nonspatial something (we know not what), "a counterform that can metaphorically be called spatial by virtue of the seeming irrelevance of time to its structure and to the order of its growth" and that undertakes "to approximate the nontemporal quality of experience" (p. 106). When he counters Lessing by suggesting that "the logical ranges of the arts are not necessarily their effective ranges" because the mind is active in shaping its perceptions and is hence able to suspend disbelief when pictures are drawn in words, Holtz implies some qualification of Lessing's antithesis of space and time as logically discrete categories. But beyond that he refuses to go, explicitly rejecting Frank Kermode's efforts to explain spatial form as a special case of time, a clear requirement of the Kantian analysis of the categories.

The useful intuition behind the theory of spatial form arises not from the need to account for a general retreat from temporality in literature, but from the frontal assault that *Tristram Shandy,* like much later poetry and fiction, makes upon the essence of phenomenal time at the center of what the eighteenth century called human nature. To be sure, narrative in the old sense has given way to new patterns with a different logic, but they are nonetheless temporal. It is especially important to distinguish between a rejection of an inadequate model of time as a sequence of now-moments and a total rejection of temporality. Holtz, on the contrary, agrees with Frank in claiming that "modern writers . . . have . . . attempted to transcend the time logic implicit in language and to force an apprehension of their verbal artifices in a moment of time rather than as a sequence of moments—to achieve a form that renders with a feeling of simultaneity a complex set of relationships, just as the visual arts present objects juxtaposed in an instant of 'time" (pp. 101–02). There are three serious consequences of getting at the problem in this way. The first is of more theoretical than practical importance in a discussion of fiction, namely, that the foregoing analysis encourages one to throw the baby out with the bath-water. By confusing temporality in general with sequential presentation, one is led to reject the very dimension of a character's being without which he would have no consciousness whatever, for the phrase "nontemporal apprehension," as earlier discussion has shown, is simply contradictory. It is only by virtue of the ec-static, time-forming function of consciousness, which arranges its simultaneous conceptual field into the temporal modes of past (antecedents), future (project), and present (execution), that transcendence comes to be and any apprehension whatever becomes possible. The second consequence that follows from categorically rejecting temporality is prominent in Sterne criticism: one is asked to see "Tristram's nontemporal, spatial narrative mode . . . as an evasion of the threat of death, the ultimate problem of time" (Holtz, p. 138). By using the term *nontemporal* for what is in fact a more complex spatial metaphor for a more complex temporality, one is tempted to interpret Tristram's general attitude toward time as negative and escapist. Third, confusing the spatial metaphor with the denial of time leads one to reject "the time logic implicit in language" and thereby seriously to bias the further enquiry into the character of language, specifically, the parallels between, on the one hand, the dia-chronic character of language which yet admits of unlimited synchronic richness and, on the other, the temporal self which is a self by virtue of its capacity, at each moment in its history, to hold simultaneously in mind its total history and its open horizon of future possibilities.[17]

The present interpretation of *Tristram Shandy* as phenom-enological reflection enables one to see why the rival metaphors of the picture and the journey become unusually problematic in the book. The concern with space and time and even with narrative technique itself, as has been said already, appear as divisions within the general ontological enquiry. Thus the relative importance of space and time must not be explored primarily as a question of literary technique as such, but as aspects of Tristram's being.

It is helpful, therefore, to reflect upon the fact that for all the tableaux in the novel, for all the characters interrupted and suspended in midair while other events occur in what is to be understood as the same time, for all the visual detailing of pose and gesture, space does not enter the novel as an in-dependent theme.[18] The reason is evident: space is the domain of the empirical and Tristram's method is not empirical. Inso-far as he must study life in Shandy Hall as part—and that a very large part—of his project, he does so empirically and thus spatially. The splendid tableau in which Mrs. Shandy stands for five minutes and eight chapters outside the parlor door, finger to her lips, listening intently while two scenes proceed simultaneously is a case in point:

———holding in her breath, and bending her head a little

17. For the bearing of this temporalism on language, see chapter 4 below.

18. Tristram's neglect of space contrasts, for example, with the sensitivity of Jane Austen's characters to private as opposed to public spaces. See Francis R. Hart, "The Spaces of Privacy: Jane Austen," *Nineteenth-Century Fiction* 30 (December 1975), 305–33; and on the phenomenology of space see Gaston Bachelard, *The Poetics of Space,* trans. Maria Jolas.

downwards, with a twist of her neck———(not towards the door, but from it, by which means her ear was brought to the chink)———she listened with all her powers. . . .

In this attitude I am determined to let her stand . . . till I bring up the affairs . . . to the same period. [V.v. 357–58]

While she stands thus at rapt attention, Walter and Trim respond in contrasting rhetorical styles to the fact of Bobby's death, the one on the other side of the parlor door, the other below stairs in the kitchen. The effect of such scenes to give the comic illusion of several actions moving simultaneously is well understood.[19]

Another example, this one a picture of Walter's despair at the news that Tristram's nose has been crushed "as flat as a pancake to his face" by Dr. Slop's forceps, demonstrates Walter's instantaneous response to the news: "———Lead me, brother *Toby,* cried my father, to my room this instant."

The moment my father got up into his chamber, he threw himself prostrate across his bed in the wildest disorder imaginable, but at the same time, in the most lamentable attitude of a man borne down with sorrows, that ever the eye of pity dropp'd a tear for.———The palm of his right hand, as he fell upon the bed, receiving his forehead, and covering the greatest part of both his eyes, gently sunk down with his head (his elbow giving way backwards) till his nose touch'd the quilt;———his left arm hung insensible over the side of the bed, his knuckles reclining upon the handle of the chamber pot, which peep'd out beyond the valance,———his right leg (his left being drawn up towards his body) hung half over the side of the bed, the edge of it pressing upon his shin-bone. ———He felt it not. A fix'd inflexible sorrow took possession of every line of his face.———He sigh'd once,——— heaved his breast often,———but utter'd not a word. [III. xxix.215–16]

19. Watt, p. 293.

It should be observed in passing that scenes like this one, which happens, like so many in the novel, before Tristram could have been an actual observer, correspond nevertheless to the earliest memories of childhood which are usually just such tableaux preserved in realistic detail most of which goes unnoticed in the interpretive gaze of ordinary adult consciousness.

What needs to be added is that as common as such scenes are, they are supportive of, but distinguishable from the central focus of the novel; that is to say, they render the empirical context in which Tristram's temporal project of explicating his own being proceeds. If Tristram's view of himself were essentially empirical as his access to others is, as Locke's examination of the mind is, and as other eighteenth-century protagonists in fiction usually are, then space and "spatial form" might predominate. Instead, all "spatial" representation is subordinated to the temporal nucleus of the project, and what appears to be conflict between spatial and temporal presentation is in fact complementary.

If time is a problem of literary procedure for Tristram, that is because it is first problematic in itself. Where his presentations of other characters are often pictorial, and empirical whether pictorial or not, his most direct presentation of himself is reflexive and temporal, for, as was observed earlier, he is not thing but act. This general observation must of course withstand the challenge offered by the action of volume VII where he assumes the density of character and travels on the Continent and where his response to his temporality and impending death is a catalyst of the action. The significance of volume VII and its relation to the novel as a whole will occupy us presently; but within the account of his journey there occurs an incident that demonstrates the way his unorthodox technical management of material reveals the very core of the whole work. During his journey through Europe, he pauses at Auxerre, which he had visited in his youth while on tour with his father, Toby, Trim, Obadiah, and the rest of the family—except for his mother who was at home knitting "a pair of large worsted breeches." The party had stopped in Auxerre and at Walter's insistence visited the crypt of the abbey of St. Germain, an event which is of the utmost pertinence at the later period to the aging and consumptive Tristram. The coalescence of the two journeys in his mind at this point, like the moments of "pure time" in Proust, effectively measures the changes time has wrought upon him, but the passage is further complicated by the temporal frame in which he writes the account and is marked as the most puzzling of all the threads of his narrative:

> ——Now this is the most puzzled skein of all——for in this last chapter, as far at least as it help'd me through *Auxerre*, I have been getting forwards in two different journies together, and with the same dash of the pen— for I have got entirely out of *Auxerre* in this journey which I am writing now, and I am got half way out of *Auxerre* in that which I shall write hereafter——There is but a certain degree of perfection in every thing; and by pushing at something beyond that, I have brought myself into such a situation, as no traveller ever stood before me; for I am this moment walking across the market-place of *Auxerre* with my father and my uncle *Toby*, in our way back to dinner——and I am this moment also entering *Lyons* with my post-chaise broke into a thousand pieces——and I am moreover this moment in a handsome pavillion built by *Pringello*, upon the banks of the *Garonne*, which Mons. *Sligniac* has lent me, and where I now sit rhapsodizing all these affairs.
> ——Let me collect myself, and pursue my journey. [VII.xxviii.515–16]

The passage superbly demonstrates Tristram's researches into the temporal character of his ec-static self—that is, the self that can understand itself from a position beyond itself—for he is the unity within the relatedness of those two past moments in Auxerre, though separated by so many years, and the present moment of his writing "on the banks of the Garonne," a project which is governed by a future aim. Well might such a being need to pause to "collect" himself before pursuing his journey.

The eighteenth century is not alone in being dominated by a metaphysics of representation and by the resulting impulse to present an object world as world picture. *Tom Jones,* for all its conventional narrative structure, presents such a world picture, and, as a totality, Fielding's novel is a complete canvas in which form, line, and color are vivid to the eye. Sterne's book is not such a canvas; in fact, after numerous readings one frequently is unable to recall in pictorial fashion just where an incident or piece of dialogue occurs. By extension from Tristram's exploration of himself, one might speculate that he has deepened the analysis of world as picture to world as act or process. Clearly, Tristram is not dissatisfied with the processes of temporality; on the contrary, he has explored them so thoroughly as to expose the limits, not of the sequential order of language and the temporal dimension of life, but of pictorialism. By implication, though not thematically, he has explored the limitations of the picture as a norm and discovered that although words may be somewhat limited in their capacity to function pictorially, pictorialism itself cannot represent the essentially temporal structure of the self. Tristram is simply unable to get himself, understood as act, into a picture. What has been taken as conflict between the processes of time-bound language and those of pictorialism in the novel is actually harmony, the illusion of "spatial" presentation being reserved for the empirically accessible contexts of Tristram's being, while the direct processes of that being are mediated by the temporal language act which, not accidentally, corresponds to the sequential character of the being-act. The core of the whole issue of Tristram's temporalism, however, lies ahead in the analytic of his finitude.

The Promise of Finitude and the Horizon of Death

Within what Michel Foucault calls "the metaphysics of infinitude" the notion of finitude has a primarily negative application as though there were a principle of insufficiency at the heart of the human experience. Thus when Locke sets out to measure the tether of the understanding, or Pope to specify man's place on the chain of being, the emphasis is on human limitation rather than upon the promise of finitude. But when we consider finitude not as the limits of human being but as the delineation of its essential freedom or openness to possibility, a new path is revealed to the inner significance of temporal being.

The analytic of Tristram's finitude may begin with the most conspicuous boundary of his being, his death. The proximity of death as an obvious part of his consciousness throughout the novel confirms its thematic importance. The consumption batters his frail body throughout the book and threatens to end his life before he can finish his work, but his reflections show that long before disease makes his death seem imminent, he fully understands the inherent possibility of death. He remembers, for example, that he is expected to die at birth, a fact that is more than coincidentally related to his name, which means "sorrowful." Moreover, the deaths of others are prominent in his reflections, especially those of Yorick, Bobby, and Toby's brother officer, LeFever.

The account of Yorick's death is the central event of volume I of the novel, the book in which Tristram is at such pains to get himself born. This initial juxtaposition of origin and destiny would seem significant in itself in a work whose core is the meaning of being. The description of the dying Yorick, later an example to the dying Tristram also attended by Eugenius, is of a man whose head, like that of Sancho Panza is "so bruised and mis-shapen'd" by the blows of his enemies

> that should I recover and "Mitres thereupon be suffer'd
> to rain down from heaven as thick as hail, not one of 'em

would fit it."——*Yorick's* last breath was hanging upon his trembling lips ready to depart as he uttered this;—— yet still it was utter'd with something of a *cervantick* tone;——and as he spoke it, *Eugenius* could perceive a stream of lambent fire lighted up for a moment in his eyes;——a faint picture of those flashes of his spirit, which (as *Shakespear* said of his ancestor) were wont to set the table in a roar! [I.xii.31]

Through the scene, attention alternates between the weeping friend Eugenius and Yorick himself. The pain of dying is clearly all on one side, a sense of loss in Eugenius which might be accurately described as a deeply felt solitude. But the meaning of the event for Tristram does not reveal itself in the experience; it is not like Eugenius' sense of loss, of broken community with a kindred spirit. Tristram loses nothing. Yorick is long dead like all the others and in no way prevented by his absence from remaining a present force in Tristram's reflections. Tristram stands, like Hamlet, contemplating the tragic sense of life that is only part of what Yorick exemplifies, for he is at once "a fellow of infinite jest" and a skull "quite chap-fallen." Just as the graveyard scene reveals more of Hamlet's character than it does of the jester's, so Tristram is the focus in the novel as he remembers that "plain marble slabb" upon which was carved simply "Alas poor YORICK!" By describing the visitors who come to the churchyard to read the inscription and feel pity for Yorick, who is beyond giving offense now and appreciated by those who want solemnity in their parsons, he once again shows that the point of his reflection is the effect of death on the living, but with an unexpected richness. The difference between Tristram and the people who file by Yorick's grave and an important part of the meaning of the black page is that whereas the meaning of death is hidden from all alike, for the others, who lament with conventional graveyard sentiment, the hidden meaning of death is doubly hidden, for they conceal from themselves the fact that anything is concealed. When Tristram translates the mystery before which he stands into that page from which "the world with all its sagacity has [not] been able to unravel the many opinions, transactions and truths which still lie mystically hid under the dark veil" (III.xxxvi.226), he reveals to us in this state of suspended reading the hiddenness of the mystery and causes us to stand with him before the fact that we are all beings-toward a mysterious end.

Tristram's reflective posture before this mystery of his own being shows none of the signs of Eugenius' sorrow of St. Augustine's anguish at his friend's death; but it may remind us strongly of Augustine's summary of the effect of the experience upon him: "I became," he says, "a great problem to myself" (p. 80). For Tristram there is no sense of metaphysical abandonment either here or elsewhere in the novel; there is just this dramatic recognition, here for the first time, that for the self, whose origin is so obscure in the first volume, it is possible not to be.

In volume VII Tristram confronts his own death directly. For reasons already observed, he says his life is a journey, and then he spends most of his book giving a series of scenes which invite spatial rather than temporal analysis and which provide the empirical contexts and the synchronic structures of his essentially temporal being so as to make that temporality itself clear. But in volume VII when he travels to the Continent, he creates a universally acknowledged and critically baffling inconsistency in his presentation. By showing himself in action, running from death and thereby assuming for the only time in the novel the objective density of a character, his strategy seems to be aimed at validating the representation of his reflections by allowing us to see him in action, especially at this crucial juncture as he faces the decisive boundary of his being.

The epigraph from the *Epistles* of Pliny the Younger would seem to provide a clue to the mysterious relationship this volume bears to the novel as a whole: *"Non enim excursus hic ejus, sed opus ipsum est";* in Work's translation, "For this is not an excursion from it, but is the work itself." If the character of Tristram's endeavor in the earlier volumes has been reflexive, the plan to present himself in the flesh as a character must seem "an excursion" from the path already chosen, a new dimension of his being and, incidentally, the only one that would have been available to the methods of conventional fiction. The excursion, from his plan and to the Continent, is ostensibly provoked by his confrontation with death, and yet a substantial part of the volume is occupied with the apparently unrelated contrast between Tristram's interests as he travels and those of travel-writers.

> "Now before I quit *Calais,*" a travel-writer would say, "it would not be amiss to give some account of it."——
> Now I think it very much amiss——that a man cannot go quietly through a town, and let it alone, when it does not meddle with him, but that he must be turning about and drawing his pen at every kennel he crosses over, merely, o' my conscience, for the sake of drawing it; because, if we may judge from what has been wrote of these things . . . there is not a galloper of us all who might not have gone on ambling quietly in his own ground . . . and have wrote all he had to write, dry shod, as well as not. [VII.iv.482–83]

What have I to do with Calais or Calais to do with me?—such is Tristram's attitude. A point to be clarified, however, is how the purpose of his journey both conditions his interests along the way and justifies his satiric treatment of travel books.

Montreuil is a town that looks well "in the maps," not so well "in the book of postroads," and "when you come to see it——to be sure it looks most pitifully." What makes it worth a visit is not the abstract guidebook information about "the length, breadth, and perpendicular height of the great parish church, or . . . the facade of the abbey of Saint *Austreberte* which has been transported from *Artois* hither." These are only the concerns that appeal to a detached aesthetic curiosity. What is important about Montreuil is a more intimate human concern, specifically, Janatone, the innkeeper's daughter, not only for "all her proportions" imagined "in the wettest drapery," but for the kinship that one mortally sick feels with such a creature of change:

> ... he who measures thee, *Janatone,* must do it now——
> thou carriest the principles of change within thy frame;
> and considering the chances of a transitory life, I would
> not answer for thee a moment; e'er twice twelve months
> are pass'd and gone, thou mayest grow out like a pump-
> kin, and lose thy shapes——or, thou mayest go off like a
> flower, and lose thy beauty——nay, thou mayest go off
> like a hussy——and lose thyself. [VII.ix.490]

The point is that ordinary travelers in measuring the length, breadth, and height of the place miss Janatone.

Satire of tourists and especially of the Grand Tour had been common among the Augustans, notably in Pope's por- trait of that "accomplish'd Son" of Dullness who "saunter'd Europe round, / And gather'd ev'ry vice on Christian ground."[20] Sterne's point, as he continues with a burlesque not only of the guidebooks (VII.v) but also of the knowledge of things that have no claim on the attention of a dying man, would seem to be more profound. Nothing, says Tristram, can so please the traveler or so distress the travel-writer as "a large rich plain" which "presents nothing to the eye, but one unvaried picture of plenty." His own pleasure, when his race with death gives him the leisure, consists in "plain stories":

> ... stopping and talking to every soul I met who was not
> in full trot——joining all parties before me——waiting
> for every soul behind——hailing all those who were com-
> ing through cross roads——arresting all kinds of beggars,

20. *The Dunciad,* IV, 311–12.

> pilgrims, fiddlers, fryars———not passing by a woman in
> a mulberry-tree without commending her legs, and
> tempting her into conversation with a pinch of snuff———
> In short, by seizing every handle, of what size or shape
> soever, which chance held out to me in this journey———
> I turned my *plain* into a *city*———I was always in company,
> and with great variety too; and as my mule loved society as
> much as myself, and had some proposals always on his
> part to offer to every beast he met———I am confident we
> could have passed through *Pall-Mall* or St. *James*'s-Street
> for a month together, with fewer adventures———and seen
> less of human nature. [VII.xliii.536]

This passage is a plan for traveling, but it is also a plan for
living. In the travels of volume VII the focus is upon the way
in which his mortality governs his journey, a symbolic exploration at close range of the larger influence of his finitude
upon a life that in its pervasive temporality is also a journey.
Volume VII, in short, is not an excursion from it; it is the
work itself.

In the earlier discussion of the intentional organization of
consciousness, the principle of selection at work in the account
of his life was observed and characterized simply by the phrase
"life and opinions." but at that stage of the investigation the
principle itself might have been an arbitrary choice, except,
of course, that had he chosen to build fortifications instead of
write a book, everything would have been different for us.
Now it is possible to deepen that account by observing that, in
Tristram's view as revealed in volume VII, not all choices are
equally appropriate or authentic and that the procedure of
his whole project is guided by his attention to the finite dimensions of his own being—most determinative among them,
his mortality. This is a point of the greatest importance also because it reveals how remote from modernism Sterne is. For all
its resemblance to Heidegger's ontological categories of
"eigentlich" and *"uneigentlich"* (owned or authentic and un-

owned or inauthentic) it is old-fashioned Augustan moralism of the highest order.[21] Just as the traveler may be distracted by a host of curiosities that lie along his way, so Tristram might have been led away by a host of existential concerns that could have filled his volumes. As it is, he has no time to lose among the ordinary distractions of life. By accepting the fact of his own finitude, his effort to retrieve the essentials of his origins, to acquire the structures of his being, and to confront his ultimate destiny is guided from within. It is thus difficult to agree with the critical view that subsequent volumes might eventually have recounted what the book has been supposed to be about, the "adventures" as well as "opinions," the absence of which has often been regarded as a measure of Tristram's failure. Had Sterne lived to make such additions, the whole character of the work would have been altered thereby.

Let us now examine his exact comportment toward his old enemy, Death. The volume opens with reflections on his "good spirits" which have preserved his cheerfulness through all his years and which "when DEATH himself knocked at my door . . . bad him come again; and in so gay a tone of careless indifference . . . that he doubted of his commission———." The tone here and in the ensuing conversation with Eugenius reveals no touch of fear—only of being too occupied with living to have leisure for dying:

> for I have forty volumes to write, and forty thousand things to say and do, which no body in the world will say and do for me, except thyself; and as thou seest he has got me by the throat (for *Eugenius* could scarce hear me speak across the table) and that I am no match for him in the open field, had I not better, whilst these few scatter'd spirits remain, and these two spider legs of mine . . . are

21. The point of historical interest is not Sterne's anticipation of Heideggerian categories but how Heidegger's renovation of tradition in the effort to retrieve the being question—he is expressly not doing ethics—renews so much of that tradition in secular terms.

> able to support me——had I not better, *Eugenius,* fly for
> my life? 'tis my advice, my dear *Tristram,* said *Eugenius*
> ——then by heaven! I will lead him a dance he little
> thinks of——for I will gallop, quoth I, without looking
> once behind me to the banks of the *Garonne;* and if I hear
> him clattering at my heels——I'll scamper away to mount
> *Vesuvius*——from thence to *Joppa,* and from *Joppa* to
> the world's end, where, if he follows me, I pray God he
> may break his neck——. [VII.i.480]

It is precisely in this spirit, vigorously embracing life, that
Tristram runs, and there is nothing in it to justify the frequent claim that he evades the issue of mortality.

The importance of the theme of death in the novel has been
universally appreciated; though without having first revealed
the point at which all themes converge in the ontological
question, criticism has not described its importance quite
accurately. Holtz correctly recognizes that the novel "in a profound sense is about time . . . as a human problem," ultimately
of Tristram's own death. But he argues that "insofar as death
bulks large in the background of Tristram's account, the
actual nature of what he tells reveals an all-too-human tendency toward suppression, distortion, and deflection, a psychological evasion of temporality and its consequences" (p. 127).
The problem is admirably stated, but the conclusion is the
exact opposite of what an examination of the book as phenomenological reflection has revealed. Suppression, distortion,
evasion are precisely what would result from focusing upon
death as an empirical event—certain to come though not yet
—what Heidegger in *Being and Time* (pp. 383 ff.) calls evad-
ing the call of one's being by becoming absorbed in the
"everydayness" of existence. Instead of choosing a "distantly
retrospective" view from which he "can ignore the logic of
temporal necessity," Tristram faces two boundaries of his being: the less-familiar problem (except among children) of
one's origin and the familiar prospect of death. One may con-

jecture that the black page and the marbled page—"motly
emblem of my work!"—are indeed the emblems of these
essential boundaries of his life, the one a dark veil over the
mystery of death, the other a less than precise microscopic
portrait of the homunculus—these are of course arranged,
death first, in the order of their importance in the process of
self-interpretation.[22] But the important point is that although
Tristram was born on November 5, 1718, and is now running
for his life, the inner meaning of neither of these facts is
simply an event in the sequence of present moments that
compose his life. Instead they provide an understanding of
the dimensions of his being. The ontological meaning of death
is not a future event before which one dwells in fear as before
an environmental threat; it is an inherent possibility in the
light of which Tristram's being assumes a special value, a
value that evasive tactics would leave concealed. Thus in his
last volume he refuses a digression with the remark,

> I will not argue the matter: Time wastes too fast: every
> letter I trace tells me with what rapidity Life follows my
> pen; the days and hours of it, more precious, my dear
> *Jenny!* than the rubies about thy neck, are flying over our
> heads like light clouds of a windy day, never to return
> more——everything presses on——whilst thou art twist-
> ing that lock,——see! it grows grey; and every time I kiss
> thy hand to bid adieu, and every absence which follows
> it, are preludes to that eternal separation which we are
> shortly to make. [IX.viii.610–11]

It is true that the next chapter follows this hauntingly intense
passage by saying (in its entirety), "Now, for what the world
thinks of that ejaculation——I would not give a groat" (IX.
ix.611); but notwithstanding the shift to a tone of playful

22. The marbled page is literally an end sheet, of course. But the extensive parallels between the forms of his book and the forms of his self
suggest the further conjecture.

defiance, the remark reinforces the lament. Tristram's awareness of death is a realization that he is the kind of being for whom it is possible not to be. And the mood of that understanding is not fear; it is a vigorous affirmation of life, though not, to be sure, the victorious affirmation of conquest over death, hell, and the grave that we might expect from an eighteenth-century parson's pen. As usual Tristram's view is limited to what is available to reflection alone, and in contemplating the ceasing to be, he embraces being in the same way as we appreciate home in a foreign country.

Death was an event in store for him before his reflections on it; but possibility is more than a future certainty, and that *more* is the freedom to make a possibility one's own by an act of appropriation or choice. On the principle of the priority of the possible it is the utmost possibility of his being which, accepted as his own, provides the ultimate perspective on the meaning of that being and the central concern that provides its wholeness. Thus when he is about to describe the seige of Lille, the climactic moment of Toby's bowling green battles, he interrupts to steal an elegiac look ahead to the deaths of both Trim and Toby for whom he has such affection and admiration. Hence, he casts the moment of their greatest happiness against the prospect of their deaths. The effect upon him, and upon us, is an intensifying of the value or the happiness of that day along with something of the exhilaration that comes with the sense of living on the edge. As Toby and Trim play at war, a representational war, so Tristram plays at life, a representational life, in the spirit of the jester-parson. But what gives tone to the game, what gives it such special zest, is the implicit choice of the limitations of the being that he is, the omnipresence in the field of play of beginning and ceasing and of struggling against obstacles along the way. How flat by contrast is Walter's detached, abstractionist account of death as "nothing but the separation of the soul from the body." The mystery concealed within the black page is itself concealed from him. The limits of his own understanding are beyond his ken, and in that phrase "nothing but" is hidden everything about death that is worth attending to, namely, its whole concrete meaning. In volume V when word of Bobby's death arrives, Walter, characteristically taking the world for granted, sits mapping Bobby's progress across Europe only to be baffled by the revelation, which of course he is not open to, that not even existence is to be assumed. One suspects that beneath his myriad of words, the essence of whose function is to reveal rather than conceal meanings, Walter hides a vague apprehensiveness from himself: "There is no terror, brother *Toby,* in its looks, but what it borrows from groans and convulsions ――――and the blowing of noses, and the wiping away of tears with the bottoms of curtains in a dying man's room. . . . 'Tis terrible no way――――for consider, brother *Toby,*――――when we *are*――――death is *not;*――――and when death *is*――――we are *not*" (V.iii.356).

Tristram is much more puzzled by the inexplicable than Walter because he is alive to the wonder of things:

> But mark, madam, we live amongst riddles and mysteries ――――the most obvious things, which come in our way, have dark sides, which the quickest sight cannot penetrate into; and even the clearest and most exalted understandings amongst us find ourselves puzzled and at a loss in almost every cranny of nature's works. [IV.xvii.293]

In grasping the truth of his own being and confronting the mystery of things, there is in him a spirit of resoluteness reinforced by the intrinsic humility of the comic spirit that affirms his finitude and reaches beyond its boundaries.

Nothing in this point of view suggests that Tristram is in love with dying or even unafraid of it, though I do not hear fear in his words or in the tone of his voice. The case for his fear of death has surely been exaggerated. There is persuasive evidence to the contrary beyond the exchange with Eugenius already cited. Early in volume VII he expresses the wish that he might "stipulate with death" that he not die "before [i.e., in the presence of] my friends."

> I never seriously think upon the mode and manner of this great catastrophe, which generally takes up and torments my thoughts as much as the catastrophe itself, but I constantly draw the curtain across it with this wish, that the Disposer of all things may so order it, that it happen not to me in my own house——but rather in some decent inn——at home, I know it,——the concern of my friends, and the last services of wiping my brows and smoothing my pillow, which the quivering hand of pale affection shall pay me, will so crucify my soul, that I shall die of a distemper which my physician is not aware of. . . . But mark. This inn, should not be the inn at *Abbeville* [where he is lodged at the moment]——if there was not another inn in the universe. [VII.xii.492]

It is the tone of the passage that must be judged. He speaks forthrightly of the "catastrophe" that "torments" his thoughts, but he seems resigned, without being indifferent, to the inevitable. One who sought to evade the reality of death would manage to avoid reflections of this kind. Tristram does not evade thinking on death—but, please God, not now, and not under circumstances that would trouble his friends.

Toward the end of the volume, some measure of health regained and Death outstripped for a time, his tone grows almost casual. He moves *"at my own leisure*——for I had left Death, the lord knows——and He only——how far behind me. . . .——Still he followed,——and still I fled him——but I fled chearfully——still he pursued——but like one who pursued his prey without hope——as he lag'd, every step he lost, softened his looks——why should I fly him at the rate?" (VII.xlii.534). Again there is no impulse to conceal the truth from himself: only God knows by how much he has escaped and how much time remains, but at least he has the leisure, as the volume closes, to enjoy the Provençal song and sunburnt mirth of Nannette and wonder why a man "could not . . . sit down in the lap of content here——and dance, and sing, and say his prayers, and go to heaven with this nut brown maid" (VII.xliii.538).

Tristram's mood, at this moment at least, parallels the tenor of one of Yorick's best-known sermons. Yorick takes as his text the remark from Ecclesiastes, "It is better to go to the house of mourning than to the house of feasting." Directly Yorick responds, "THAT I deny . . . for a crack-brain'd order of Carthusian monks, I grant, but not for men of the world." As the sermon unfolds, joy is said to foster temptation, especially "when we take a view of the place in that more affecting light in which the wise man seems to confine it in the text, in which, by the house of mourning, I believe, he means that particular scene of sorrow, where there is lamentation and mourning for the dead."[23] Such contemplation leads to the virtue that alone justifies the text. One other brief passage might be cited. In "God's Forbearance Abused" the imminence of death is offered as bringing moral stability to life: "For though, in our fond imaginations, we dream of living many years upon the earth;——how unexpectedly are we summoned from it? ——How oft, in the strength of our age, in the midst of our projects,—when we are promising ourselves the ease of many years?—how oft, at that very time, and in the height of this imagination, is the decree sealed, and the commandment gone forth to call us into another world?"[24] In the novel the imminence of death restrains more than one wreckless impulse. When Tristram predicts the advent of a new paganism with the momentary enthusiasm of a confirmed sensualist, he suddenly checks himself: "but where am I? and into what a delicious riot of things am I rushing? I——I who must be cut

23. Sterne, *The Sermons of Mr. Yorick,* I, 19 and 31.
24. Ibid., II, 206.

short in the midst of my days, and taste no more of 'em than what I borrow from my imagination" (VII.xiv.495). This is also the restraint that, at the end of volume VII moves Tristram to leave Nannette and dance it away to *"Perdrillo's pavillion"* where he will write "uncle *Toby's* amours——I begin thus——END of SEVENTH VOLUME" (VII.xliii.538).

Reflection upon the other dimensions of Tristram's finitude provides him with further understanding of his possibilities for being which are simultaneously the delineation and the promise of his being. All the domestic misadventures and the intellectual limitations one suffers under in such a family of "originals" make him a problem to himself. His social, intellectual, and even historical horizons, in being formulated in his mind, are not escaped, but they are transcended just as the self becomes responsible for itself by taking up that reflexive position beyond itself. In understanding his situation he brings it to language and thereby takes possession of what had been in possession of him. Just as a possibility was said to be more than a future certainty when it is embraced as one's own, so a limitation is more than a current restriction when it is brought into the light of understanding. In this point lies the secret of Tristram's pursuit of clarity. "Man has to live in the world which is his field of existence. The situation which he needs is not given to him ready made. He has to situate himself, that is, to plan his own situation. For this reason he must create clarity in his field of existence."[25] Beyond this more or less practical need for clarity there always lies the further mystery articulated in the first sentence of Aristotle's *Metaphysics:* "All men by nature desire to know."[26]

The obstructions that lie in the way of his book likewise make it a problem to itself. In one dimension it is a book quite

---

25. Remy C. Kwant, *Phenomenology of Language,* p. 261.
26. Trans. W. D. Ross, in *The Basic Works of Artistotle,* ed. Richard McKeon, p. 689.

literally about the problems involved in writing a book of its own type. The difficulty of revealing one's whole mind in a single moment, though not resolved by "spatial form," paradoxically is resolved by frantically trying to tell everything at once and failing, just as, in the analogous region of the self, recognizing one's finitude and doggedly reaching beyond those inviolable boundaries brings them under one's own rule. Word chains cannot paint pictures with their richness of synchronic texture; yet by the magic of illusion they do. And word pictures cannot convey the diachronic process of temporal experiences; yet without them the social context which uncovers ontological structures would be mere vacancy. Words themselves are unruly: they will not hold shape; yet they do finally say just what Tristram wants them to say. Thus, in a serious offense against Cartesian maxim, the book doubts its own medium, the medium without which it could not doubt. And finally, the obstacles that one encounters in writing one's "life and opinions" are mirror images of the perplexities one faces in living it. Judging from the vigor and skill with which Tristram resolves his numerous authorial dilemmas and the gusto he brings to the game, "one would think I took a pleasure in running into difficulties of this kind, merely to make fresh experiments of getting out of 'em. . . . What! are not the unavoidable distresses with which, as an author and a man, thou art hemm'd in on every side of thee——are they, *Tristram*, not sufficient, but thou must entangle thyself still more?" (VIII.vi.545).

4

The Nexus of Word and World

We have now arrived at a point from which it is possible to see that when Tristram takes language for his theme, his reasons are more radical than a mere ontic[1] concern of a writer with the obstacles he inevitably encounters in his medium in the course of a day's work. To say that he is preoccupied with his craft is true so far as it goes; but it reduces language to something he thinks about and leaves the word *per se* outside the circle of his project and language as a theme unrelated to all the other concerns of the work. As we observed of the reflections on time, his primary interest is not in philosophical themes in themselves or with practical problems like making words hold their referential shapes. Those are regional problems that fall within the scope of his ontological concerns and which make those concerns aesthetically accessible. It is true that in writing his life, he makes of it a complete language system, a linguistic universe so to speak; but his real interest is in language as part of the continuum of his conscious being, not merely as a medium for conveying that life to others. This chapter therefore will ask what makes the problem of language an essential part of his more general investigation of the region of his own consciousness and what the reflexive method reveals about the character of language

1. Heidegger uses the term *ontic* to refer to an enquiry about an immediate object or thing, whereas he calls that enquiry "ontological" which investigates the meaning of its being.

itself. If we make the assumption common to both the eighteenth and twentieth centuries that the application of language to the realm of subjectivity differs in no essential way from its application to objective things and events, that the former is even derived from the latter as though language first reproduced objective reality and then reproduced subjective reality on the model of its dealing with the objective, then we will miss the significance of Tristram's reflections which arise from the peculiar contiguity of these domains. As the contours of this thesis become better defined it will also become clear why, rather than formulating sharp and clear concepts of the nature and function of language, Tristram reflects on the position it occupies in his life as a whole, another in the constellation of themes in the region of his general enquiry. This chapter will show, then, that as Tristram reflects on his own relation to language and seeks to retrieve the act of thinking that informs the speech of others, he turns away from the empirical view that he has inherited from Locke and eighteenth-century theory generally, adopting instead a style of analysis that may now be called Orphic or hermeneutic.

Language as Object

The empirical procedure of taking language as a mundane thing dominates in Tristram's historical situation. He is born into a world where rationalistic thought has already dissolved the old systems of communal myth and set the abstract Cartesian ego against an abstract world of object. His is a world that threatens to shrink to the boundaries of the individual ego, where intellectual isolation has almost wrecked communal life, where every man tends to become enclosed in a cage of his own subjectivism and his view of the world is appropriately labeled his hobby-horse. Most everyone in the novel has his hobby: Toby has his science of fortifications;

Dr. Slop, his obstetrics; Walter, his ludicrous systems of thought, except that his horse is more ass than the "sporting little filly-folly" that Tristram finds relatively innocent. Such specialization of interests causes the breaking up of language into separate provinces of quasi-private meaning that constitute the intellectual isolation of the characters. Walter spends an hour and a half arguing to Mrs. Shandy the advantages of accepting the services of Dr. Slop rather than those of the midwife, but to no avail, for the hapless Mrs. Shandy has no hobby-horse and hence, in Walter's view, no ideas whatever, no peg to hang a single inference on: " 'Cursed luck!' says my Father, '. . . for a man to be master of one of the finest chains of reasoning in nature,——and have a wife at the same time with such a head-piece, that he cannot hang up a single inference within side of it, to save his soul from destruction' " (II.xix.147). Nor does he succeed any better with Toby: when he undertakes to explain the learned "solutions of noses," Toby answers irrelevantly, "Can noses be dissolved?" (III.xli.239). For Toby hears only those words that can be related to his own grid of private ideas. These prevailing conditions in Shandy Hall illustrate the Lockean conviction that the listener can only find in words the meaning he has the ability spontaneously to put into them, which for the Shandys is usually the wrong meaning.

However dissatisfied Tristram may come to be with the treatment of language as object, his understanding nevertheless begins with book III of the *Essay* where Locke claims that "words are the sensible signs of ideas, and the ideas for which they stand are their proper immediate meaning." Accordingly, language is a system of signs arbitrarily chosen to represent, not things directly, but the ideas which in turn may signify things. The word has no intrinsic relation to what it signifies, and thought, in itself, does not need word. Hence, Locke is troubled by "the imperfection of words":

> . . . *words in their primary or immediate Signification, stand for nothing, But The* Ideas *in the Mind of him that*

> *uses them* . . . yet they [men] in their Thoughts give them
> a secret reference to two other things. *First, they suppose*
> *their Words to be Marks of the* Ideas *in the Minds also of*
> *other Men, with whom they communicate.* . . . *Secondly,*
> Because *Men* would not be thought to talk *barely* of their
> own Imaginations, but of Things as really they are; there-
> fore they *often suppose their Words to stand also for the*
> *reality of Things.* [III.ii.2, 4–5]

The model Locke has in mind is a system in which a word
corresponds exactly and without remainder to the "idea" in
the mind of the speaker and conveys that sole meaning to the
listener. Such a correspondence between word and idea presupposes, of course, direct connection between the idea in
the mind and the "real essence" of the thing to which the
idea refers. Unhappily, the lack of conformity of idea to thing
and of word to idea causes perpetual misunderstanding and
guarantees an intellectual isolation of the man whose thoughts
"are all within his own Breast, invisible and hidden from
others" (III.ii.1). The resulting need to control meaning by
definition as though it were the only security against the
deceptions of words is a notion that Tristram examines in
several important passages.

In fact, he has little use for definition, for when Eugenius
"pointing with the fore finger of his right hand to the word
Crevice, in the fifty-second page of the second volume of this
book of books," says "here are two senses," Tristram steps up
to him, lays his hand on his breast, and replies, "to define——
is to distrust." To define is to remove the word from its normal
environment by marking out rigid borders, and whatever
may have been said about Tristram's difficulties with words,
he does not distrust language.[2]

---

2. As Merleau-Ponty points out, "an entirely defined language . . .
would be sterile." The significance is "open," idiosyncratic, according to
the speaker's own sense, or else there "would be no acquisition on the
level of thought" (*Consciousness and the Acquisition of Language*, p. 52).

This exchange with Eugenius is set in The Chapter Upon Noses, the context of which is my great-grandfather's haggling over my great-grandmother's demand of "three hundred pounds a year jointure" in exchange for "two thousand pounds fortune." Her argument is, "Because . . . you have little or no nose, Sir." At this point Tristram breaks off the bargaining to discuss a definition with us:

> Now, before I venture to make use of the word *Nose* a second time,——to avoid all confusion . . . it may not be amiss to explain my own meaning, and define, with all possible exactness and precision, what I would willingly be understood to mean by the term: being of opinion, that 'tis owing to the neglience and perverseness of writers, in despising this precaution . . . That all the polemical writings in divinity, are not as clear and demonstrative as those upon *a Will o' the Wisp,* or any other sound part of philosophy, and natural pursuit.

Already doubt has entered into this Lockean procedure in the characterization of theoretical disputes as delusions; but the point to mark is that care in definition is not a guarantee of clarity in thought. Thus, continues Tristram, "unless you intend to go puzzling on to the day of judgment,"

> . . . give the world a good definition, and stand to it, of the main word you have most occasion for. . . .
>
> In books of strict morality and close reasoning, such as this I am engaged in,——the neglect is inexcusable; and heaven is witness, how the world has revenged itself upon me for leaving so many openings to equivocal strictures, ——and for depending so much as I have done, all along, upon the cleanliness of my reader's imaginations. . . . I define a nose, as follows,——intreating only beforehand, and beseeching my readers . . . for the love of God and their own souls, to guard against the temptations and suggestions of the devil. . . . For by the word *Nose,* throughout all this long chapter of noses, and in every

part of my work, where the word *Nose* occurs,——I de-
clare, by that word I mean a Nose, and nothing more, or
less. [III.xxxi.217–18]

Quoting this well-known passage at length stresses its implicit
acknowledgment that definitions, whatever practical help
they may be, do not reach the depths of verbal meaning. By
the time we come upon Tristram's mock definition it has
ceased to matter how the definition is formulated. He clearly
exults in the capacity of words to respond to the shifts and
turns of a context and to serve ends other than conveying
information in the indicative mood. If the language were
considered from the perspective of a purely formal system, the
ambiguity in the meaning of "nose" in this passage might be
said to arise from the opposition of the other words in the
context. But even in this example one can detect what will
be clearer in other instances, namely, the prior ontological
condition of meaning.

Since definition as Locke conceives of it overlooks the relation of word to verbal context, Tristram finds it largely
useless and undesirable. When he sets out to give the
"memoirs" of "uncle Toby's courtship of widow Wadman,"
he refuses to give us "a description of *what love is*," either by
"its parts" or by enquiring "whether love is a disease," or
"whether the seat of it is in the brain or liver." Those ques-
tions he leaves to his father and concludes, "I am not *obliged*
to set out with a definition of what love is." He will trust
instead to "what I have in common with the rest of the world.
. . . Let love therefore be what it will,——my uncle Toby fell
into it." To understand why we are then told to "call for pen
and ink" and paint the widow "as like your mistress . . . as
unlike your wife as your conscience will let you" is to see
that to grasp the meaning of Toby's falling in love requires
an interpretive act which consists of entering imaginatively
into his sentiments and hence of imagining a lady as attrac-

tive to us as the "concupiscible" widow is to him. Likewise in the case of the word *love:* what is needed is the experience itself, not a definition, or should we be supposed to lack the experience, as we lack experience of the fortifications that Toby would explain, then metaphor must situate love within what is accessible to us.

That language is something more complex than a set of ciphers that convey information is indicated in the parlor when Walter receives the letter announcing Bobby's death. The misfortune sets Walter's tongue loose on a sequence of as graceful eloquence as ever afforded relief to a tormented breast. The "entire set" of "fine sayings" that philosophy provides on the subject of death "rushed into my father's head." In the middle of his recitation, however, he mistakes a word and is called down by Toby:

> "Kingdoms and provinces, and towns and cities, have they not their periods? and when these principles and powers, which at first cemented and put them together, have performed their several evolutions, they fall back."——Brother *Shandy,* said my uncle *Toby,* laying down his pipe at the word *evolutions*——Revolutions, I meant, quoth my father,——by heaven! I meant revolutions, brother *Toby*——evolutions is nonsense.——'Tis not nonsense——said my uncle *Toby.*——But is it not nonsense to break the thread of such a discourse, upon such an occasion? cried my father——do not——dear *Toby,* continued he, taking him by the hand, do not——do not, I beseech thee, interrupt me at this crisis.——My uncle *Toby* put his pipe into his mouth. [V.iii.353–54]

What this exchange reveals is that Walter's language does not function just to transmit information by means of signification. His quotations are not referential. When Toby takes his pipe out of his mouth and says nothing more than "Brother *Shandy,*" Walter shows that he is already aware of the mistake he has made. The person who is so often annoyed with other people's abuse of his words is impatient at the interruption because his stream of eloquence is a way of giving form and articulation to his feelings, and from it "he got great ease." He is not merely conveying information, is not even interested in being understood in that sense. Walter's rhetoric is like a melancholy song welling up in his being; and in this context the difference between "evolutions" and "revolutions" is negligible, and clearly no justification for so untimely an interruption.

Another example which demonstrates the inadequacy of empirical theory to account fully for language is the great comic scene between Toby and Mrs. Wadman where she, having exhausted all clandestine means of determining the exact nature of "the monstrous wound upon his groin," decides upon the assault direct. Tristram closely observes the misunderstanding and isolation that occur when language is mistaken for an empty shell that lacks the power to convey the speaker's field of consciousness. The characters only listen to the external sound of the words, not to the speaking that informs the words. Toby promises to satisfy Mrs. Wadman: "You shall see the very place Madam." But she somehow misunderstands the exact signification of the word *place*. When Toby sends Trim out of the room (for a map in fact) and, returning to the sofa, says, "You shall lay your finger upon the place," the incongruity of their ideas requires an authorial translation. As these extraordinary lovers attend more to words than to what is uncovered by them, Tristram shows that the meaning of words can be found only by discovering their roots in the cognitive field of the speaker. The whole scene, he tells us, "shows what little knowledge is got by mere words—we must go up to the first springs." We will postpone for the moment asking where we are to look for these "first springs" (by which he may be understood to refer to the sources of meaning itself) in order to examine how Tristram exposes the roots of signification.

It is not only that Tristram sees an expressive as well as an informative function for language. There is nothing especially provocative in that, though it does mark an advance on Locke. His own intentions even when brought to language in the indicative form serve many different and often simultaneous aims; he informs us about his life, expresses his own sense of his being, tries to persuade us even of absurdities, stirs a sense of pity, excites to laughter. He obviously understands that language is rich enough to accommodate these complex uses. But among characters whose misunderstanding of the word contributes substantially to the general condition of impotence, he never tires of exploiting the comic possibilities of misunderstanding, which on the empirical model suggest the vast inadequacy of language itself. If word is merely an external container for idea, a passive shell informed by the thinking subject but lacking meaning in itself, then, as Merleau-Ponty points out in summarizing the weakness of this position, the thinking subject is not a speaking one.[3] Whatever theoretical doubts may be raised about the character of the word, about one thing there can be no question: Tristram speaks and in speaking he understands that we have the power to catch another's thought from his words and to think what we had not thought before. If words can induce meanings that are new to us, they must be more than signs for ideas that we already have. Tristram shows in practice that the power of words to trick those who trust them naively is also their power, properly used, to reveal more than conventional meanings.

There is an important contrast between Tristram's exposing, on the one hand, the differences in universes of discourse among the Shandys as so many failures to achieve universality and, on the other, his taking an interest in the individuality of each character's language as a particular view of the

---

3. *The Essential Writings of Merleau-Ponty,* ed. Alden L. Fisher, p. 188.

world and a clue to the mystery of human language itself. Criticism has taken the former to be his attitude and gone on to argue that language is at fault. Moglen expresses the widely held view: "The nominalism which is only suggested by Locke is extended by Sterne until language is revealed to be at the root of the chaos, the confusion, and the misunderstandings of everyday life and intellectual discourse."[4] The truth seems to be that Tristram's exuberant play with the family hobby-horses discovers in each language—Toby's, Walter's, Slop's— a unique view of the world, and he does so not by means of the formal traits of the language but by virtue of what is said in each. One is reminded that when Wilhelm von Humboldt asserts that each language contains a particular view of the world, he means that in learning a language, conceived as an entity independent of one's own being, one acquires thereby a particular relationship to the world that is peculiar to that language. Gadamer suggests that the deeper truth in his statement is that "language has no independent life apart from the world that comes to language within it" (p. 401). By observing the various worlds that are brought to presence among the Shandys and the conflicts among them, Tristram is led to extraordinary clarity about the nature of the word.

In order to observe by how much Tristram outstrips the conventional view, we may return for a moment to an example alluded to earlier. When Walter unwittingly uses a metaphor of the seige in the midst of those expostulations one evening upon the domain of truth, Toby supplies his own meaning:

> the word *siege* ... open'd his ears,——and my father observing that he took his pipe out of his mouth, and shuffled his chair nearer the table, as with a desire to

---

4. P. 152. Cf. Traugott who says the novel is about the faults of language and Lanham who admits that Sterne may be "the last great defender of the classical word" (p. 76) but only "in its pleasure-giving rather than its truth-telling function" (p. 71) since language tricks and deceives us.

profit,——my father with great pleasure began his sentence again,——changing only the plan, and dropping
the metaphor of the siege of it, to keep clear of some
dangers my father apprehended from it.

'Tis a pity, said my father, that truth can only be on
one side, brother *Toby*,——considering what ingenuity
these learned men have all shewn in their solutions of
noses.——Can noses be dissolved? replied my uncle
Toby. [III.xli.239]

There are alternative ways of looking at this passage. If we
focus narrowly upon the exchange between the two men, we
see only another comic instance of the mechanism of association and of the fatal imperfections of words. Accordingly,
Toby's hobby-horse, his semiprivate language, appears to be
an imposition of his own categories of experience upon the
world. The point to mark in taking the passage in this way
is not that words lack the capacity to reveal meaning, but that
the word *siege* at once reveals a part of Toby's world and
thereby conceals what Walter wishes to reveal. But when we
widen our focus on the scene and observe Tristram in the
process of observing—making, that is, the crucial and dis-
regarded distinction between the protagonist and his family—
a different theme stands out. Tristram, whose life has been
so tortured by the consequences of intellectualist assumptions,
sees the relation of word to the structure of Toby's consciousness and that not in the word *siege* alone, but in his modest
uninterest in the theory of noses as well. Tristram sees the
world imposing on the subject (Toby) and demanding, in
vain, that he adapt to what is disclosed from without, in short,
that he understand. The word should penetrate the intentional arc of Toby's experience, and its meaning rise in
dialectical relation to the personal aura of his world. If it did,
the word would be, as Merleau-Ponty says, "an act of transcending . . . , an instrument for conquest of self by contact

with others,"[5] but it requires the disposition to listen and the will to understand. Toby's interpretation is coherent, but only with his own closed universe of discourse. What lies outside the intentional field of that closed system is simply not there for him. Thus it is he and not language that fails to achieve the universality required for understanding.

It is obvious from this example and the others that Tristram does not follow Locke in treating language as though it were an autonomous domain, detached for purposes of analysis from lived meaning. As we share Tristram's point of view on the exchange between Toby and the widow, it is obvious that their words are not uprooted abstractions, signs of ideas "invisible and hidden from others," as Locke says, even though the exchange would appear to illustrate such a view. Furthermore, they are not characters necessarily locked within the prisons of their own subjectivism, reaching out to each other by means of that system of fortuitous, acoustically expressed words. Tristram sees, and we see, that their words are embedded in their concrete lives, that the continuity must be maintained between their language and the source of meaning, and that our understanding of their misunderstanding demonstrates the power of language to reveal the intelligibility of the encounter between a person and the whole of his lived experience contained in the cultural horizon that he calls his "world." The problem is not the imprecision of words, finally, but the ineffability of lived meaning. Though his method is different, Sterne follows in the steps of Rabelais, his most esteemed predecessor, in burlesquing the reduction of word to the status of just another object in a world full of things.

A common satirical theme in Rabelais is the disengaging of words from the act of speaking in order to establish them

5. *Consciousness and the Acquisition of Language*, p. 63.

as autonomous objects, spatial and visual, as when Friar John uses several hundred epithets for Panurge and what begins as speech becomes a textual list in which the "saying" ceases and the speaker disappears. An even more ludicrous and pertinent example is the scene in the fourth book where Pantagruel hears the anguished cries of the warring Arimaspians and Nephelibates, preserved in ice since the preceding autumn and released to air and ear by the warm breeze of spring. Pantagruel throws handfuls of still frozen words down on the deck of the ship before Panurge where they look "like striped candy of various colors. We saw there throaty words, quartz-green words, azure words, sable-colored words, golden words, which, when they had been heated a little between our hands, melted away like snow; and we could really hear them, but we could not understand them, for they were in a barbarous tongue."[6] Such a comic device points up the absurdity of reducing words to mere objects and thereby overlooking their source of meaning in a lived context; moreover, it is a device that paradoxically appears in a book which, despite its illusion of spoken language, presupposes that lived meanings are recoverable from texts that are clearly objects. In a similar example in the novel, Walter loses patience with a sentence on noses in an Erasmus colloquy because it will yield up no subtleties of meaning either literal or allegorical, nothing but plain sense, however vigorous the exegesis. Conventional methods of interpretation having failed,

> he had got out his penknife, and was trying experiments upon the sentence, to see if he could not scratch some better sense into it.——I've got within a single letter, brother *Toby*, cried my father, of *Erasmus* his mystic meaning.——You are near enough, brother, replied my uncle, in all conscience.——Pshaw! cried my father,

6. *The Uninhibited Adventures of Gargantua and Pantagreul*, trans. Samuel Putnam, p. 620.

> scratching on,——I might as well be seven miles off.——
> I've done it,——said my father, snapping his fingers.——
> See, my dear brother *Toby*, how I have mended the sense.
> ——But you have marr'd a word, replied my uncle *Toby*.
> ——My father put on his spectacles,——bit his lip,——
> and tore out the leaf in a passion. [III.xxxvii.230]

The roots of signification, clearly, will not be recovered by empirical experiments on texts, however refined the methods.

Tristram's attack upon the objectification of language is more radical than the simple denial and parody that has so far been demonstrated. In fact he deepens Locke's criticism of the instability of the word by experimenting with the complete disruption of signification. The absurd consequences of treating language as an autonomous domain are explored, for example, in the story of the nuns of Adoüillets, which has been studied with care by Richard Lanham who notes the hints of lesbianism and of antireligious sentiment in it. We are left adrift, however, not only by the fragmented character of the story but by its concealed relation to Tristram's own project. Here, as elsewhere, to speak of his satire against the Roman Church is to point out what is certainly true but what hardly scratches the surface of its full meaning. A closer reading will bring to light that its real bearing is on the problem of language and indirectly thereby on the larger configurations of the novel. The Rabelaisian character of the episode is announced in the first sentence where the abbess is said to have sought a remedy for her knee through "prayers and thanksgiving, . . . invocations to all the saints in heaven promiscuously," and "particularly to every saint who had ever had a stiff leg before her" (VII.xxi.504). This is no instance of casual licentiousness in Sterne; it is carefully related in theme and detail to other episodes in the work. Only in the next volume, for example, can one see in retrospect the resemblance between the fair Beguine who "fomented" Trim's wounded knee "with her hand night and day" (VIII.xx.572) and the novice who is "troubled with a whitloe in her middle finger, by sticking it constantly into the abbess's cast poultices." The bawdy is essential in presenting the abbess as more concupiscent than religious and more concerned with her physical than her spiritual well being. That is the first of the incongruities we notice in the episode: what the nuns are shown to be, their inner reality as persons, bears no resemblance whatever to the tradition whose external signs of allegiance they show to the world. Thus the satiric point, though if that were the whole point, the story would be an incomplete jest and one not really pertinent to Tristram's story.

Signs play a conspicuous part in the tale. As the nuns leave their convent for "the hot-baths of *Bourbon*," they "laid their hands saint-wise upon their breasts——look'd up to heaven ——then to them [the other nuns]——and look'd 'God bless you, dear sisters.' " Halfway through the journey the muleteer's wine skin is empty and, spying "a little tempting bush over the door of a cool cottage" (the sign of a tavern), he "gave the mules . . . a sound lash, and looking in the abbess's and *Margarita*'s faces (as he did it)——as much as to say, 'here I am'——he gave a second good crack——as much as to say to his mules, 'get on'——and so slinking behind, he enter'd the little inn at the foot of the hill" (VII.xxi.505–06). When the abandoned mules, whose impotence is more than hinted at, stop halfway up the hill, the episode focuses upon the point of the story, and one important enough to justify its lewdness, namely, the discontinuity between speaking and being, under the sign theory of language. The immediate problem is to persuade the mules to move by shouting singularly inappropriate obscenities at them and yet without sinning thereby, since the plight of the nuns instantly convinces them, as they show in the first of two linguistic orgies, that they will be "ravish'd and die unabsolved." Turning casuist in a manner that reminds us of similar instances of self-deception in Walter, they decide to divide the sinful words between them, a syllable to each, and they speak the forbidden words in what they clearly regard as a delicious crescendo of verbal debauchery which, whatever its effect on the nuns, has none on the mules who "do not understand" (VII.xxv.510).

Now the abbess's strategy is carefully described: it is to detach the power of signifying from the power of a more profound speaking. The lashes the muleteer had given the mules, though intended to deceive, nevertheless gave articulation to the intention in which they arose, and his "speaking" was thus founded in lived meaning. The coarse words of the nuns, by contrast, are spoken so as to serve a utilitarian purpose without revealing any lived meaning whatever. This is only one of numerous instances in the book where mute gesture speaks louder than the noise of words. The dark irony is, of course, that language is always more than the acoustically expressed word, and the nuns' plan for avoiding sin reveals their real state of moral being. The meaningless signs they give the world, "clad in white, with their black rosaries hanging at their breasts," show that they no longer appreciate the unity of word and being, and when accordingly they attempt to use words as ciphers, the words betray what they are most anxious to conceal. The sterility of the whole enterprise is stressed by making the particular words lewdly rather than creatively sexual, spoken to mules, creatures who "take advantage of the world, inasmuch as their parents took it of them——and they not being in a condition to return the obligation *downwards* ... they do it ... which way they can" (VII.xxi.507). The ironic self-deception that results from this effort to uproot language from its ground in lived experience leaves the nuns stranded in their impotence and us in possession of a preliminary insight into the mode of being of language as embodying the intentional experience of the speaker.

Like Rabelais, Tristram is not merely concerned with the risk of ordinary verbal confusions. Those are commonplace.

He is concerned with a common misunderstanding about language itself, a corollary of which is a misunderstanding of the self. In a number of important passages he subjects word as sign to close scrutiny by disrupting their significations. In the Chapter upon Whiskers at the opening of volume V a perfectly ordinary and respectable word is borne along through a shifting context until it is brought to "the beginnings of concupiscence," is ruined forever, "absolutely unfit for use." The bearing of this chapter of the novel has never been adequately explained, and to do so one must consider the passage "Upon Whiskers" in relation to its context where Tristram inveighs against plagiarism in words borrowed from Burton and then adds, "this leads me to the affair of *Whiskers*——but, by what chain of ideas——I leave as a legacy in *mort main* to Prudes and Tartufs, to enjoy and make the most of" (V.i.343).

In the brief but important introduction to the Fragment upon Whiskers in which, as James Work shows, plagiarism is attacked in a plagiarism, Tristram contrasts a journey with a "madcap postillion" and his "two mettlesome tits" who "flew like lightening" from Stilton to Stamford with the "eight *heavy beasts*" who "drag'd——drag'd the London wagon. The former put into his head the thought confirmed by the latter, that there are two ways of using the literary works from which one borrows. One can, like the laboring beasts, drag out the *"relicks of learning . . . by main strength,"* forever "adding so much to the *bulk*——so little to the stock"; or one can refuse "to go sneaking on at this pitiful——pimping——pettifogging rate" and, like the postillion's courageous horses, use those noble "powers which dart him [man] from earth to heaven in a moment," transforming his borrowings by a "miracle" of imagination into something that increases the "stock" of learning. Inspired by the thought that the postillion has raised in his mind, Tristram makes a vow: "I will lock up my study door the moment I get home, and throw the key to it ninety feet below the surface of the earth, into the draw-well at the back of my house." Hence that key at the bottom of his well shuts him out of his library, though not apparently from his writing, and keeps him from plagiarizing; at the same time it opens to him the miracle of transformation that can occur when the learning of others, made his own, is brought to new life by being made to speak for him.

The introductory passage ends with a wish that every imitator may be struck with "the farcy for his pains" (what Dr. Johnson defines as "the leprosy of horses") and may be thrown with his kind into "a good farcical house, large enough to hold——aye——and sublimate them ... all together" ("to sublimate" is "to exalt; to heighten; to elevate").[7] Presumably, then, Tristram is contemplating their metamorphosis from lumbering, heavy beasts into "mettlesome tits." "This leads me," he concludes, "to the affair of Whiskers."

The fragment itself shows how the word *whiskers* at the court of the Queen of Navarre becomes obscene because of "accessory ideas" which "leave prints of themselves about our eyes and eye-brows" and which "we see, spell, and put ... together without a dictionary." Thus when the Lady La Fosseuse says of the Sieur de Croix, with whom five of the ladies-in-waiting have already fallen in love, "But he has no whiskers," pronouncing the word in a "soft and low" but articulate voice, "with an accent which ... implied something of a mystery," the ladies, "looking close at each others prints," break into a laugh and ruin the word for the whole court of Navarre. Tristram reflects on the whole matter:

> The best word, in the best language of the best world, must have suffered under such combinations.——The curate of *d'Estella* wrote a book against them, setting forth the dangers of accessory ideas, and warning the

7. Samuel Johnson, *A Dictionary of the English Language.*

> Navarois against them. . . . The evil indeed spread no
> further then,——but have not beds and bolsters, and
> night-caps and chamber-pots stood upon the brink of
> destruction ever since? Are not trouse, and placket-holes,
> and pump-handles——and spigots and faucets, in danger
> still, from the same association?——Chastity, by nature
> the gentlest of all affections——give it but its head——
> 'tis like a ramping and a roaring lion.
>   The drift of the curate *d'Estella's* argument was not
> understood.——They ran the scent the wrong way.——
> The world bridled his ass at the tail.——And when the
> *extreams* of DELICACY, and the *beginnings* of CONCUPIS-
> CENCE, hold their next provincial chapter together, they
> may decree that bawdy also. [V.i.347–48]

The problem as Tristram clearly sees is not in the words themselves but in their use. If they speak at all, they do so as more
than ciphers with a single, clear reference.

On the surface it would appear that Tristram has demonstrated how unreliable and deceptive words are. If *whiskers*
is a name which can gradually shift its significance or in a
more extreme case even lose it entirely, until it becomes in-
determinate and unintelligible, then Locke might well be
suspicious of words. Accordingly, eighteenth-century scien-
tists ask what the term *motion* names and baffle themselves
trying to find the corresponding thing, and down to our own
day people ask about the self or about language as though
they were essentially substantial things rather than acts. As
we may now see, Tristram does not make that mistake with
regard to either the self or language.

The Lockean sign theory also assumes that as a name each
word in a sentence has its own separate signification and that
context has nothing to do with that meaning. In the introduction to *A Treatise Concerning the Principles of Human
Knowledge* Berkeley had already raised this objection against
Locke (pp. 17–18), but in the Chapter upon Whiskers Tris-

tram dramatizes the point by dissolving the designated meaning of the word in its context without following Berkeley's theoretical expedient of rejecting the distinction between language and the world. In fact, for all his interest in subjectivity, Tristram rarely concerns himself with the question of the kind of being attributable to the world; it is simply regarded as the environment for human being which is articulated in speech.[8]

What the passage under examination actually demonstrates is that the disruption of reference is a necessary possibility of language rather than its weakness or its abuse, for it exemplifies the transformation of a relic of past speech into a living word, the very miracle that Tristram speaks of in the introductory paragraphs of the chapter. It is the power of "whiskers" to change and to reveal the intentional focus of the speaker's thought just as the static textual relics in Tristram's library must be changed if they are to become part of the temporal presence of speech.

One is now prepared to understand that obscure connection between the issue of plagiarism and the body of this chapter. Reproducing the "relicks of learning" is to appropriate only the fossilized shell of the primitive language act. Tristram must lock up his study and allow his sources to speak through his own intentions as the word at the court of Navarre is allowed almost to lose its identity and be brought to "the beginnings of concupiscence." Volume V, in which the episode occurs, is preceded by three pertinent epigraphs. The first and second are from Burton: "If I shall say anything too facetious, you will judge me indulgently"; and "If anyone should censure my writings as lighter than becomes a divine or more satirical than becomes a Christian——not I, but Democritus said it" (Democritus is not only remembered as the laughing philosopher but also is noted for finding

---

8. This fact argues persuasively against Tristram's alleged idealism.

truth at the bottom of a well). The third of the epigraphs, altered from the Second Council of Carthage, says, "If any priest or monk know jesting words, exciting laughter, let him be damned"—not merely "rebuked" as the original says. The world may condemn both Tristram's plagiarism and his Chapter upon Whiskers, but if we look below the surface, not at the words themselves but at what is uncovered by them, we shall see that there is nothing here of what the first epigraph calls "too facetious" nor any "jesting words" for which, according to the third, a priest should be damned.

Indeed, as is so often the case, his most licentious passages stress a point of grave moral wisdom. The problem at the court of Navarre is not the language, which is alive and well; it is that meeting of delicacy and concupiscence, shrewdly made to share the same psychological territory, that is responsible for the Lady Baussiere's mounting the palfry of her imagination and ignoring every obligation of religion, charity, and kinship. When in the Queen's oratory "the host passed by——the Lady *Baussiere* rode on"; at the plea of a suffering kinsman, "Cousin, aunt, sister, mother——for virtue's sake, for your own, for mine, for Christ's sake remember me——pity me——the Lady *Baussiere* rode on." The power of the word that moves the Lady Baussiere to ignore her whole duty as a Christian is also the power of the word in Tristram's use to move us to an understanding, not of the Lady Baussiere alone, but of the word itself.

Three propositions about Tristram's views of language should now be clear: (1) his interest in the subject arises as part of the general investigation into the nature of his own being—hence his initial approach to the language question is at a more primitive level of enquiry than the empirical; (2) the apparent weakness in language cannot be corrected by means of definition as Locke believes but by a recovery of the meaning of language itself; and (3) since language cannot be understood as a set of signs divorced from their ground in the life experience of the speaker, one must attend to the ground of signification itself in order to understand. The passages in which Tristram disrupts signification have pointed in a provisional way toward an alternative view that may liberate him from the verbal sterility of the Shandys. The next step is to investigate what may justly be referred to as the retrieval of the power of the word and ultimately its relation to the being of things and speaking subjects.

Language as Event

Notwithstanding the numerous variations in the conception of language through the centuries, from Aristotle to twentieth-century linguistic science, language has been generally conceived as a coherent system of signs for communicating meanings by pointing to things—to the subject of discourse in Aristotle, to empirical objects in Ockham, to our ideas of those objects in Locke. Wilhelm von Humboldt is often credited with having revived another ancient view for the modern world by distinguishing between language as *ergon* or product and language as *energia* or act.[9] There had always been dissenting voices, of course, that harked back to the gathering motion of the ancient *logos* in Heraclitus or the Gospel of St. John. St. Augustine, for example, describes how language came to occupy a central place in his own consciousness:

> The older people did not teach me by suggesting the words to me according to any definite method of instruction, as was the case a little later with the alphabet; rather, with my own mind which Thou gavest me, O Lord, I wished to make known with divers grunts and sounds and with divers gestures the meanings within my heart, so that my will would be obeyed. But, I did not succeed

9. Cf. Michel Foucault, *The Order of Things*, p. 291.

with all things which I desired nor with all the people from whom I desired them. I would fasten it in my memory, when these people called something by name and when, at this sound, they made a bodily movement toward it. I would observe and keep in mind that this thing was named by this sound which they uttered, when they wanted to indicate the thing. Their desires became evident from their bodily gestures (the natural speech of all mankind), which reveal the disposition of the mind, in regard to things sought, possessed, rejected, or avoided, by a facial expression, by a nod, by a movement of the eyes or some other part of the body, and by the tone of voice. As to these words that were used in their own places in different sentences and which I frequently heard, I gradually learned what things they were the signs of, and, when my lips had become accustomed to these expressions, I now expressed my desires by means of them.

In this way I exchanged with the people among whom I lived the signs which were the expressions of my wishes. I advanced into the stormy society of human life, subject to the authority of my parents and the control of older people. [*Confessions,* pp. 14–15]

It is not especially surprising that this passage should bear close resemblance to Tristram's approach in the light of Sterne's familiarity with the Church Fathers, with homiletic literature, and with biblical exegesis. Furthermore, based on an approach immediately available at any time to one's intimate experience as speaker and hearer, it is the viewpoint that one would naturally occupy prior to cultivating the more artificial and abstract methods of empiricism.

There are three important points of comparison between the passage from Augustine and Tristram's perspective. First, neither relies on formal analysis of instances of language; each turns his gaze instead on the function of language in the acts of his own consciousness. Such a reflexive strategy aims at grasping the essence of language as a privileged faculty of the consciousness for which there are meanings and which is able to bring those meanings to articulation in various ways. The two broad alternatives available to Tristram, in general the same advanced in the twentieth-century debate between structuralist and phenomenological theories of language, are to approach the subject by means of the formal preconditions of language on the one hand and on the other, to study the act of speaking. It is to Sterne's credit that Tristram shows interest in both. The significance of the word *whiskers* is either sustained or undermined by the other words in the context, ultimately by the whole language system, and by shifting the context, he causes the signification to shift.[10] But clearly the issue at the core of his concern with linguistic vitality is how meaning itself arises in experience and comes to articulation in speech, the realm of the intuitive foundations of meaning that is concealed from view in empirical analysis. His most direct access to that realm is reflexivity; one's awareness of the self and its processes, specifically language, already presupposes a communal existence. Self-reflection by its own nature reveals more than what is peculiar to some fictitious solipsism. And thus, the second point of resemblance between Tristram and Augustine is the social character of language. As a social phenomenon, it comes into existence not through the teaching of a table of signs as if one could understand by thinking the meanings of words in a discursive manner, but as it "gathers" the thing into a discrete entity by the aid of that natural language of

10. Merleau-Ponty recounts a comparison of words to historical institutions introduced by Michel Breal (*Semantics: Studies on the Science of Meaning*): "Parliament was originally a court of justice. It began with the right of recording royal edits, but progressively acquired the right of remonstrance. In the eighteenth century, we find it at the point of becoming an organ of political opposition. Similarly, the word that has been introduced to signify one thing loses its original meaning and acquires another" (*Consciousness and the Acquisition of Language,* p. 96).

countenance, eye, limb, and voice as used by the speaking community. Thus the word provides the intuition of the discrete thing and secures it within the horizon of intelligibility. The third resemblance is the relation of word to intentionality. Augustine says that the name brings the thing into the presence of consciousness along with the affections that pertain to its place in human existence. Thus the thing comes to consciousness with its meaning already intact and facilitates one's purposive dealings with his world, what he calls "the stormy society of human life."

As a first step in achieving his own understanding of the prior conditions of language and its articulation, Tristram makes himself a master of what may be called the nonword—the expression of meaning in gesture, pose, even silence—by reflecting both on the phenomenon of language as rooted in primitive realms of meaning and on the impulse toward articulation which underlines speaking. The profound human capacity for revealing meaning, for saying, is exemplified in the dilemma that confronts Toby when he returns to his brother's house in London to recover after being wounded at the seige of Namur. Owing to Walter's kindness, a continual stream of "fresh friends and inquirers" call to help "begile the pain" with an hour's "chat by his bedside." The need to discourse upon the battle in which he received the wound presents such insurmountable difficulties to Toby's powers of eloquence that he can not extricate himself from "the scarp and counter-scarp,——the glacis and covered way,—— the half-moon and revelin,——[so] as to make his company fully comprehend where and what he was about" (II.i.82). So "sadly bewilder'd" by difficulties in keeping his discourse upon fortifications "free from obscurity," he is struck one morning by the scheme of mounting a large map of Namur on a board to aid his explanations. The "true cause" of Toby's problem with language, Tristram assures us, "is the unsteady uses of words which have perplexed the clearest and most exalted understandings. . . . 'Twas not by ideas,——by heaven! his life was put in jeopardy by words" (II.ii.86–87). The dilemma is developed fully enough for the reader to see for himself exactly the sense in which words or their "unsteady" uses are at fault; for Toby tries to make himself understood by cataloguing the fortifications by their obscure, technical names rather than describing the concrete human event of his misfortune. Later, after Toby is reduced to a state of as great perplexity by the quantity of his maps as he had been by the obscurity of his words, Trim provides yet another expedient by suggesting the use of the bowling green for what, in its genesis, is an extension of Toby's powers of language. When he has trouble with words, he resorts to visual alternatives—first maps, then the bowling green—and his choice, for all the hobby-horsical satisfaction he gets from it, is a quixotic retreat from the spontaneous articulation of meaning in the spoken word to a fossilized meaning embedded in an object language like that of the projector at Lagado who carries the things he wishes to converse about on his back for ready and unambiguous reference without the mediation of words.

Toby's impulse to speak, like Walter's in the funeral oration and like Tristram's throughout the novel, bears comparison with Samuel Beckett's character Watt who gnaws on the marrowbone of language and reveals a desire that words "be applied to the situation":

> Looking at a pot, for example, or thinking of a pot, at one of Mr. Knott's pots, of one of Mr. Knott's pots, it was in vain that Watt said, Pot, pot. . . . For it was not a pot, the more he looked, the more he felt sure of that, that it was not a pot at all. It resembled a pot, it was almost a pot, but it was not a pot of which one could say, Pot, pot, and be comforted. . . . Not that Watt desired information, for he did not. But he desired words to be applied to his situation, to Mr. Knott, to the house, to the grounds, to his

duties, to the stairs, to his bedroom, to the kitchen, and in a general way to the conditions of being in which he found himself. [*Watt*, p. 81]

As Toby spends his days enacting the battles *a posteriori,* he is using extraverbal means to articulate a need more primitive than the wish to convey information, the urge to articulate the condition of being in which he finds himself.

This universal impulse to speak, brought to fruition in a game of toy soldiers, is only one in a long series of reflections on forms of nonverbal articulation. It is Trim alone of all the characters in the novel who is said to be *"Non Hobby-Horsical per se"* (II.v.95). He is successful in communicating with all the other characters whether in the pose he adopts for reading Yorick's sermon in the parlor, the ability to come to an amorous understanding with Mrs. Wadman's maid Bridget, or to reduce the company to tears with a single gesture.

In the kitchen scene, where Obadiah announces Bobby's death, the initial focus is on the servants' various hobby-horsical responses as Obadiah's words fall within the intentional arc of their consciousness, and their verbal responses are bits of dangling conversation, one might say, from an empirical perspective. Tristram comments, "Well might Locke write a chapter upon the imperfections of words." Then Trim enters and makes his moving funeral oration, and the sequence of Tristram's presentation invites reflection upon much more than the famous gesture. In the first of two accounts the reader is not admitted to the full visual and temporal dimensions of the gesture of the hat, dropped to express death: "Are we not here now, continued the corporal, (striking the end of his stick perpendicularly upon the floor, so as to give an idea of health and stability)——and are we not——(dropping his hat upon the ground) gone! in a moment!——'Twas infinitely striking! *Susannah* burst into a flood of tears," and the other servants "melted" at the gesture. This time Tristram provides only Trim's words, the gestures as bare uninterpreted facts, and the effects on Trim's audience. But it is clear that the intentionality of each of the hobby-horsical servants has stumbled against something that violates his focal orientation, an instance of what Husserl calls the "intentional transgression." Tristram insists upon the importance of our reflection on the event, for "I perceive plainly that the preservation of our constitution in church and state . . . may in time to come depend greatly upon the right understanding of this stroke of the corporal's eloquence." The object of this all-important "right understanding" is the nature of meaning itself, the obscuring of which would issue in the collapse of the value standards of the whole culture. Tristram says twice, "We are not stocks and stones" but creatures with bodies and senses by virtue of which meaning comes to be; we are "men cloathed with bodies, and governed by our imaginations." It is by the mediation of one's bodily presence in the situation that the gesture calls for meaning. "The scene invites me to become its adequate viewer, as if a different mind than my own suddenly came to dwell in my body, or rather as if my mind were drawn out there and emigrated into the scene it was in the process of setting for itself."[11] The meaning is neither in Trim's gesture nor is it something that the servants add to the gesture as though the meaning were in mind before the gesture which calls for it to arise. Meaning is a function of a person's engagement as a physical, emotional, imaginative being with the world in which he is. This reflection excludes two widespread assumptions about the nature of meaning: it is not something inherent in the event itself; nor is it something that one constructs as a subjective quality and adds to the event. The advent of meaning is a more primitive event than the rational subject-object schema can account for.

11. Maurice Merleau-Ponty, *Signs*, trans. Richard C. McCleary, p. 94.

Gesture, Tristram says, is an even more effective way of
conveying meaning than words, for "the eye . . . has the
quickest commerce with the soul,——gives a smarter stroke,
and leaves something more inexpressible upon the fancy,
than words can either convey——or sometimes get rid of."
It might also be observed that the more primitive and spontaneous the mode of articulation, the more convincing it is,
but the correlative limitation on gesture is that it is so intimately bound to its native environment that it tends not
to retain its content of meaning when transferred to other
circumstances. One may use language, as the rhetorical tradition does, with such calculation of effect as to distort or even
ignore the meaning that is ostensibly being expressed. This
accounts for the power of Trim's gesture for freedom in the
flourish of his stick and the explanation of Tristram's cir-
cumcision to Bridget by extending his forefinger along the
table and cutting the edge of his hand across it.

After the explanation of the power of the gesture, Tristram
repeats the dramatic climax of the scene with the full revelation of its potency, in words, of course:

> ——"Are we not here now!"——continued the corporal,
> "and are we not"——(dropping his hat plumb upon the
> ground——and pausing, before he pronounced the
> word)——"gone! in a moment?" The descent of the hat
> was as if a heavy lump of clay had been kneaded into the
> crown of it.——Nothing could have expressed the senti-
> ment of morality, of which it was the type and fore-
> runner like it,——his hand seemed to vanish from under
> it,——it fell dead,——the corporal's eye fixed upon it, as
> upon a corps,——and *Susannah* burst into a flood of tears.
> [V.vii.362]

Richard Lanham has correctly pointed out that the effect
of the scene is a sense of "accomodation, acceptance . . .
cohesion . . . community," though he finds in the gesture no
more than a "mechanical hat trick" (pp. 61–62). Trim's suc-

cess in articulation derives from the community in mortality which reemerges as a healing force when the universal human meaning of death is articulated and appropriated for communal contemplation. Tristram insists upon the reader's attention to the oration because it is about the problem of meaning; it seeks to recover the basis of the intelligibility of things in a household where everything, including the death of the heir apparent, is slipping into unintelligibility.

Tristram's sensitivity to nonverbal articulations of meaning through physical responses in gesture and attitude of body, serves to demonstrate that it is impossible for a conscious being not to convey meanings in such ways. Walter gives a clear statement of this fact in discussing the kind of tutor that would be suitable for Tristram: "I maintain ... that a man of sense does not lay down his hat in coming into a room,——or take it up in going out of it, but something escapes, which discovers him" [VI.v.414–15]. Again and again Tristram contemplates scenes in which bodily attitude reveals character, mood, and intention: Walter trying to retrieve his handkerchief or lying across the bed; Mrs. Shandy at the parlor door; Toby knocking the ash from his pipe; Trim reading the sermon.

It must be observed in passing, however, that Tristram recognizes the same capacity for ambiguity in gestures that he finds in words. Thus when Walter and Toby discuss the effects of a birth in a house upon all the women in it, Walter, who has failed to get any satisfactory information from Susannah about her mistress, complains that all of them "from my lady's gentlewoman down to the cinder-wench, becomes an inch taller ... and give themselves ... airs." Toby prefers to think

> that 'tis we who sink an inch lower. . . . 'Tis a piteous burden upon 'em, continued he, shaking his head.——
> Yes, yes, 'tis a painful thing——said my father, shaking

> his head too—but certainly since shaking of heads came into fashion, never did two heads shake together, in concert, from two such different springs. [IV.xii.284–85]

As Tristram sees, the gesture effectively works as a means of entering simultaneously into the contradictory sentiments: the meaning is in the gesture as the meaning of music is in the sound. And as the meaning of the gesture is implicit in the subjective and intersubjective situation, so is thought implicit in word.

Another type of nonverbal articulation that interests Tristram, as he contemplates the preconditions of speech, is vocal patterns of intonation and stress. When Mrs. Wadman and uncle Toby discuss the merits of having children, he can think of no favorable arguments that she, without mentioning the factor of age, has not already answered,

> unless it be the pleasure which it has pleased God——
> A fiddlestick! quoth she. . . .
> Now there are . . . an infinitude of notes, tunes, cants, chants, airs, looks, and accents with which the word *fiddlestick* may be pronounced in all such causes as this, every one of 'em impressing a sense and meaning as different from the other, as *dirt* from *cleanliness*. . . .
> Mrs. *Wadman* hit upon the *fiddlestick*, which summoned up all my uncle *Toby's* modest blood into his cheeks——so feeling within himself that he had somehow or other got beyond his depth, he stopt short.

Toby then proposed marriage, took up the Bible from the table, and read, as it chanced, the passage on "the siege of *Jericho*" (IX.xxv.635). Patterns of sound are even capable of leading to understanding without saying anything determinate. For Locke the referents of words are ideas, but for Tristram words can reach the understanding without the mediation of any ideas at all. He professes to have trouble translating Slawkenbergius's Tale:

> What can he mean by the lambent pupilability of slow,

low, dry chat, five notes below the natural tone,——
which you know, madam, is little more than a whisper?
The moment I pronounced the words, I could perceive
an attempt towards a vibration in the strings, about the
region of the heart.——The brain made no acknowledgment.——There's often no good understanding betwixt
'em——I felt as if I understood it.——I had no ideas.
[IV.i.273]

The most profound of nonverbal articulations that Tristram studies is silence, an extraordinarily dense form of
expression that may lend assistance to speech, as when it
intensifies the presence of what was just spoken or holds out
the promise of what is about to be said. Such "external"
silences are unusually important in Sterne as extensions of
ordinary punctuation, most frequently taking the form of
dashes of various lengths. At its most significant, however,
silence is a corollary of the sense of finitude already discussed.
When Walter responds to the mashing of Tristram's nose at
birth and retires to his bedroom where he falls across the bed
"in the wildest disorder" and "in the most lamentable attitude," he "sigh'd once,——heaved his breast often,——but
utter'd not a word." And for "a full hour and a half" Toby sits
beside the bed in a silence that is laden with Walter's misery
and his own sympathy. Though this "internal" silence is
treated comically—Tristram uses the occasion to provide
some fifty pages of the lore of noses (including Slawkenbergius's Tale) which serve to define the silence—the silence is
nevertheless a yielding, if an unwilling one, before something
beyond Walter's control and an expression of defeat in his
perpetual efforts to bring the world under the dominion of
his own theories.

In Elizabeth's case silence may be observed as a weapon of
rhetorical battle as potent as any in the Shandy arsenal. Walter
suggests a caesarean delivery to spare his son's cerebellum
from being crushed by "470 pounds averdupoise acting perpendicularly upon it," but "seeing her turn as pale as ashes

at the very mention of it . . . he thought it as well to say no more of it" (II.xix.153). The facial expression is the most conspicuous means by which Mrs. Shandy conveys her response, but her silence, the failing to speak, is the positive assertion of a not-speaking which repeatedly defeats all Walter's verbal strategies. So effective is she, in fact, that it is difficult to understand why she has been accused of lacking understanding, of being tranquilly submissive in her "placid denseness," "a universal blank" with a "guileful and deformed mind" "unrippled by thought."[12] The debate that Walter holds in his beds of justice on the question of putting Tristram into breeches exemplifies the effectiveness of Elizabeth's strategy of keeping the peace in Shandy Hall by refraining from speaking. The scene makes no obvious use of silence, for she speaks her agreement to both sides of every trivial question, completely alive to Walter's tricks to draw her into the debate. What is important about it is Tristram's sense of what she does not say, of the dimension of silence that lies behind her words, for it is her peculiar way of relating herself to her domestic world, a way of maintaining herself in the combative milieu of her environment.

> WE should begin, said my father, turning himself half round in bed, and shifting his pillow a little towards my mother's, as he opened the debate——We should begin to think, Mrs. *Shandy,* of putting this boy into breeches.——
> We should so,——said my mother.——We defer it, my dear, quoth my father, shamefully.——
> I think we do, Mr. *Shandy,*——said my mother.
> ——Not but the child looks extremely well, said my father, in his vests and tunicks.——

12. Henri Fluchère, *Laurence Sterne: From Tristram to Yorick,* trans. and abridged Barbara Bray, p. 246; Traugott, p. 49; Holtz, p. 71. This traditional, unsympathetic view of Elizabeth has been corrected by Ruth Marie Faurot, "Mrs. Shandy Observed," *Studies in English Literature* 10 (1970), 579–89.

———He does look very well in them,———replied my mother.———

———And for that reason it would be almost a sin, added my father, to take him out of 'em.———

———It would so,———said my mother:———But indeed he is growing a very tall lad,———rejoined my father.

———He is very tall for his age, indeed,———said my mother.———

———I can not (making two syllables of it) imagine, quoth my father, who the duce he takes after.———

I cannot conceive, for my life,———said my mother.——— Humph!———said my father.

(The dialogue ceased for a moment.) [VI.xviii.437]

Elizabeth's defensive strategy of not speaking to the issue demonstrates her understanding that the way to beat a person who argues for victory is never to join the issue.

When Walter holds her to the terms of the marriage articles, forcing her to give birth in the country, she answers all his arguments in favor of the man-midwife passively, silently, "like a woman," and his skill in disputation is confounded. If she must submit to the terms of the contract, she will trust her life to the care of the woman whose experience and success are well-established rather than submit herself to a hobby-horsical projector like Dr. Slop, the human consequences of whose science are not established. Her practical wisdom prefers tradition to novelty where human life and well-being are at issue, and that practical wisdom speaks decisively by remaining silent. One who listens only to what she says will find her "scarcely alive," but one who listens to the unspoken context of her few words, as Tristram does, will feel the potency of the silence that is part of speaking.

As a final example of the use of silence we may return to the black page, for here Tristram exemplifies the silent dwelling before the mystery of his own finitude which makes him able to receive what is worthy of being said. Parallel to the silence behind his mother's slight verbal gestures is Tristram's silent listening to his own being, the background to the speaking of his book. The genuine speech that reveals rather than conceals meaning begins in such an attending to the encounter between one's self and one's world which speaks within the realm of one's finitude. In reflecting upon Walter's unnatural contortion, that "transverse-zig-zagery" of body brought about in the effort to retrieve his India handkerchief from his right coat pocket with his left hand, his right being already occupied in "taking off his wig," Tristram comments on the primordial occurrence of meaning: "the circumstances with which every thing in this world is begirt, give every thing in this world its size and shape;——and by tightening it, or relaxing it, this way or that, make the thing to be, what it is——great——little——good——bad——indifferent or not indifferent, just as the case happens" (III.ii. 158). This passage and the stress he places on Trim's kitchen oratory shows that Tristram is not just interested in linguistic as opposed to nonlinguistic meanings; in his effort to discover the relation of word to his own being process, he is seeking a limiting concept of meaning itself. In doing so he maintains the continuity of language and the source of meaning. His silence before the mystery of death is a submissive yielding to what one can only wonder at or be awed by, a deference he pays to what he is not the source of. And the secret of understanding is being open to meaning and consists in this standing reticently, patiently, receptively before the inaccessible. Meaning as an intersubjective event arises in this yielding as a reaching out to others, Walter, Toby, Yorick, who require this silence in order to reach him.

Walter listens only to words as things, not to what is uncovered by them; he is not open to the style of life and thought that informs another person's words. When he listens to Trim read Yorick's sermon which should speak directly to him on the power of self-deception, his remarks show that his

concern is with literary surfaces rather than with the meaning
that informs them: Walter interrupts after the first sentence
("Trust!——Trust we have a good conscience!") by observing, "Certainly, *Trim*, ... you give that sentence a very im-
proper accent; for you curl up your nose, man, and read it
with such a sneering tone, as if the Parson was going to abuse
the Apostle" (II.xvii.123–24). Trim is right and Walter is
wrong, of course, for that tone of abuse is one of the uncon-
ventional qualities common in Yorick's sermons. At the end
Walter remarks, "Thou hast read the sermon extremely well,
Trim. ... I like the sermon well ... ——'tis dramatic,——
and there is something in that way of writing, when skilfully
managed, which catches the attention" (II.xvii.140–41). The
"stile and manner of it" pleases Walter, but the meaning remains hidden from him because he listens *to* rather than
through the words.

At the core of Tristram's strategy in discovering how speech
is connected with other modes of articulating meaning is the
examination of contexts in which meaning does not originate
in words but in which the whole thematic field of consciousness is embodied in the act of articulation. Thus in the middle
of Yorick's sermon when Dr. Slop mentions the sacraments,
Toby asks,

> Pray how many have you in all ... ——for I always for-
> get?——Seven, answered Dr. *Slop*.——Humph!——
> said my uncle *Toby;* tho' not accented as a note of ac-
> quiescence,——but as an interjection of that particular
> species of surprize, when a man, looking in a drawer,
> finds more of a thing than he expected.——Humph! re-
> plied my uncle *Toby*. Dr. *Slop,* who had an ear, under-
> stood my uncle *Toby* as well as if he had wrote a whole
> volume against the seven sacraments.——Humph! re-
> plied Dr. *Slop,* (stating my uncle *Toby*'s argument over
> again to him)——. [II.xvii.129]

In that single monosyllabic gesture the whole of Toby's protestant consciousness wells up, a complete world of meaning is brought to light. The repetition of the same monosyllable from the opposing side, and the tables are turned, another and contradictory world of experience spoken into being. Words obviously name particular things and thereby make them available in conceptual space; but in this case the "word" is stripped of the power of naming in order to reveal an additional dimension, namely, its function in exposing the horizon of understanding in which particulars are named. Thus, to use an extraneous example, the word *Pequod* not only names a ship but calls up a particular adventure, a forgotten way of life, the mood, even, of the sea; it is the unsayable *Gestalt* of meaningfulness, the unity of world and things and word without which the word would mean nothing. "Humph!" omits the sign function and stresses only the polyphonic presentation of such a world of consciousness. Unlike Locke and the Royal Society for whom word and speech are founded in preestablished meanings, Tristram has grasped an implicit relationship between saying and being, and the result is his ability to retrieve the mysterious, submerged unsaid in Toby's utterance. His experiments with the power of words to reveal or to bring being into presence are complemented by others which demonstrate the power to conceal or to return meaning to the void of undifferentiated being. When one listens with understanding to language, as Tristram does but as the Shandys in general do not, one attends to this context of world speaking silently within every word.

The final step in Tristram's reflections on the word, then, is to grasp the sense in which language not only articulates world by the "gathering" motion that brings undifferentiated being into the opening of conscious presence but also is in some way constitutive of the phenomenal world in which meaning arises and thereby becomes the locus of Tristram's being. The passage from St. Augustine stressed how the process of naming gathered the booming, buzzing confusion of undifferentiated being into specific things. It is within the aura of language that the determinacy of a preobjective sensory manifold is translated into a cultural space in which both subject and object come to be. What is meant by the claim that for Tristram the structure of language is hermeneutic is that meanings do not ground words; words ground meanings. Tristram does not simply convey his "life and opinions" in language; he articulates them for himself as well, and he can do so because he has language which delineates a conceptual horizon and differentiates things within that horizon, both self and other.

Locke had assumed that language functions primarily as a tool to convey information, and he thereby concealed the intuitive foundations of meaning. But reflexive rather than empirical investigation shows that language does not just facilitate communication; it establishes the phenomenal horizon in which speakers and things spoken of are constituted. Tristram realizes himself in the encounter with the world that is given by language. The superficial sense in which his being is linguistic in so far as he is a character in a book of words, then, parallels the ontological sense in which as a person he lives, moves, and has his being in the space established by words. The misfortunes under which he suffers arise in part from the Shandean way of abusing words, but his reflections which are efforts to comprehend his disunified existence have led him to an understanding of the essential unity of the act of being and the act of speaking. He is a victim of the uncreative word only in the sense that his ancestral community is cut off from the poetic being of the word by having embraced the cipher theory. Walter remarks that "the highest stretch of improvement a single word is capable of, is a high metaphor," but he adds, "——for which, in my opinion, the idea is generally the worse, and not the better" (V.xlii.405). Metaphor to him is not a new emergence of meaning but mere rhetorical ornament. By means of his re-

flexive method Tristram overcomes the sterility of this view,
and the result is the triumph of the poet.

The relative merits of definition and metaphor as linguistic
ideals may be summarized in the passage where love is defined

> alphabetically speaking, [as] one of the most
>   A gitating
>   B ewitching
>   C onfounded
>   D evilish affairs of life—the most
>   E xtravagant

and so on through "R idiculous" which should have gone
before "S tridulous." But, as Walter remarks, "You can
scarce . . . combine two ideas together upon it, brother *Toby*,
without an hypallage"——What's that, cried my uncle
Toby. The cart before the horse, replied my father" (VIII.
xiii.551–52). Love is an experience that confounds the logical
insistance upon keeping horses in front of carts and for which
definitions can be provided. In fact, Tristram's list is successful only because it is set in the context of his own inclination
to let his overheated imagination run upon some "earthly
goddess" with the aid of "inflammatory" metaphors of warm
fur caps and fingers in pies. It is not the alphabetical definition that explains the susceptibility that he is attributing to
himself and Mrs. Wadman but the metaphors that give substance to the definition. In the words of Merleau-Ponty: "The
empirical use of already established language should be distinguished from its creative use. Empirical language can only
be the result of creative language" (*Signs,* p. 44).

The conventional view that the success of the novel is
Sterne's alone, that his protagonist remains comically bound
in the shallows and absurdities of his family, underrates
Sterne's actual achievement. It is not the story of an effort at
autobiography which fails; it is the story of an effort that is
a spectacular success, an intellectual enquiry pursued in the
healing comic spirit which uses words to create the world, the

life, the opinions, and to bring to clarity and into the domain of Tristram's freedom, the marred being that he is. Along the way, he has his troubles with words, that "fertile source of obscurity," but the final result is that he makes words do anything he wishes. He delineates the boundaries of his own being by reaching beyond the restrictions of his own finitude, and he is able to bring the character of language into focus by trying to push it beyond the limits of its capacity even as the sonneteer expresses the ineffability of his mistress's beauty by complaining of the weakness of his own powers of expression.

In the discussion of intersubjectivity we saw that Tristram's rhetoric was simultaneously reflexive and nonreflexive, directed to himself and to his audience. We feel in the immediacy of his thought processes and in the baroque cadences of his sentences, the spontaneity of his discovering patterns of meaning in the act of speech. Although he is writing a book, he understands the primordial form of language to be spoken rather than written, temporal rather than spatial. The priority of speech to writing was still understood by the traditionalists of the eighteenth century who often express hostility to books, as in Sterne's parody of the format of the book when he encourages his reader to fill in blank pages for himself. The contrast is obvious in Dr. Johnson who is at least as important as a conversationalist as he is as a writer and his biographer who is compulsively textual, perpetually "boswellizing" the world into the shape of the written page. One would expect the issue to be especially clear to Sterne, the expert at pulpit rhetoric, engaged in the silent enterprise of writing a novel.

A number of Tristram's themes coalesce in his championing the spoken word. Speech, like human nature, is essentially temporal, "a response to the living moment."[13] The empirical analysis which he rejects appeals to language as an essentially

13. Walter Ong, *The Presence of the Word*, p. 57.

visual, textual thing which, as Plato protests, falsifies the essence of wisdom,[14] though it enhances the possibility of verification in the sense required of historical objectivism and ultimately implements the tyranny of "facts." Walter Ong remarks that *"sound is more real or existential than other sense objects, despite the fact that it is also more evanescent.* Sound itself is related to present actuality rather than to past or future. It must emanate from a source here and now discernably active, with the result that involvement with sound is involvement with the present, with here-and-now existence and activity" (pp. 111–12). Merleau-Ponty points out that written modes like vision, by presenting a field, invite analysis of the field and dissection of the observers, whereas oral modes are synthetic, uniting the listening group into an audience.[15] Where the process of bringing a world to presence is the normal function of speech, it tends to be interrupted by the act of writing. As Ricoeur puts it, "The constitution of the sign as sign presupposes the break with life, activity, and nature."[16] But Tristram's rhetoric is calculated to preserve the immediacy of experience by maintaining the illusion of speaking to a present audience. Tristram's relationship with his readers presupposes the efficacy of the spoken word to establish the community of audience, but an audience of conversants; it constitutes a public or communal field of reference; and since his speaking is his life, it reveals his being as a conversation within which the domain of objec-

14. "Letter VII," *The Platonic Epistles,* trans. J. Harward, 341b–43c. Also see the close of the *Phaedrus* where Socrates contends that writing is not a substitute for the spontaneous play of mind in dialectic and should be treated with caution since it tends to encourage idolatry rather than convey truth.

15. It is interesting to note that there seems to be no word in English for a group of spectators that suggests a unity arising in the act of common seeing as *audience* does for a group of auditors.

16. Ricoeur, "Husserl and Wittgenstein," in *Phenomenology and Existentialism,* ed. Edward N. Lee and Maurice Mandelbaum, p. 216.

tivity is established. Language thus unites us in a manner that sharply contrasts with the prevailing condition at Shandy Hall where the attitude toward language presupposes that it is a set of tools in stock for signifying preestablished meanings and where the alienated condition of persons is exactly suited to that view. The Shandys' failure to come together in conversation, to dwell in a common world established by communal speaking as the servants do in the kitchen scene, contributes to Tristram's concern with the problem of language and provides the measure of his success as a speaker. In the writing that is "but a different name for conversation" where he listens to us and to his own words, to the silent language of his own being and his world, including even the Shandys' failure to ground their speech in listening—he speaks to us, and in doing so listens to his own words, and in that linguistic space encounters his own being in the manner of appropriation.

The Congruency of Rhetoric and Thought

Having accounted for the character of the language act and the underlying theory of meaning as Tristram understands them, we may turn to the principles of organization that govern his efforts to inform and persuade his audience. The actual rhetorical patterns of the novel have been studied in detail,[17] but an important question that has had little attention is yet another way in which Tristram studies his father's excesses and arrives at a clearer position of his own, namely, the age-old conflict between rhetoric and thought which first occupied Socrates and Plato in the debates with the sophists. Lanham has correctly set the topic of rhetoric

17. See especially William J. Farrell, "Nature versus Art as a Comic Pattern in *Tristram Shandy*," *English Literary History* 30 (1963), 16–35; also see Graham Petrie, "Rhetoric as Fictional Technique in *Tristram Shandy*," *Philological Quarterly* 48 (1969), 479–94.

in the novel in this ancient context, specifically against the background of "Sophistic assumptions about man and society" (p. 30). The purpose here will be to investigate that background as a means of discovering in Tristram's understanding a movement beyond the respective positions occupied by Locke and Walter Shandy to the essentially conjunctive character of eloquence and thought.

In the three speeches on love in the *Phaedrus,* Plato examines three broad types of attitude that one may take toward language as a rhetorical implement, and the three correspond closely to the respective attitudes of Locke, Walter, and Tristram.[18] The first is by the sophist Lysias and is recounted to Socrates by Phaedrus who is enamored of the eloquence of the speech. It defends the proposition that the disinterested nonlover is to be preferred to the lover because, in following a prudential policy of what "is most conducive to [his] own interest," he is more reliable and constant, freer of that "malady" which makes him "unable to control himself" (*Phaedrus,* 221). The nonlover, whose type is common in the world, for there are "many more nonlovers than lovers," is devoted to the "objective." Moreover his freedom from personal bias is supposed to make him the firmer friend and the more adaptable companion because he does not jeopardize one's position in the world by attracting undesirable public attention. The rhetorical parallel to the nonlover, praised in Lysias's speech, is the neutral, workaday language which provides an objective account of the world, untarnished by the prejudices of affection. The Royal Society had advocated just such a literal, prosaic language free of the ornaments of rhetoric, unencumbered with those irrational, emotional

18. I am indebted to Richard M. Weaver's discussion of how the speeches on love in the *Phaedrus* are integrated with larger themes of the dialogue: "The *Phaedrus* and the Nature of Rhetoric," in *Philosophy, Rhetoric, and Argumentation,* ed. Maurice Natanson and Henry W. Johnstone, Jr., pp. 63–79.

meanings that are unrelated to the significative function. Lysias is condemning what Locke calls "that powerful instrument of Error and Deceit. . . . If we would speak Things as they are," Locke continues, "we must allow, that all the Art of Rhetoric, besides Order and Clearness, all the artificial and figurative application of Words Eloquence hath invented, are for nothing else but to insinuate wrong Ideas, move the Passions, and thereby mislead the Judgment" (*Essay*, III.x.34). As Traugott observes, Locke "rigorously forgot the passions in his theory of belief" (p. 81); but just as Lysias does not forget to encase his speech in eloquent diction, Locke does not purge his language of metaphors, those instruments of error and deceit. Sterne may have been "easy in his Lockean orientation" (Traugott, p. 56), but he decisively reduces Locke's criticism of rhetoric to absurdity in the character of Walter whose uncritical attitude toward himself and his intellectual theories makes him the dupe of his own passions and the approximate parallel of the selfish lover in Socrates' rebuttal of Lysias's speech.

Socrates attacks Lysias dialectically in an ironic argument which claims that "the non-lover has all the advantages in which the lover is accused of being deficient." The heart of the playfully serious argument, in brief, is that the lover is guilty of exploitation. Because he is "the victim of his passions and the slave of his pleasure," he must insure to himself the delight of his lover by jealousy "reducing him to inferiority," especially by denying him the wisdom of "divine philosophy" and keeping him "wholly ignorant." Furthermore, the selfish lover will deprive his beloved of the physical training, the friends, the kinsmen, and the wealth that might make him strong and less dependent. The lover may make an agreeable companion while he loves, but when his passion cools and the object of his interest changes, he abandons the person whom he has ruined and becomes "a perfidious enemy." The implicit parallel of the base lover in the dialogue is the base rhetorician, against whom under the name *sophist* Plato argued so persuasively that a stain was left on the word *rhetoric* that the efforts of Aristotle, who sought to make it a mode of thought, and all his descendants, not excluding Quintilian, have not successfully eradicated. For all that effort, the skill of the rhetorician, his great distinction, from Athens to Madison Avenue, has remained what he can *do* with language rather than what he can *say* or understand. Yet the *Phaedrus,* as we shall observe presently, offers the grounds of reconciliation between eloquence and thought and in doing so reveals the understanding that Tristram himself reaches.

In the novel Walter's posture as orator closely approximates that of the base lover in several respects. Although Walter is in partial agreement with Locke's view of language, especially in regretting metaphor as an abuse while making frequent use of it, in his character "Sterne developed the forlorn frustrations implicit in Locke's theory, and back into the resultant void marched the passions—with all rhetorical ostentation" (Traugott, pp. 81–82). The result is a vigorous exposure, no less serious for its comic mode, of the exploitative character of rhetoric in the service of aggressive egotism, for Walter seeks to be the ruler in the oral economy of Shandy Hall. We have already observed examples in which he ignores truth and talks for victory, but the crucial instance occurs where Tristram carefully aligns Walter's funeral oration in the parlor with Trim's in the kitchen—

> two orators so contrasted by nature and education, haranguing over the same bier.
> My father a man of deep reading——prompt memory ——with *Cato,* and *Seneca,* and *Epictetus,* at his fingers ends.——
> The corporal——with nothing——to remember—— of no deeper reading than his muster-roll——or greater names at his finger's end, than the contents of it.

The one proceeding from period to period, by metaphor and allusion, and striking the fancy as he went
along, (as men of wit and fancy do) with the entertain-
ment and pleasantry of his pictures and images.

The other, without wit or antithesis, or point, or turn,
this way or that; but leaving the images on one side, and
the pictures on the other, going strait forwards as nature
could lead him, to the heart. O *Trim!* would to heaven
thou had'st a better historian! [V.vi.359]

Trim's simple language of nature can speak volumes in a
single gesture that makes death universal and personal;
whereas Walter's words are chosen to serve his passion, to
express his grief (or disappointment), and to establish his
control over the situation as he undertakes to convince Toby,
ostensibly, himself in fact, that death is nothing. In the middle
of his oration when he quotes "*Servius Sulpicius's* consolatory
letter to *Tully*" by way of Burton, he speaks of returning from
Asia. Toby, unaware that he is quoting, is surprised to hear
it and asks "what year of our Lord was this?——'Twas no
year of our Lord, replied my father.——That's impossible,
cried my uncle *Toby*.——Simpleton! said my father,——
'twas forty years before Christ was born" (V.iii.355). As
rhetorician he is unconcerned with what his words actually
say, and when he is taken at his word, he responds with out-
rage, and insults Toby. Walter uses language as Plato's selfish
lover uses the beloved, as a tool of his own egotism. From this
circumstance there follow two consequences of the greatest
importance which function in his role as rhetorician but
which also broach the issue of impotence in the novel. The
first is the negation of the word, its dissociation from truth,
that is implicit in his rhetoric; the second is his attitude toward man, an anthropology that his self-conscious calculation
in the use of language betrays.

Walter's practice tends to abuse the integrity of the word,
to violate the pact with the world that is implicit in his and

all other speaking, for language is, as Merleau-Ponty puts it, "the vow to retrieve the world" (*Signs*, p. 95). When Trim recites his catechism, Walter delights Yorick by observing, "——SCIENCES MAY BE LEARNED BY ROTE, BUT WISDOM NOT," and goes on to wager "aunt *Dinah*'s legacy, in charitable uses" that Trim lacks "any one determinate idea annexed to any one word he has repeated." In response to the challenge to interpret the commandment to honor parents, Trim shows what firm hold on the concrete world underlies his rote learning: it means "allowing them . . . three halfpence a day out of my pay" (V.xxxii.393). Walter's spontaneous wager in the interest of charity, by contrast, is a hollow gesture unconnected with the concrete world and understood as conferring no obligation. The same point is made in a more general way in the discussion of Ernulphus's curse where Tristram adopts the pose of critic to ridicule the critics' concern with the superficial and exterior dimensions of a work to the exclusion of what it actually says. Nothing is said in this passage about the meaning of the curse, about the way it deals with reality (the person cursed), except for a single remark that refers only to surfaces, but in which Tristram uses ironic understatement to expose the prevailing moral blindness: "there is something of a *hardness* in his manner, ——and, as in *Michael Angelo,* a want of grace,——but then there is such a greatness of *gusto!*" What the Shandys appreciate in the curse is "an orientality" of copious invention that "we cannot rise to." The brunt of the irony is born by Dr. Slop who uses the curse to avenge himself on Obadiah for tying up his "green bays bag" of obstetrical instruments with twenty knots and causing him to slash his thumb instead of the strings with his penknife. Walter mischievously offers him the use of Ernulphus's text commenting that "a wise and just man . . . would always endeavour to proportion the vent given to the humours . . . to the size and ill intent of the offence upon which they are to fall," there having been no ill intent on Obadiah's part at all. And Toby adds, *"Injuries come only from the heart"* (III.x.169). The difference between the exterior shell of words and the spirit that informs it in Dr. Slop's usage is pointed up first by the absurd affair of *borrowing* a curse as though the curse consisted of the marks on the page. In addition Tristram dramatizes the issue in a satiric thrust at critics whose solicitude is only for "th' Exactness of peculiar Parts." By way of example there is Garrick's soliloquy measured by the stopwatch, the book judged by "rule and compasses," the epic compared with "an exact scale of *Bossu's*," and the grand picture which matches none of the masters; Tristram adds, "I would go fifty miles on foot, for I have not a horse worth riding on, to kiss the hand of that man whose generous heart will give up the reins of his imagination into his author's hands" (III.xii.181–82). Toby assumes in all simplicity what Tristram's reflections have revealed in rich complexity: that to use the word is to act upon the world.

Anthropologically, Walter bears out the famous assertion of Protagoras that "man . . . is the measure of all things, of the existence of things that are, and of the non-existence of things that are not,"[19] in which statement the root fallacy of the sophist lies exposed, namely, that there is no "in between," no realm of becoming, no potency in a thing to change. John Wild's succinct analysis shows how the sophist ignores the structure of change, thereby reducing the dynamic unity of the world with its ontological distinction between agent and patient to ontologically equal entities with no "bond of potency."[20] If things are what they are, fully realized and hence not engaged with each other in a hierarchy of becoming, then all beings are coordinate, for without potency

19. *Theaetetus,* 152.
20. "Husserl's Critique of Psychologism: Its Historic Roots and Contemporary Relevance," in *Philosophical Essays in Memory of Edmund Husserl,* ed. Marvin Farber, p. 34.

a world of process is reduced to an inventory of things existing, like marbles in a bag, without intrinsic cohesion. It is
finally contradictory to make man the measure of all things:
he must either be simply another of those unrelated beings,
causally determined and unable to measure anything, or he
must be related to other things from within the hierarchy
of potency and, by means of understanding, able to function
as agent within the process, governed or measured by a
superior agency. Thus *externally* man is set over against
nature, according to the sophist, while *internally* reason is
degraded from the power to understand and give form to the
instincts and desires, to a principle within the soul merely
equal to the passions. In the place of a creative unity of
powers is substituted an uneasy compromise of opposing
forces, the ultimate result of which is that reason, having lost
its natural authority, becomes the tool of the passions.

These issues are pertinent because Walter is not simply
given to making speeches; Tristram's almost exclusive
description of him in rhetorical terms, as though his
argumentative hobby-horse were the very center of his being,
demonstrates that rhetoric is the clue to his whole character.[21]
In volume I where Tristram discusses the theory of that
"strange kind of magick bias" whereby "good or bad names"
become "irresistibly impress'd upon our characters and conduct," he provides the first description of his father as rhetor:

> he was born an orator;——Θεοδίδακτος.——Persuasion
> hung upon his lips, and the elements of Logick and
> Rhetorick were so blended up in him,——and, withall,
> he had so shrewd a guess at the weaknesses and passions of
> his respondent,——that NATURE might have stood up
> and said,——"This man is eloquent." In short, whether
> he was on the weak or the strong side of the question,
> 'twas hazardous in either case to attack him. [I.xix.51–52]

21. Petrie, p. 481.

Graham Petrie remarks that "he never talks *to* anyone; he either talks *at* them or allows them to eavesdrop on his self-communings. But he needs always to be aware that someone is listening to him" (p. 486). His skill and passion in arguing either side of a question demonstrates that his particular blend of logic and rhetoric subordinates the former to the latter and reduces logic to an arsenal of argumentative weapons in the service of the ego rather than a means to understanding and truth. In volume V where Walter displays his oratorical skills on the occasion of Bobby's death, Tristram explores his ruling passion in greater detail:

> My father was as proud of his eloquence as MARCUS TULLIUS CICERO could be for his life, and for aught I am convinced of to the contrary at present, with as much reason: it was indeed his strength——and his weakness too.——His strength——for he was by nature eloquent, ——and his weakness——for he was hourly a dupe to it; and provided an occasion in life would but permit him to shew his talents, or say either a wise thing, a witty, or a shrewd one—(bating the case of a systematick misfortune)——he had all he wanted.——A blessing which tied up my father's tongue, and a misfortune which let it loose with a good grace, were pretty equal: sometimes, indeed, the misfortune was the better of the two; for instance, where the pleasure of the harangue was as *ten,* and the pain of the misfortune but as *five*——my father gained half in half, and consequently was as well again off, as it never had befallen him.
>
> This clue will unravel, what otherwise would seem very inconsistent in my father's domestick character; and it is this, that in the provocations arising from the neglects and blunders of servants, or other mishaps unavoidable in a family, his anger, or rather the duration of it, eternally ran counter to all conjecture. [V.iii.352]

Of all the dark tendencies in Walter's character none is darker than his inclination to subordinate all of nature to his rhetorical interests, and yet he remains an essentially comic character who butts his head against an intractable world and leaves the world none the worse for it. When his hopes for a colt from his favorite mare are dashed by what he takes to be Obadiah's mismanagement of the affair,

> My mother and my uncle *Toby* expected my father would be the death of *Obadiah*——and that there never would be an end of the disaster.——See hear! you rascal, cried my father, pointing to the mule, what you have done!——It was not me, said *Obadiah*.——How do I know that? replied my father.
>
> Triumph swam in my father's eyes, at the repartee—— the *Attic* salt brought water into them——and so *Obadiah* heard no more about it. [V.iii.352–53]

Since the disruptive tendencies in Walter's character are being stressed here, it is important to observe that his aggressive egotism is mitigated by his comic stance. Numerous examples show that he is not too serious to play.

The most important point to mark about Walter as rhetorician is that language is not a way to truth, a means of understanding his world and his own being. "There was not a subject in the world upon which my father was so eloquent, as upon that of door-hinges.——And yet at the same time, he was certainly one of the greatest bubbles to them, I think, that history can produce: his rhetoric and conduct were at perpetual handy-cuffs" (III.xxi.203). His speaking does not rise out of a silent, rational attending to the world; it is an imposition of his own rationalistic concepts upon things. Like the ancient sophist who could not account for change, Walter makes no effort to achieve ontological understanding, to see things as they are. It is as though the world of becoming, which is the concern of philosophy, had been banished into the abyss of nonbeing. The unimportance of the being question which occupies Tristram so extensively is ironically pointed up in the example of the white bear. He uses the bear to exemplify to Yorick the doctrine that "the whole" of the intellectual world "entirely depends ... upon the auxiliary verbs." The irony is that these are the very parts of the language that express the ways in which one can be related to the dynamic processes of being. The verb "to be" is prominent in the list, of course, although what "to be" says is exactly what is being ignored in Walter's claim that having so much as seen a white bear is irrelevant to one's ability to talk at length about one. "Now, by the right use and application of these, continued my father, in which a child's memory should be exercised, there is no one idea can enter his brain how barren soever, but a magazine of conceptions and conclusions may be drawn from it" (V.xlii.406). Walter exemplifies the consequences that follow from the dissociation of speaking and being, of word and world.

One of the strongest arguments for the protagonist's having arrived at a more satisfactory understanding of rhetoric is the clarity with which he explores the exploitative behavior of the man whose aim is to rule in the realm of words rather than enlist in the service of truth. On the surface it is not at first so obvious, however, that Tristram differs much from his father. Like him, he has the marks of the contending orator; although he is writing a book, he is essentially oral in his linguistic orientation, devoted to the temporal and synthetic use of language. At times he is even combative like his father—though for signally different ends. It is Toby whose position in relation to language offers the most conspicuous contrast in that he must resort to space in order to "speak." In this respect he is the representative of objectified, visualist culture, essentially passive, where the others are devoted to vigorous rhetorical and dialectical competition.[22] The specific

22. On the traits of personality fostered by a visual culture, see Ong, pp. 130–38.

difference between Walter and Tristram is the latter's use of rhetoric in the service of understanding, which also allows an accommodation of the oral word, the center of communal life, to the textual word.

The third speech in the *Phaedrus* is, like the second, spoken by Socrates, and its object is to provide the accommodation of rhetoric and truth. We learn that there are four types of divine madness, "prophetic, initiatory, poetic, erotic," each inspired by its appropriate god and superior to ordinary sanity. "The attachment of the non-lover, which is alloyed with a worldly prudence and has worldly and niggardly ways of doling out benefits, will breed in your soul those vulgar qualities which the populace applaud, will send you bowling round the earth during a period of nine thousand years, and leave you a fool in the world below." The selfish madness of the base lover is a derangement, says Socrates (an aberration, we might say), but the madness of the inspired lover is "the greatest of heaven's blessings," for by bringing its own instincts and desires under control it entertains "no feelings of envy or jealousy" and tries "to make him [the beloved] as like as possible" the god who inspires it. The bearing of this final speech upon rhetoric is that the same instrument that seeks to move the listener for exploitative motives may be used in the service of truth, indeed must be so used, for Socrates has Rhetoric advise on her own behalf, "arrive at the truth first, and then come to me. . . . I boldly assert that mere knowledge of the truth will not give you the art of persuasion." The famous myth of the chariot dramatizes the point in Socrates' own speech: having arrived at the true position by means of dialectic, he uses the allegory to move Phaedrus to share his view, thereby surpassing Lysias, the defender of rhetoric, at his own game.

Petrie has shown that Tristram's rhetoric, unlike Walter's, "is never abstract and never purely formal; it concerns itself with human beings and with the means of describing, persuading, amusing and convincing them." He uses it as a way to "sort out the details of his story and to present it to his audience in some kind of coherent form . . . to persuade the audience to adopt the attitudes towards the characters and events of his story which he wishes them to have" (pp. 485, 489). In the light of what has already been said about the protagonist and his readers, the point will be made sufficiently clear by a single example. When Tristram proposes to translate "the tenth tale of the tenth decad" from Slawkenbergius, he discusses the problem of saying the unsayable in a passage that mixes facetiousness and that spontaneity of thinking that carries the credibility of the involuntary gesture. The tale is "The Intricacies of *Diego* and *Julia*" and it gives "a whimsical view of the involutions of the heart of a woman."

> . . . how this can ever be translated into good *English,* I have no sort of conception.——There seems in some passages to want a sixth sense to do it rightly.——What can he mean by the lambent pupilability of slow, low, dry chat, five notes below the natural tone,——which you know, madam, is little more than a whisper? The moment I pronounced the words, I could perceive an attempt towards a vibration in the strings, about the region of the heart.——The brain made no acknowledgment.——There's often no good understanding betwixt 'em.——I felt as if I understood it.——I had no ideas.—— The movement could not be without cause.——I'm lost. I can make nothing of it,——unless, may it please your worships, the voice, in that case being little more than a whisper, unavoidably forces the eyes to approach not only within six inches of each other——but to look into the pupils——is that not dangerous? [IV.i.273]

The actual conceptual content of the story remains obscure as Tristram explains his responses to the tone of the text he claims to be trying to translate. The intimacy of his relationship with the reader as he sits listening to that tone and puzzling over its mysterious effects has a high level of credibility because we are participants in the enquiry—and it makes no difference that the whole episode is facetious. Tristram is articulating his own processes as he turns his text this way and that, trying to reach an understanding. We are neither "eavesdropping" nor being "talked at"; we are being drawn into that play of mind.

In the earlier discussion of Tristram's careful construction of a community of discourse with his audience, it was observed that his rhetoric is both reflexive (that is, a narrative which interprets himself to himself by means of his transcendence) and oriented toward an audience with whom he seeks to establish a "familiarity" that "will terminate in friendship." (I.vi.10–11). The fact that his rhetoric aims at understanding the real nature of the self that he is, shows that his rhetoric and thought are not simply complementary, but essentially conjunctive. Given the intersubjective character of the self, his search for a true or authentic relationship to himself is complemented by his efforts to establish an intimacy with his readers, and that relationship with the audience is necessary to both the dialectical and the rhetorical aspects of his project to make sense of his life. He does not, therefore quite agree with Socrates' view in the *Phaedrus* that rhetoric is necessary for conveying the truth once it is acquired; he goes beyond that by making it part of the means of arriving at truth, a component in the process of which anything is assimilated in the act of interpretation. Discovery and expression are therefore, as in Quintilian, the same process, and Tristram's thought and his rhetoric are one.

Where empiricism is interested in the representative function of the sign, *Tristram Shandy* meditates the event of meaning from which signification derives. When it is approached by means of reflection, language reveals itself as essentially synthetic rather than analytic; the aim of the word is interpretation rather than representation. Tristram studies language in the human act of speaking and as a clue to the ontology of the being who speaks. In his meditations, as in St. Augustine's, we are carried up to those "first springs" of meaning where we discover that it is by grace of the word that we have a phenomenal world. The temporal depth of transcendence enables him to speak, and in speech beings stand forth from the undifferentiated background of being. In the being-space thus opened by language, in the domain of the word, the self and its phenomenal world come into presence in a prereflective unity. In that being-space of language, furthermore, the various horizons of Tristram and his audience coalesce, and for us the thesis with reference to the word reinforces the thesis with reference to the self. All speaking is an interpreting, and since the phenomenal self arises in the hermeneutical encounter with the other, it is as though Tristram came to be in a conversation that has already begun before he appears and that extends beyond him even to this discussion of his book. Thus language may be said to give Tristram himself or to be the locus of his being, which at bottom is a conversation.

Having clarified the finite, temporal structure of that being and its interpretive function, we may now turn back to the original occasion of the enquiry which made Tristram's being a problem to him and ask what difference all these reflections make to a child of wrath, decrepitude, and mistake, cast so untimely into the "scurvy and disastrous world." The answering will be a reflection on the Shandy malaise and the modern world and an act of appropriation which is an inalienable part of the interpretive process.

5

Tristram's Sorrow: The Crisis of European Life

This study has argued that Tristram is quite literally and in good faith writing his "life and opinions" by exploring the foundations of his selfhood rather than recounting, as most fictions do, the existential concerns that might occupy his ordinary life. All his digressions are in both substance and manner of presentation necessary and coherent constituents of this essentially ontological project of interrogation which brings to the fore the involvement of the intentional structure and communal character of consciousness, the syndrome of time, finitude, and death, and the coincidence of speech, rhetoric, and truth in the processes of Tristram's being. It is also within the horizon of this project that we come to the climactic theme, the impotence that mars all the prospects of the family, his own creative aspirations, and even the future of his world. The place of this theme in his project is different from those which have guided us through the earlier stages of our researches, however: in seeking to understand the Shandy malaise we largely emerge from the ontological enquiry and return to the conventional level of discussion that has traditionally occupied Sterne criticism. What will be new here is the richer setting of the existential concern with the psychic health and creative life of the family that is provided by the being question, the contribution of "true Shandeism" to the ideal of creative life, and the fresh perspective that our path back to the fulness of being offers on the form of the novel as a whole.

Melvyn New has observed that the metaphor of creativity is the unifying idea of the whole work from the concern with procreation to "the whole of man's physical and intellectual efforts to propagate himself and his ideas." Without agreeing that the theme gives the book its deepest principle of unity, one is obliged to agree that the issue of creativity permeates it. With Bobby's death in volume IV, Tristram's position in the family changes: "FROM this moment I am to be considered as heir-apparent to the *Shandy* family——and it is from this point properly, that the story of my LIFE and my OPINIONS sets out; with all my hurry and precipitation I have but been clearing the ground to raise the building——and such a building do I forsee it will turn out, as never was planned, and as never was executed since *Adam*" (IV.xxxii.336). It is as heir to the Shandys that the irony of his name reaches its fullest proportions: had Walter succeeded in getting to Mrs. Shandy's chamber in time to have him named Trismagistus, he would thereby have been associated with creative power; but Walter's unskillfulness at getting into his breeches and Susannah's leaky memory testify to the general incompetence of the family that makes the sorrow in the name Tristram more appropriate for the child that is destined to be its last representative.

It has been demonstrated already that Tristram's program for his book is to bring clarity to that complex problem, his life, for he is, as Walter's lament puts it, the "child of wrath! child of decrepitude! interruption! mistake! and discontent!" (IV.xix.296). But the burden of his heritage is not simply the sexual impotence of his family; their enigma is a symbol of a general cultural malaise that may justifiably be called, and that we are in fact encouraged to see as, the crisis of western life, so large are the implications of the novel. A preliminary concern of this chapter will be to explore the full extent and significance of the impotence or, in more general terms, the paralyzed affectivity that has marked every Shandy for several generations. The larger investigation will be into the condition of the modern world and the causes of its illness as reflected in the novel with particular attention to its future prospects. The discussion will finally turn to the grounds for hope, without which the comic spirit of the novel would suffer, and to discovering what resources of healing are available to the inhabitants of Shandy Hall, the general features of which, rather than fully justifying the critical comparisons between Sterne and twentieth-century existentialism and absurdist literature, affirm the conservative, Augustan qualities of Sterne's mind and art.

The Shandy Malaise

The Geographical and Historical Dimensions of the Problem

It is first necessary to establish that the domestic circumstances of the family are typical of their world at large. As Tristram reviews the family history, it is a story of noses: Walter

> would often declare, in speaking his thoughts upon the subject, that he did not conceive how the greatest family in *England* could stand it out against an uninterrupted succession of six or seven short noses.——And for the contrary reasons, he would generally add, That it must be one of the greatest problems in civil life, where the same number of long and jolly noses following one another in a direct line, did not raise and hoist it up into the best vacancies in the kingdom.——He would often boast that the *Shandy* family rank'd very high in king *Harry* the VIIIth's time, but owed its rise to no state engine,——he would say,——but to that only;——but

> that, like other families, he would add,——it had felt the
> turn of the wheel, and had never recovered the blow of
> my great grandfather's nose.——It was an ace of clubs
> indeed, he would cry, shaking his head,——and as vile a
> one for an unfortunate family, as ever turn'd up trumps.
> [III.xxxiii.220–21]

Walter's view is reductionist in that he gives priority to the
proportions of the physical organ of generation in tracing
the fortunes of the family; but Tristram's appropriation of
Walter's account suggests the core of truth in this comic
passage. The fortunes of the family are taken to parallel the
fortunes of the nation. The family flourished in the sixteenth
century, but fell into a decline at the time of the civil wars,
for Tristram's great-grandfather had "little or no nose"
(III.xxxi.217) and yet it was an inch longer than his father's
had been (III.xxxii.219)—Sir Roger, that is, who wore the
jackboots at the battle of Marston-Moor (III.xxii.205). As we
learn later, "in all our numerous family, for these four generations, we count no more than one archbishop, a *Welch*
judge, some three or four aldermen, and a single mounte-
bank——In the sixteenth century, we boast of no less than a
dozen alchymists" (VIII.iii.542). The decline is evident from
men of learning with access to the great mystery of things to
a few functionaries of church, state, and trade. If the life of
the family, specifically its creative capacity, corresponds to
the life of the nation, then the spiritual conditions in Shandy
Hall require careful analysis. But the extent of the crisis is
not limited to England. In a variety of ways the scope of the
problem is established as coextensive with European culture, most notably by Slawkenbergius's Tale and by Tristram's experiences on the continent in volume VII.

Slawkenbergius's Tale[1] reinforces the historical point made

1. Criticism has not dealt very satisfactorily with the Tale. William
Freedman accounts for its presence by a chain of contingencies: Walter
translated it because noses interested him greatly because of the family

by the family history for it explicitly associates the effect of Diego's nose upon the Strasburgers with Luther and the Reformation: "such a cause of restlessness and disquietude, and such a zealous enquiry into the cause of that restlessness, had never happened in *Strasburg,* since *Martin Luther,* with his doctrines, had turned the city up-side down" (IV.255). Moreover "the two universities of *Strasburg*——the *Lutheran* . . . and the *Popish* . . . were . . . employing the whole depth of their knowledge . . . in determining the point of *Martin Luther's* damnation" (IV.260–61). The resemblance between the polemical struggles of Nosarians with Antinosarians and the intellectual battles of the novel make it appropriate that the Tale should be Walter's favorite among Slawkenbergius's Decads. It seems to be Slawkenbergius's interpretation that the loss of the city to Louis XIV in 1681 was owing to the same condition that made it readily accept reformed doctrines by about 1523, namely, curiosity, cast here in the form of the epistemological problem: how does one know the truth about the stranger's nose? The hobby-horsical accounts divide both learned and unlearned among themselves. The medical faculty disputes naturalistically over the nose and its possible place in the design of nature; the logicians argue about death, an issue that is said to be "closer to the point" (some take an abstract naturalistic position that death is "nothing but the stagnation of the blood" while others argue the equally abstract traditional view that "Death is the separation of the soul from the body") (IV.259); the theologians divide into the rationalistic Popish group and the voluntaristic Lutherans among whom the question of the Real Presence is

---

history of noses which comes up because of the accident to Tristram's nose at birth (p. 279). True enough, but associational patterns alone cannot reveal the inner coherence of these or any of the other digressions. John Stedmond finds parallels between the Tale and Tristram's story which are "inexact but suggestive" (p. 105).

scarcely concealed. The vulgar meanwhile debate the facts of the case, but "every *Strasburger* had the intelligence he wanted" (IV.257). The conspicuous question in all the disputes is the central issue of modern thought: the nature, limits, and test of knowledge. The parody is of the reductionist tendency inherent in all specialized systems, legal, medical, logical, or what have you; none provide valid accounts of the world. But it is important to note that the satire in no way precludes knowledge of the real. The satire itself works on the presumption that there is a standard for knowing which the Strasburgers do not measure up to and which Tristram and his audience share.

The social disorder, the ultimate collapse of the city, is caused by what no citizen pauses to reflect upon, namely, their idolatry of the organ of procreation belonging to a man who has himself been on a pilgrimage to the Promontory of Noses in the service of a higher ideal, of love for his mistress Julia. The result is that the whole city is disarmed for any creative work whatever. Diego, like the Shandys of Harry VIII's time, has the stature of a character from romance, whose creative capacity is symbolized by the appurtenance of the nose. The implication is that the fall of the city, "the true springs of this and such like revolutions," is the disposition to indulge one's curiosity about matters that are not one's real concern. The futile debates do not reveal the real source of the Strasburgers' fascination with the nose, whether real or not, as reflection on their preoccupation might have done. Their own sterility, demonstrated in the haggling, is expressed in that concern with the symbol of fertility as is Walter's and, in a different way, Tristram's own throughout the novel. The Tale, therefore, not only restates many thematic concerns of the opening volumes; it extends the spiritual crisis of Shandy Hall to the Continent and, by association with the Reformation and the epistemological question, locates the Shandy malaise within a general crisis of

modern western life, the implications of which Tristram seeks
to bring to light.

The historical scope of Tristram's thought extends outward
into the future when he considers the state of the culture half
a century hence. In reproving his readers for preferring
accounts of the dimensions of the parish church at Montreuil
to the dimensions of Janatone, Tristram says the readers may
take the former themselves since all is as the builders left it
and, "if the belief in *Christ* continues so long, will be so these
fifty years" (VII.ix.490). A bit later after a reference to his
own times as "the latter days" when "David prophetically
foresaw" the *"grand tour,* and that restless spirit for making
it . . . would haunt the children of men" (VII.xii.492), he
enters into the calculations of Lessius and Franciscus Ribbera
on the size of hell. He scorns "the cold cautiousness of one of
those little souls from which *Lessius* . . . hath made his estimate, wherein he setteth forth, That one *Dutch* mile, cubi-
cally multiplied, will allow room enough, and to spare, for
eight hundred thousand millions, which he supposes to be as
great a number of souls (counting from the fall of *Adam*) as
can possibly be damn'd to the end of the world." Franciscus
Ribbera makes a different calculation of the area that will be
required for such a number, but

> he certainly must have gone upon some of the old *Roman*
> souls, of which he had read, without reflecting how much,
> by a gradual and most tabid decline, in course of eigh-
> teen hundred years, they must unavoidably have shrunk,
> so as to have come, when he wrote, almost to nothing.
>
> In *Lessius's* time, who seems the cooler man, they were
> as little as can be imagined——
>
> ——We find them less *now*——
>
> And next winter we shall find them less again; so that
> if we go on from little to less, and from less to nothing, I
> hesitate not one moment to affirm, that in half a century,
> at this rate, we shall have no souls at all; which being the

period beyond which I doubt likewise of the existence of
the Christian faith, 'twill be one advantage that both of
'em will be exactly worn out together. [VII.xiv.494–95]

The disorder that is represented under the sign of Shandy
impotence is geographically as large as Europe, historically
as old at least as the Reformation with which it bears close
kinship, and as bleak as the prospects of the family when
Tristram, anticipating the demise of Christian culture, dies
without heirs.

Structural Implications

The issue of creativity comes to the fore in the final volumes
of the novel and in such a way as to raise the question of their
unity with the earlier parts of the book. This has, of course,
been a bone of contention for years. There is nothing new
in the claim that Tristram's interest in Toby's experiences
is a means of learning more about himself.[2] Toby is directly
responsible for the clause in the marriage contract about Elizabeth's making a journey to London "upon false cries and
tokens" which indirectly contributes to the misfortunes of
Tristram's birth, and he is indirectly responsible for the
window accident as well. However, these are all external
matters that hardly touch the inner significance of the relation between Toby and his nephew about which there is still
considerable obscurity.

In 1940 James Work argued in his introduction to *Tristram Shandy* (pp. xlviii-xlix) that there are two narrative
sequences, the tale of Walter's household, including Tristram's birth, and the story of Toby's adventures. Later, Rufus
Putney stressed the formal design of the five and a half
volumes devoted to the first narrative line while regarding

2. Overton Philip James, *The Relation of "Tristram Shandy" to the
Life of Sterne*, p. 135.

the shift to Toby as a change in design and a weakness (p. 163). Then Wayne Booth dramatically extended appreciation of the plan of the work as a whole by marshalling both external and internal evidence to prove that there is no change in plan and that the two lines of development are thoroughly intertwined:

> Sterne planned the structure of the book as an elaborate and prolonged contradiction of his title-page. For this purpose, one major shift of attention, if sufficiently surrounded with a multiplicity of minor shifts, is all that is needed: begin by pretending to tell the life and opinions of Tristram Shandy and end by telling the amours and campaigns of Uncle Toby, concluding the whole account four years before the birth of your hero.[3]

Booth's argument effectively silences the complaint of generations that the book is "without plan or order."[4] What it does not settle is the precise character of that order. The claim that the title page is contradicted by the structure and that the story belongs to Toby requires decisive proof; in fact, all of Booth's evidence, thorough as it is, is consistent with the thesis developed here that Tristram's reflective clarification of the conditions of his own existence requires the careful examination of his genetic community, especially as it explicates the specific conditions which result in his ill-fated conception, birth, and the sequence of accidents that mar his chances in the world. The prominence of Toby in the early volumes, the anticipations of his story as the "choicest morsel," the finality of volume IX and all its parallels with volume I support the conclusion that Tristram's "life and opinions," not Toby's, are completed by the ninth volume and its apt summary of Obadiah's problem with the bull, of Toby's affair with Mrs. Wadman, and of the whole unfortunate

3. Wayne C. Booth, "Did Sterne Complete *Tristram Shandy?*" *Modern Philology* 48 (1951), 180.

4. Walter Bagehot, *Literary Studies*, II, 104; quoted in Booth, p. 172.

sequence of Tristram's problems beginning with the first
Sunday night in March 1718—all summarized as a story of
"A COCK and BULL."

It is true that in both the early and the late volumes that the
"work is digressive, and it is progressive too"; it is but another "master-stroke of digressive skill" that Toby's story
advances Tristram's own which figures as prominently as
ever, "one wheel within another" (I.xxii.72–73). There is
positive evidence that even in the midst of his own story Toby
is the smaller wheel. Although volume IX "is almost entirely
concerned with these amours and describes them *in their entirely*," as Booth says, the truth of the matter is that Toby's
story is more nearly the occasion of volume IX than its focus.
It is not primarily about him at all. The amours merely provide the most conspicuous opportunity in the recent history
of the family for Tristram to investigate the general problem
of dissociated affectivity as a dimension of his own misfortunes. His insistence upon letting "people tell their stories
their own way" invites close scrutiny of his strategy at this
crucial point. He carefully juxtaposes his own experience
both as writer and as traveler against Toby's story and
manages the latter in an unusual way that signals his intention. The narrative sequence has been gradually "mended"
until he is "able to go on with my uncle *Toby*'s story, and my
own, in a tolerable straight line" (VI.xl.473). Melvyn New
finds the more direct strategy "hardly in his favor—the line
is straight enough, but in the wrong direction, as Tristram
moves further and further away from his own 'life and
opinions.' "[5] But by this point in the novel the central investigation with its regional enquiries is sufficiently clear so that

5. "Sterne and Henry Baker's *The Microscope Made Easy*," p. 103, n.
2. Elsewhere New argues that "the growing disorganization and dissolution of Tristram in his study is here dramatically epitomized in the
structure of the work; retreating . . . into the past, Tristram is turned
completely around and, to the end of Volume IX, never regains his
bearings" (*Laurence Sterne as Satirist*, p. 163).

the numerous digressions required to reveal, for example, the global field of Toby's character, are no longer needed. He is free to move forward, as he has promised so often, in the examination of what can go wrong with the kind of creature he has discovered himself and the people in his community to be. Thus he announces in volume VI, "WE are now going to enter upon a new scene of events" which requires that other matters be left behind: "Let us leave, if possible, *myself:*—— But 'tis impossible,——I must go along with you to the end of the work" (VI.xx.442). Then he launches his most direct and extended account of himself by devoting all of the seventh volume to his tours of the Continent, thereby demonstrating that he has no intention of telling someone else's story to the exclusion of his own.

Volume VIII, as part of Toby's story, is largely preparatory; its theme is love, developed by means of contrasting points of view, especially Walter's, Trim's, and Toby's, as we shall see when we study the characters individually. Volume IX opens then with Toby and Trim marching on Mrs. Wadman's house under the watchful eyes of Walter and Elizabeth. Trim encourages (and delays) his master with the story of his brother Tom. First, Trim "unwarily conjured up the Spirit of calculation with his wand" and the "flourish" expressive of freedom; whereupon he "conjured him down again" with the obscene tale of Tom's sausage courtship with the Jew's widow in Lisbon. Tristram then devotes four chapters (xii-xv) to a digression on the problem of writing a work balanced "betwixt wisdom and folly" thereby stationing himself prominently in Toby's adventure (so prominently, in fact, as to interrupt the suspense of the story repeatedly). What he feels the need of in his work at this point is something of fancy, wit, or pleasantry: "The only difficulty, is raising powers suitable to the nature of the service" (IX.xii. 614). Since "FANCY is capricious——WIT must not be searched for——and PLEASANTRY (good-natured slut as she is) will not come in at a call, was an empire to be laid at her feet," one must find some way of coping with the difficulty on his own. "——The best way for a man, is to say his prayers ——" unless, as presumably happens in Tristram's case, "it puts him in mind of his infirmities and defects as well ghostly as bodily." He gets no help from reflecting on the faculties of the soul, none from restraining the body "by temperance, soberness and chastity," and none from the theological virtues since the courage gained from "faith and hope" is annulled by "that sniveling virtue of Meekness." What works better in overcoming dullness "in ordinary cases . . . when I am only stupid . . . Or . . . I am got . . . into a cold unmetaphorical vein of infamous writing" is to shave and to "dress myself from one end to the other of me, after my best fashion" (IX.xiii.615–16). Tristram explains the effect of his procedure in a conceit that parallels the process of his book in that, while shaving, a man is engaged in studying his own reflection in a mirror: ". . . as every man chuses to be present at the shaving of his own beard . . . and unavoidably sits overagainst himself the whole time it is doing . . . ——the Situation . . . has notions of her own to put into the brain.——" Thus "a rough-bearded man," perhaps because his beard takes longer to cut, "might be carried up by continual shavings, to the highest pitch of sublimity."

The apparent object of this digression, placed in the middle of Toby's courtship, is to associate Tristram's inconstant powers as an artist with Toby's less than vigorous manner of wooing the widow. Although he has been promising through several volumes that his treatment of the affair will "turn out one of the most compleat systems . . . of love and love-making, that ever was addressed to the world" (VI.xxxvi.466), he now complains, "though I have all along been hastening towards this part of it, with so much earnest desire, as well knowing it to be the choicest morsel of what I had to offer to the world, yet now that I am got to it, any one is welcome to take up my

pen, and go on with the story for me that will——I see the
difficulties of the descriptions I'm going to give——and feel
my want of powers" (IX.xxiv.627). The interruption, which
incidentally serves to keep him clearly in view, shows his
spirits flagging at this juncture, and he writes an Invocation
to the "Gentle Spirit of sweetest humour" in which he claims
that as he traveled through France and Italy, "my uncle
Toby's amours running all the way in my head, they had the
same effect upon me as if they had been my own." This tendency is toward the coalescence of Tristram's state of mind
with his uncle's, especially when on the Continent the French
girls run in his head and make him feel that kinship poign-
antly despite the surface difference between Toby's modesty
and his own lust. The parallel is reinforced by the story of
"poor Maria," gone mad from disappointed love when her
banns were forbid by a vicious curate. The interlude showing
Tristram's sympathy with the damsel in distress bears comparing with Toby who is afraid of women "unless in sorrow
or distress; then infinite was his pity; nor would the most
courteous knight of romance have gone further . . . to have
wiped a tear from a woman's eye" (IX.iii.602–03). Tristram
hears the girl's sad music, leaps from the chaise in which he
is traveling, and rushes to her. When a glance of her eyes
associates him with her goat, he is struck with "the humblest
conviction of what a *Beast* man is." In this remark worthy of
his father, he rejects the spirit of comedy: "I would not have
let fallen an unseasonable pleasantry in the venerable pres-
ense of Misery, to be entitled to all the wit that ever *Rabelais*
scatter'd——and yet I own my heart smote me, and that I so
smarted at the very idea of it, that I swore I would set up for
Wisdom and utter grave sentences the rest of my days——and
never——never attempt again to commit mirth with man,
woman, or child, the longest day I had to live" (IX.xxiv.631).
The sentiment is of Toby's kind, and in associating himself
with gravity Tristram opposes entirely the comic spirit and
whatever wisdom it offers.

Meanwhile Toby and Trim march up to the widow's door; but instead of getting Toby's confession that *"he was in love"* as he sits down (xviii) and his equally brief proposal of marriage (xix), we are dropped suddenly into the famous scene in which Mrs. Wadman enquires about the exact place of the wound. It demonstrates Toby's fatal "modesty," as Tristram calls it, and the widow's aggressiveness, neither of which are so clear in the delayed chapters. Tristram is not interested in the narrative for its own sake but in the underlying psychic forces which in some way help him understand himself. Therefore, he follows the chapter on the wound (xx) with an examination of the widow's motives and strategy, explained with the help of Slawkenbergius's account of how a woman in search of a husband stops one ass after another and thrusts her hand into his pannier to discover what is inside (xxi). Then comes a chapter investigating how the purposes of nature "bungle it" in creating "a married man," specifically applied to Toby:

> with regard to my uncle *Toby*'s fitness for the marriage state, nothing was ever better: she had formed him of the best and kindliest clay——had temper'd it with her own milk, and breathed into it the sweetest spirit——she had made him all gentle, generous and humane——she had fill'd his heart with trust and confidence, and disposed every passage which led to it, for the communication of the tenderest offices. [IX.xxii.626]

There are deeper issues here than a mismatching of modesty and sexual aggressiveness, but the point at the moment is Tristram's skipping over materials which in Toby's story would be pertinent, and signaling his strategy by leaving the chapters blank. The account of the adventure is eventually completed, but conspicuously subordinate to and shaped by Tristram's central purpose. By announcing his intention to recount events linearly, then suspending narrative links as important as Toby's confession of love and his proposal, meanwhile studying the psychic causes of incompatibility and juxtaposing all of this with his own case in the Invocation, Tristram makes an explicit comparison of the story as it would be told if it were actually Toby's with the story that is told of his own life.

The overall effect of this narrative strategy is to associate the issue of artistic creativity in Tristram with that of sexual vigor in Toby and, within the region of this riddle to make problematic the relation of sentiment, modesty, passivity, and a mood of seriousness with the incapacity that troubles all the residents of Shandy Hall. The important question, therefore, is how the central theme of volumes VIII and IX contributes to Tristram's understanding of himself and his world and thus completes the project announced on his title page. For that we must consider the contrasting points of view in the family, not only on the question of love that surfaces on the occasion of uncle Toby's affair, but the full range of psychic aberrations that have a place in the riddle of Tristram's life.

Pathology of the Family

Tristram's most extensive examination of the failure of creativity which touches his life so intimately centers, of course, in the brothers Shandy who divide between them the traits of the modern intellectual and the modern man of feeling. Under the scrutiny of the book both are recognized as suffering from specific kinds of psychic fragmentation. As has already been remarked, Walter demonstrates the bent of the modern thinker, who from the perspective of the Augustan satirist, Tristram himself, and, by our day, not a few others, is perpetually engaged in an aggressive egotism of reckless speculations that "twist and torture everything in nature to support his hypothesis," an unequivocal expression of the will to power, relieved in the novel from time to time by those winning lapses into good-natured affection and

rhetorical joking and by Tristram's comic spirit which tends
to allay all vices in the telling. Tristram's representation of
his father's science shows that his intellectualism is an aberration, first, in the egotism and, second, in the abstractionism
inherent in all his thinking.

In the first case Walter, like both Descartes and Locke,
assumes a detached, unconditioned ego at the center of a
world that is already constituted. He never enquires how
there comes to be an ego in a context; and the practical consequence of this theoretical omission is that he overlooks that
primordial affective and conceptual engagement with the
world that conditions all thought. Hence he neglects his own
inherent intentional bias and proceeds to reason the world
into the shape of his own proclivities. This uncritical egotism
and seriousness about himself at the center of all Walter's
theorizing is one of the most prophetic insights in the book,
for at the core of the character is an attitude that threatens
to reduce reality to an inventory of objects at the mercy of
his own manipulative will to power in exactly the fashion
that has since been the achievement of technological thought.
As analysis of the intellectual conditions that were to lead to
the spirit of technology and the general exploitation of
nature, the portrait is as profound as Swift's study of Laputa.
A brief example will demonstrate how the closed systems of
Walter's aggressive thought, untempered by the more relaxed
intentions of Tristram's comic spirit, serves the uncritical
interests of his own ego. When he refuses to allow Mrs.
Shandy to lie in in London, he fears the opinion of the world
—not the danger to his wife, observe—should any misfortune
result. So he argues to himself that the "publick good" is
concerned in the question: "the body national" is like "the
body natural" in that the "flow of population and wealth"
to London is like the flow of "blood and spirits" to the brain.
The resulting "stoppage of circulation" threatens "a state
apoplexy," an ill consequence to be avoided presumably by

Mrs. Shandy's giving birth in the country. The vicious circularity and self-deluding character of this procedure consists in the unreflective assumption that as a thinking subject one occupies an unconditioned, absolutely neutral perspective, immune therefore to the inherent biases without which, in fact, no consciousness would be conceivable.

The second point about Walter's science is closely associated with this egotism. In *The Crisis of the European Sciences,* as we have seen, Husserl describes how physics since Galileo has constructed a mathematical universe based ultimately upon the experience of perception and supposed to explain the perceptual world. Instead of explaining the concrete world of ordinary life, physical systems conceived in mathematical terms have been substituted for the actual processes of what in the strictest sense is the *real* human world. Tristram's characterization of his father is in part a *reductio ad absurdam* of the process Husserl describes. Walter supposes that his theories about names and noses, auxiliary verbs and childbirth provide accounts of the ordinary world, when in fact he substitutes misfit theoretical constructions for the existential world and thereby loses his ability to deal effectively with that concrete human reality. Tristram indicates how clearly he understands his father's self-delusion when he says that "it is the nature of an hypothesis, when once a man has conceived it, that it assimilates every thing to itself as proper nourishment; and, from the first moment of your begetting it, it generally grows the stronger by every thing you see, hear, read, or understand" (II.xix.151). Thus it happens that Walter creates a theoretical world in the place of the existential world of squeaking parlor doors that nonetheless persist in interrupting his naps. Nowhere is this feature of his intellectual life clearer than in his projected Tristrapaedia which, as Tristram says, "My father spun, every thread of it, out of his brain." He has been frustrated in three points that are most material to the welfare of his offspring and the future prospects of the family: the damage to the seat of the understanding inevitably sustained by "470 pounds averdupoise acting perpendicularly upon it" in natural childbirth, the christening in which the little Shandy is "Tristram'd" with the most contemptible and abhorred name in all Christendom, and the accidental foreshortening of "that precious part of him" upon the well-being of which part the entire future hope of the family depends. Hence it is that Walter, "baffled and overthrown in all his little systems and wishes," places such importance on Tristram's education. "Prejudice of education," in Walter's unexamined and deeply prejudiced view, *"is the devil"* and must be resisted with all the spirit that one uses in avoiding "the clack of nurses and . . . the nonsense of the old women." He is, of course, defeated in this scheme as he is in all the others by something gone awry in his intellectuals; Tristram comments, "the misfortune was that I was all that time totally neglected and abandoned to my mother; and what was almost as bad, by the very delay, the first part of the work, upon which my father had spent the most of his pains, was rendered entirely useless,——every day a page or two became of no consequence" (V.xvi.375).

Nor is this feature of Walter's character an isolated phenomenon; it is in some measure a class phenomenon. It is bound thereby to the world of utilitarian work. He is retired from trade, no longer obviously engaged with the world on a practical, economic level. The advantage is that we observe him as he is, not as he bends to the necessities of the public world. What this specification of class reveals is an attitude of mind that is as typical of his theoretical speculations in retirement as of his trade in Colman Street. Just as the merchant's dealing with the world subordinates the world to his own calculations, so the utilitarian thinker employs thinking as a tool to achieve his own aims. Walter's detached, theoretical point of view bears the marks of the abstractionism of his class. What he uncritically exemplifies to Tristram's critical eye is the new philosophy that Descartes envisions in the *Discourse:* "it is possible to attain knowledge which is very useful in life, and ... instead of that speculative philosophy which is taught in the Schools, we may find a practical philosophy by means of which ... we can ... render ourselves the masters and possessors of nature."[6] By assuming that his theoretical stance is unconditioned, by failing to see, that is, that even theoretical behavior presupposes some affective disposition and attunement of the understanding to the subject contemplated, Walter becomes the dupe of those very fugitive motives which he implicitly denies. Thus his theoretical speculations, his hobby-horses, are not "sporting little filly-follies"; they are vicious expressions of the will to power and of a presumptuous and reckless epistemology which contribute directly or indirectly to the atrophy of every creative mode of life and portend—if the gravity of the phrase may be forgiven—the abolition of man or, in Tristram's phrase, the extinction of the human soul. Such a serious characterization of Walter's position is justified because his character is one of the earliest, most prophetic, and meticulous studies of the type of person who, in preferring the tree of knowledge to the tree of life, promulgates an anthropology which would later lose sight of its own finitude and undertake the unlimited control of nature and even of man.

Walter and Toby, taken as dual intellectual influences on Tristram, have been interpreted as representatives of rival philosophic positions: Walter resembles the rationalist who is made absurd by an inability to manage the unification of his concepts with the materials of sense, while Toby resembles an empiricist who fails to give any conceptual coherence to his sensory manifold.[7] Such a fracturing of the two compo-

6. *The Philosophical Works of Descartes,* trans. Elizabeth S. Haldane and G. R. T. Ross, I, 119.

7. Wilfred Watson, "Sterne's Satire on Mechanism: A Study of *Tristram Shandy*" (Ph.D. diss., University of Toronto, 1951), chaps. II and III.

nents of knowledge would provide a vivid illustration of Kant's aphorism, "Thoughts without content are empty, intuitions without concepts are blind." If such a simple diagrammatic relationship obtained, Tristram as artist might add the third element of cognition in the Kantian analysis, namely, the power of imaginative synthesis by means of which alone it is possible to pass from momentary sensation to human understanding. Such a scheme of analysis not only simplifies the characters, but it fails to recognize that the issues of the novel are more extensive and more radical than the problem of knowledge.

If Walter, the intellectualist, serves to illustrate the mental aberrations of the household, Toby, the sentimentalist, illustrates its affective deformity. In the man of feeling with the wound upon the groin sexuality has been so totally displaced that it is allowed only unconscious expression in his general association with sexual innuendo throughout the book, in the visual patterns of his fortifications which resemble the organs of reproduction, in the location of his "belov'd mistress" the bowling green concealed from view by hedges and shrubs and capable of raising an immoderate blush in his cheeks, in the tendency of his eye to be arrested by crevices in walls. His counterpart, the widow Wadman, that true "daughter of Eve" and unblushing devotee of the flesh, exemplifies the opposite consequence of the fragmentation, for lewdness, of which there is plenty in the book, is as much a symptom of the displacement of libidinal energy and as essential a part of the human decay of Tristram's world as in Toby's "modesty." One is reminded that for Blake in *The Four Zoas* the fallen state reveals itself first in the dissociation of Tharmas or sexual instinct, the instinct for wholeness. The lapse that has occurred in Albion results in a self divided and tormented by loneliness and self-consciousness. The Shandy malaise, as has been noted already, is both intellectual and affective. The traditional association of hobby-horses and concupiscence from their first introduction in the company of Dr. Kunastrokius suggests that the problem is single and disruptive of the whole psyche. In fact, Tristram has recognized what Plato argues in the *Symposium*, namely, that eros is the life force in every civilized art and science; and with unflagging energy he exposes its sublimation and repression in all dimensions of life in his father's house and his own culture. The dissociation is clearly exemplified in Toby's cerebral devotion to the arts of war and his inability to understand the human consequences of either real battles or the game of toy soldiers on the green. He is the new man of feeling who can comprehend neither the "pains of labour" nor the "deaths of thousands" but who can sympathize with a fly.

One of the major emphases of volume VIII is the contrast between Toby and Trim and Toby and Walter on the matter of love. Trim tries without success to tell the story of "the King of *Bohemia* and his seven castles," for Toby's interruptions defeat the intention completely. But when he chances to mention his having been in love, Toby is instantly alive to that tale: "So, thou wast once in love, *Trim!*" With only a few interruptions he positively encourages the corporal to recount the story of the fair Beguine, which, overheard by Mrs. Wadman concealed in her arbor, provides her with a suitable opportunity to open her own assault upon Toby. Trim's affair with the Beguine is but one of several indications that the infirmity of the Shandys, however widespread geographically and historically, is most conspicuous among educated classes. Trim's ability to speak, his understanding of the commandments, his capacity for making love to Bridget (with some damage to the Dutch drawbridge), all indicate that the unhealthy condition of his culture has not destroyed his aptitude for action though his forte is intensity of feeling without intellectual discrimination. The world has left him wounded to be sure, but with a wound on the knee, not upon the groin like those that have impaired the creative powers of his social superiors in one way or another. Thus when Toby admits that he is in love and proposes to tell Mrs. Wadman "civilly," Trim advises, "I would begin, an' please your honour, with making a good thundering attack upon her, in return——and telling her civilly afterwards!" (VIII.xxviii.581). In volume IX the contrast becomes even more vivid when Toby's modest proposal to Mrs. Wadman is followed by Trim's forthright love-making to Bridget, the total lack of intellectual and emotional compatibility of the former couple exactly reversed in the latter.

In the contrast between Walter and Toby, the fragmentation from which both suffer reaches greater clarity because Walter is able to articulate and even defend it as an ideal. The importance of the contrast is signaled by Tristram's remark, "There is nothing shews the characters of my father and my uncle *Toby*, in a more entertaining light, than their different manner of deportment, under the same accident," namely falling in love.

> My father, as appears from many of his papers, was very subject to this passion, before he married . . . he would never submit to it like a christian; but would pish, and huff, and bounce, and kick, and play the Devil, and write the bitterest Philippicks against the eye that ever man wrote. . . .
>
> In short during the whole paroxism, my father was all abuse and foul language, approaching rather towards malediction——only he did not do it . . . with *Ernulphus's* policy——for tho' my father, with the most intolerant spirit, would curse both this and that, and every thing under heaven, which was either aiding or abetting to his love——yet never concluded his chapter of curses upon it, without cursing himself in at the bargain, as one of the most egregious fools and coxcombs, he would say, that ever was let loose in the world.
>
> My uncle *Toby*, on the contrary, took it like a lamb

——sat still and let the poison work in his veins without
resistance——in the sharpest exacerbations of his wound
(like that on his groin) he never dropt one fretful or dis-
contented word——he blamed neither heaven nor earth
——or thought or spoke an injurious thing of any body,
or any part of it; he sat solitary and pensive with his pipe.
[VIII.xxvi.578–79]

In the process of instructing Toby on the subject, Walter distinguishes two kinds of love: one "rational," one "natural";
the former, "ancient——without mother——where *Venus*
had nothing to do"; the latter, "begotten of *Jupiter* and
Dione" which "partakes wholly of the nature of *Venus*"
(VIII.xxxiii.587). In effect, he consigns the body and consciousness to totally different dimensions of being, even as
Descartes in Meditation III undertakes to bring his mind to
full life by lulling his body to sleep. Tristram, in fact, remarks
that Walter is fond of "libelling . . . the desires and appetites
of the lower part of us" (VIII.xxxi.584). In the discussion of
Walter as rhetorician, it was observed that his view of man,
like that of the sophists, tends to elevate passion by displacing
reason, and yet he seems to exalt reason here. Although one
hesitates to give Tristram credit for seeing the implications
fully, it is evident that Walter conceives of reason and passion
as rival forces of equal status, thereby ignoring the ancient
structure whereby reason as active agent was understood to
give form to passion. The rivalry that Walter describes implicitly exalts passion, degrades reason, and prepares the way for
the position of Hume that reason is and ought to be the slave
of the passions, a view that Walter unwittingly exemplifies in
that his rationalistic theories are really instruments in the
service of his desires, the desire especially to annihilate rhetorical opposition.

This bifurcation of his own being hints at the abstractionist
character of the family impotence which is a physical articulation of the human condition of Tristram's world at large. In

Walter's purely cerebral dissertation on the two kinds of love, he claims that "the first, which is the golden chain let down from heaven, excites to love heroic" and "to the desire of philosophy and truth——the second, excites to *desire,* simply ——." Both Yorick and Elizabeth object, and her agreement with the parson goes a long way to establish her as generally more sound in principle than her husband:

> ——I think the procreation of children as beneficial to the world, said *Yorick,* as the finding out the longitude——
>
> ——To be sure, said my mother, *love* keeps peace in the world——
>
> ——In the *house*——my dear, I own——
>
> ——It replenishes the earth; said my mother——.
>
> But it keeps heaven empty——my dear; replied my father.
>
> ——'Tis Virginity, cried *Slop,* triumphantly, which fills paradise.
>
> Well push'd nun! quoth my father. [VIII.xxxiii. 587–88]

The doctrine that sex is sin, attributed by Blake to what he calls "deists," has made its mark on the Shandys, and Walter defends the principle itself. His rationalist response to passion is forthrightly summarized by the penultimate speech of the novel, and its importance to a correct understanding of the "life and opinions" of his son is implied by the fact that all points of view are represented in the scene, all the major characters assembled, as Booth says, "to listen to the final statement about a cock-and-bull story" (p. 175).

> ——THAT provision should be made for continuing the race of so great, so exalted and godlike a Being as man ——I am far from denying——but philosophy speaks freely of every thing; and therefore I still think and do maintain it to be a pity, that it should be done by means of a passion which bends down the faculties, and turns

> all the wisdom, contemplations, and operations of the soul backwards——a passion, my dear, continued my father, addressing himself to my mother, which couples and equals wise men with fools, and makes us come out of caverns and hiding-places more like satyrs and four-footed beasts than men.

In this climactic statement of what lies at the heart of the Shandy malaise, which Tristram has been attempting to isolate through nine volumes, Walter even finds evidence for his view in the ordinary behavior of people, though without noticing the circularity of his argument, that to decry passion is to create the impulse to secrecy which he interprets as evidence that passion is dishonorable.

> . . . wherefore, when we go about to make and plant a man, do we put out the candle? and for what reason is it, that all the parts thereof——the congredients——the preparations——the instruments, and whatever serves thereto, are so held as to be conveyed to a cleanly mind by no language, translation, or periphrasis whatever?

He goes on to ask why the weapons of war which destroy life are considered glorious when the instruments of procreation will not bear thinking upon: "——The act of killing and destroying a man . . . you see is glorious——and the weapons by which we do it are honourable." At that point Yorick, who so admires the gallantry with which Walter defends the most untenable theories that "though he would often attack him ——yet could never bear to do it with all his force" (VII. xxxiv.588), this time rises "to batter the whole hypothesis to pieces" but is interrupted by Obadiah with his story of a cock and a bull, and the book ends (IX.xxxiii.645). The loss of what Yorick would have said is no real loss; his view, the moral norm, has been implied all along.

It is possible to argue that Tristram sees the crisis of European life primarily as a male phenomenon, that his mother, lacking the abstractionist mentality of the male Shandys, contributes to him the bent for analyzing the crisis. He is, after all, "the son in the flesh of a woman who cannot catch an implication and a man who tortures all reality to fit a hypothesis."[8] He is as capable of working with abstractions as his father, but he is also able and willing, like his mother, to catch the drift of thought and the structure of values behind the sound of words.

The position of Mrs. Shandy in Tristram's reflections on the general problem of creativity should lead to some reevaluation of her importance in the novel and of the relative ability of Shandy women to take decisive and effective action. Her reputation, as was observed earlier, has been damaged by her husband's low opinion of her intellectuals although she is neither entirely without understanding nor completely ineffective at influencing the course of life in the family. Walter's criticism of her, that "she is not a woman of science" (VI.xxxix.472), must not be misunderstood as constituting a final evaluation of the quality of her understanding. Tristram is proceeding to the "memoirs" of uncle Toby's amours, and Mrs. Shandy interrupts Walter's musing "about the hardships of matrimony" with the announcement, "——My brother *Toby* . . . is going to be married to Mrs. *Wadman*.——Then he will never, quoth my father, be able to lie *diagonally* in his bed again." The response is quite as lacking in pertinence to the real drift of Elizabeth's thought as her responses usually are to his statements. But Walter expects more than he offers:

> It was a consuming vexation to my father, that my mother never asked the meaning of a thing she did not understand.
> ——That she is not a woman of science, my father would say——is her misfortune——but she might ask a question.——

8. Lehman, p. 250.

> My mother never did.——In short, she went out of
> the world at last without knowing whether it turned
> *round,* or stood *still.*——My father had officiously told
> her above a thousand times which way it was,——but
> she always forgot.

Tristram goes on to explain that conversation was impossible
between them beyond "a proposition,——a reply, and a rejoinder." Elizabeth is responding in this example to a major
change in the domestic life of the family. In a remark that
shows some affection for Toby, though it is perhaps more
ambiguous toward Mrs. Wadman, she says, "If he marries,
'twill be the worse for us." Walter promptly disagrees, "Not a
cherry-stone . . . he may as well batter away his means upon
that, as any thing else," to which Elizabeth rejoins, "To be
sure" and drops the subject. This is not the behavior of the
obviously simple woman that she is usually understood to be;
it shows instead a degree of practical wisdom in maintaining
domestic tranquility that deserves respect rather than contempt. As for the interest in science in general and the motion
of the earth in particular, the Shandy world is exactly four
miles round, and it makes not a whit of difference to the life
of the family how much science she has.

Not only does a close reading of the passage above show
that Elizabeth comes off rather better than Walter, but Tristram consistently satirizes the progress of modern learning of
the kind his mother lacks:

> My fellow labourers and associates in this great harvest
> of our learning, now ripening before our eyes; thus it is,
> by slow steps of casual increase, that our knowledge physi-
> cal, metaphysical, physiological, polemical, nautical,
> mathematical, aenigmatical, technical, biographical, ro-
> mantical, chemical, and obstetrical, with fifty other
> branches of it, (most of 'em ending, as these do, in *ical*)
> have, for these two last centuries and more, gradually
> been creeping upwards towards that Ακμή of their per-

fections, from which, if we may form a conjecture from the advances of these last seven years, we cannot possibly be far off. [I.xxi.64]

The ultimate result of this improvement in knowledge will be to "put an end to all kinds of writings whatsoever, and since an end to the need for writing will bring an end to the need for reading and, in turn, an end to all knowledge "as war begets poverty, poverty peace," the whole cycle will begin anew. Tristram's considered view differs clearly and substantially from the fashionable optimism of his day.

Elizabeth's success in controlling Walter where she cares to is no less than a tradition among the Shandy women. In the Chapter Upon Noses where Tristram's great-grandmother and father haggle over the size of her jointure, Tristram stresses the consequences of the female victory over the impotent Shandy males: his great-grandmother outlives both his great-grandfather and grandfather to collect her jointure from Walter, "a hundred and fifty pounds half yearly" for twelve years. The evidence seems to indicate that the women, like the servants, are not immune to, but less effected by, the Shandy malaise than the men. On such important issues of concrete life Elizabeth defeats all the rhetorical subtleties Walter can marshal in defense of his cause, and she does so without ever entering the debate, by standing her ground in eloquent silence. That is not to say that one is wholly convinced of Elizabeth's effectiveness as an agent of action. Tristram (appropriating a line from Moral Essay II), describes all the Shandy women: "the SHANDY FAMILY were of an original character throughout;——I mean the males,——the females had no character at all,——except, indeed, my great aunt DINAH, who, about sixty years ago, was married and got with child by the coachman" (I.xxi.65). Tristram is referring to a particular constitution of the mind," as Dr. Johnson defines "character" in this sense, a specifically intellectual formlessness along with an affective indifference in the Shandy women that is an important dimension of the story he wants to tell. That her influence upon his own development should have been so slight, especially in light of the fact that "I was all that time totally neglected and abandoned to my mother" (the time during which Walter was busy simultaneously writing the Tristrapaedia and missing his chance to use it), testifies to her complicity in the uncreative life of the family. The general formlessness of her mind is matched by an absence of passion which together make her responses to major events like the misfortunes that befall Tristram and the death of Bobby irrelevant to Tristram's main purpose of conveying his life to us by presenting the people, forces, and events that have shaped and misshaped that life. Mrs. Shandy is generally too passive to exert any formative influence on her son, but hers is an important part of the family pathology.

Elizabeth is thus in no way exonerated from responsibility for the impotence of the family; she is implicated in the general sterility, both physical and spiritual, that afflicts life at Shandy Hall. Her famous Sunday night indifference, the interruption of Walter's domestic duty, and her association of his sexual prowess with a run-down clock implicate her in the common intellectual and affective malaise. Beyond Walter's mechanistic interpretation of the ill effects of the clock upon Tristram's character, the episode demonstrates the casual indifference: her affective disposition toward the universe and life in general, if one may so characterize the religious sense of dependency, is equally neutral. We learn in the first volume that she is a papist, but Tristram's manner of telling us is by a hint so obscure as not to be noticed until he quarrels with "Madam reader" for missing it. Her religion, in short, makes no difference whatever in the atmosphere of secularism that prevails in the family and that is largely unrelieved except by Parson Yorick's usually ineffectual influence. Dr. Slop's ill-tempered theological polemics at least contribute to the intellectual delineation of his character, though his Catholicism is a fossilized, mindless dogmatism as decadent in its way as the religious paraphernalia that encrusts the licentiousness of the lesbian nuns of Andoüillets. Elizabeth, we see, is as unconcerned with her own religion as with Walter's hypotheses and embraces. At the end of volume VIII when the two of them are walking down to Toby's house "to countenance him in this attack of his" upon Mrs. Wadman, my mother wishes she could "look through the key-hole" at the lovers "out of *curiosity*." Walter "ungraciously" retorts, "Call it, my dear, by its right name . . . and look through the key-hole as long as you will." Then conscience-stricken at having made an insinuation so concupiscent, he chances to catch her eye, and Tristram interprets:

> a thin, blue, chill, pellucid chrystal with all its humours so at rest, the least mote or speck of desire might have been seen at the bottom of it, had it existed——it did not. . . . My mother——madam——was so [lewd] at no time, either by nature, by institution, or example.
>
> A temperate current of blood ran orderly through her veins in all months of the year, and in all critical moments both of the day and night alike; nor did she superinduce the least heat into her humours from the manual effervescencies of devotional tracts, which having little or no meaning in them, nature is oft times obliged to find one. [IX.i.599–600]

Thus Tristram explains his mother's general frigidity; then— and the point is of great importance—he quotes in the tone of endorsement his father's "tragicomical . . . prediction, 'That I should neither think, nor act like any other man's child, upon that very account.' "

To understand this revision of Mrs. Shandy's character aright, one must observe how much more appropriate such a picture of fragmentation and indifference is for the larger view Tristram is offering of an uncreative world than could be found in a character with a congenital lack of intelligence.

Mrs. Shandy has the natural endowments to live creatively, but, like all the characters in her world (excepting Yorick to some extent and to a lesser extent Trim), she lacks the psychic cohesiveness that makes a creative life possible. In this way she contributes substantially to Tristram's reflections upon the condition of his own being and those of his culture.

So relentless is Tristram's pursuit of understanding that he exposes his own soul even more fully than those of his departed relatives. It is his future, his possibilities for living an integrated life that are inseparably tied to the prospects of his cultural atmosphere. After predicting that within fifty years the Christian faith and the human soul will have disappeared, Tristram exclaims, "Blessed *Jupiter!* and blessed every other heathen god and goddess! for now ye will all come into play again, and with *Priapus* at your tails——what jovial times! ——but where am I? and into what a delicious riot of things am I rushing? I——I who must be cut short in the midst of my days" (VII.xiv.495). It has been argued that this pagan worship of Priapus is Tristram's real element and his answer to the failure of Christianity.[9] The momentary tone of sensual abandon, like his toying with Nannette at the end of volume VII, when taken in conjunction with the prominence he gives to the whole problem of love, at least suggests the nearly pagan state of his affections. It will be remembered, however, that the real conditions of his existence, specifically his finitude, call him away from Nannette to the more important work he has set for himself. While on the Continent he makes a pilgrimage to the tomb of the two lovers which he expects to be "as valuable as that of *Mecca,* and . . . little short, except in wealth, of the *Santa Casa*" (VII.xxxi.521–22). The episode suggests the importance he attaches to love, but the fact that the tomb is not there when he arrives implies that there is no

9. New, *Laurence Sterne as Satirist,* p. 181.

love in this neo-pagan world after all; the pursuit remains, but sexuality is debased by both its exaltation and its denial. Unlike Bobby, whose weakness was in the head, Tristram's is in the groin, as foreshadowed by the accident in the nursery and verified in the bedroom scene with Jenny:

> ———Do, my dear *Jenny*, tell the world for me, how I be-haved under one [of the disasters of life], the most oppres-sive of its kind which could befall me as a man, proud, as he ought to be, of his manhood———
> 'Tis enough, said'st thou, coming close up to me, as I stood with my garters in hand, reflecting on what had *not* pass'd. [VII.xxix.517–18]

The public admissions of sexual inadequacy show that passion becomes impotent quite as easily as does the intellect when it is exalted to a position of supremacy in the psyche. Such a recognition on Tristram's part hardly constitutes an endorse-ment of the quality of life that is likely to survive the disap-pearance of Christian culture. Far from celebrating the coming of the new paganism that he finds in himself and forecasts for the world, his remark about the disappearance of the soul and his examination of this dimension of his world offer a prospect of a human wasteland. Yet the novel is one of the greatest works of comedy in the English language, in part because its matter and its manner are one; the vision of man and his world, for all the serious talk about spiritual disease, is comic. To discover how that is possible and how exactly Sterne's comedy copes with such pathetic, even tragic, material will be the next task of this discussion.

It is not so, just because the bleak vision is mitigated by what J. B. Priestly called "the kinship of his [Sterne's] people" who though they "cannot share one another's thoughts . . . can share one another's feelings." The "unity of feeling, the mu-tual trust and affection, . . . so broadly and so often emphasized" goes a long way to redeem the more somber tone of life in the family.[10] However, the Shandys are dead, another reason why we cannot feel much anxiety over the consequences of their foibles upon them, but Tristram faces a future in which the grounds of trust and affection in mutual kinship do not obtain. Whatever degree of hopefulness or, failing hope, whatever confidence he can sustain for man and the future must come from some other source.

"The power to heal"

After observing that his father's "rhetoric and conduct" were "at perpetual handy-cuffs," Tristram exclaims,

> ——Inconsistent soul that man is!——languishing under wounds, which he has the power to heal!——his whole life a contradiction to his knowledge!——his reason, that precious gift of God to him——(instead of pouring in oyl) serving but to sharpen his sensibilities, ——to multiply his pains and render him more melancholy and uneasy under them!——poor unhappy creature, that he should do so!——are not the necessary causes of misery in his life enow, but he must add voluntary ones to his stock of sorrow. [III.xxi.203]

The context of this exclamation is important: it is not a comment on reason in general except where it is called "that precious gift of God." It is a lament over Walter's particular exaltation and debasement of reason. But there is hope in the passage. It implies that Walter and the others are not the helpless victims of a disorderly universe, that they might, just for the choosing, heal the wounds that cripple their lives. The foregoing analysis has claimed that the crisis, both private and public, to which Tristram's book is a response is a dual

10. "The Brothers Shandy," in *The English Comic Characters* (New York, 1931), p. 156.

problem involving the character of knowledge, as has always been recognized and, more deeply, the very nature of being human. The twin results are (1) a conception of man as a naturalized object among mundane objects whose potentiality is to be acted upon rather than to act and whose powers of interpretation, given this anthropology, do not extend to the real self available to reflection; and (2) a general paralysis which consists in granting priority to the actual over the potential, to objects over acts, to causality over freedom, to patient over agent. The exploration of the ground for Tristram's confidence in a cure for the disorder will proceed in two stages: first, the nature of the healthy state of psychic integration and, second, the character of the power by which that integration may be brought about.

Psychic Integration

Yorick is the single character in the novel who has any claim to be regarded as normative. As with every other character, events, and theme, Yorick's prominence, his presence even, must not go unquestioned; he must have an identifiable relation to the central project. The parson's position in volume I as the first character to be presented with any fulness, is not completely accounted for by his role in establishing the midwife in the community. It is not explained by the mere fact that the parson is an interesting character *per se* and one for whom Tristram has a reverence and affection equal to his idea of "the peerless knight of *La Mancha,* whom, by the bye, with all his follies, I love more, and would actually have gone further to have paid a visit to, than the greatest hero of antiquity." In fact, Tristram expressly says that his affection for Yorick "is not the moral of my story: The thing I had in view was to shew the temper of the world in the whole of this affair" (I.x.22). What emerges in this conflict between the parson and the world are the personal traits which, more than any other factors, become Tristram's point of reference for judging the world. Both Yorick's descent from the court jester and his explicit comparison with Quixote stress the extent to which he is "utterly unpracticed in the world," specifically where restraint in telling the truth is wanted:

> *Yorick* had no impression but one, and that was what arose from the nature of the deed spoken of; which impression he would usually translate into plain *English* without any periphrasis,——and too oft without much distinction of either personage, time, or place;——so that when mention was made of a pitiful or an ungenerous proceeding,——he never gave himself a moment's time to reflect who was the Hero of the piece,——what his station,——or how far he had power to hurt him hereafter;——but if it was a dirty action,——without more ado,——The man was a dirty fellow,—and so on: ——And as his comments had usually the ill fate to be terminated either in a *bon mot,* or to be enliven'd throughout with some drollery or humour of expression, it gave wings to *Yorick's* indiscretion. [I.xi.27]

The parson is not on bad terms with the world for the same reason the Shandys are; it is his misfortune to live in an epoch that prefers policy to honesty and gravity to a merry heart. At the last, "overpower'd by numbers . . . he died . . . quite broken hearted" (I.xii.30).

It has already been argued that Yorick's death serves to establish as early as the opening volume the significance for Tristram of that ultimate limit of one's being, but Yorick's death is doubly significant because in the historical scheme it is the man who represents the moral norm who lives a life quite as alien in his epoch as Quixote's was in his, a representative of a healthy style of life that makes him a misfit in an unhealthy world. He is not like Walter, Toby, Dr. Slop, Mrs. Shandy, Mrs. Wadman, or even Tristram himself, all of whom have in one way or another put on the trappings of the modern

world. Yorick more nearly belongs to the century of his Shake-
spearean ancestor than to the age of Shandy impotence. By the
time Tristram comes to write, they are all dead, of course; but
the world has passed none of them by so completely as Yorick
who was never "bubbled" by their "great wigs, grave faces,
and other implements of deceit" (III.xx.202).

The importance of the sermon on conscience has been well
established, though the positive influence of Yorick on Tristram himself has not been sufficiently stressed. In fact, the
authority of the sermon in volume II derives from the integrity of Yorick's character already established in the first volume. His is the voice and example of a Christian humanism
that has no other representative in Tristram's world but
which overlaps substantially with his own more secular understanding; this fact is supported by Yorick's large part in the
book, by the implications of the sermon on the superiority of
reason and law over conscience, and by the "Author's PREF-
ACE" on the unity of wit and judgment. The sermon, which
speaks only to the issue of moral knowledge, has implications
more extensive than ethical judgments, for it offers the alternative to the dissociation among the faculties that is characteristic of the Shandys and which would ultimately make all
knowledge inaccessible to them. The soul is not represented
as what the twentieth century takes it for, in Lawrence's
metaphor, "a dark, vast forest with wild life in it"; it is,
properly ordered, a hierarchy governed by the reason, with
complete access to its own contents by means of reflection: "If
a man thinks at all, he cannot well be a stranger to the true
state of this account;——he must be privy to his own thoughts
and desires;——he must remember his past pursuits, and
know certainly the true springs and motives, which, in general,
have governed the actions of his life." Our knowledge of the
world may be narrow, for "*hardly do we guess aright at the
things that are upon the earth, and with labour do we find the
things that are before us.* But here the mind has all the evi-

dence and facts within herself;——is conscious of the web
she has wove;——knows its texture and fineness . . . Conscience is nothing else but the knowledge which the mind has
within herself of this" (II.xvii.125–26). Knowledge of the self
is available for any who choose it, and the way is reflexivity,
the mind attending to its own processes. Yorick's posthumous
preaching in fact recommends just the method that Tristram
follows, many years later, in trying to understand and shape
his own life.

The cause of error, when one is "a greater stranger to his
own disposition and true character than all the world besides,"[11] is the displacement of reason by passion. As evidence
that this view is characteristic of Sterne's conservatism, Cash
quotes the sermon called "Felix's Behavior towards Paul":

> The judgments of the more disinterested and impartial
> of us, receive no small tincture from our affections . . . but
> in the more flagrant instances . . . 'tis melancholy to see
> the office to which reason, the great prerogative of his
> nature, is reduced; serving the lower appetites in the
> dishonest drudgery of finding out arguments to justify
> the present pursuit. [*The Sermons of Mr. Yorick*, I,
> 313–14]

For this reason conscience is not to be trusted when it tends to
excuse a questionable action. However, an accusing conscience
may be relied upon as the voice of reason which alone makes
accusations. Thus the analogy with which the sermon closes of
the court of law before which an accused act is tried:

> Your conscience is not a law:——No, God and reason
> made the law, and have placed conscience within you to
> determine;——not like an *Asiatic* Cadi, according to the
> ebbs and flows of his own passions,——but like a *British*
> judge in this land of liberty and good sense, who makes

11. *The Sermons of Mr. Yorick*, I, 54; quoted in Arthur Hill Cash,
"The Sermon in *Tristram Shandy*," *English Literary History* 31 (1964),
399.

no new law, but faithfully declares that law which he knows already written. [II.xvii.140]

The conjunction of reason and God in the passage is not only orthodox; it helps explain reflection as a limiting concept in Tristram's project: the reflexive process can bring to light what is implicit in consciousness, but it does not have access to theological accounts of the workings of consciousness. Therefore, Yorick and Tristram have somewhat different ways of describing the same phenomenon. The point of correspondence between their accounts is what naturalistically appears as the dictates of reason and theologically as the law of God. Tristram is thus able to discover the guides for life in reflection alone that duplicate the religious principles of Yorick and Sterne, and the sermon can have a singular influence upon him without loading his book with the intellectual systems of moral theology. It should be noted in passing, however, that the later sermons focus upon the essentially secular concerns of the motives of action and the naturalistic enquiry into the elements of character.[12] One is tempted to describe Tristram's position as a secularization of Christian values, but the domain of the sacred is not excluded; in fact, it is a consideration of the utmost importance in distinguishing the salient differences in the complexions of Tristram's mind and his father's.

There is in the sermon a troublesome passage about a banker and a physician, both irreligious, who, should their interest invite them to take advantage of their clients and patients with impunity, would have no moral force to counterbalance the temptation. It is difficult to see this effort to demonstrate the failure of morality without religion as making much sense—Cash says that "Sterne fails miserably in this attempt."[13] In fact, the point is treated as though it were too obvious to want explaining. This is certainly not the case.

12. Moglen, p. 66.
13. "The Sermon in *Tristram Shandy*," p. 410.

It is even less obvious how the argument, if it were intelligible, might apply to Tristram's experience. One solution seems tenable: what the argument suggests is that when one's motives for action do not lie beyond the self, when in other words man is taken as the measure of all things, one result is the subordination of all of reality to human will as in the case of Walter. In him there is no sense of awe before the unknown but only confidence in the absolute intelligibility of all things. A second result is that this egocentric, assertion of the will constitutes the sur-render of reason to passion within the soul and fosters a strat-egy of self-deception that the sermon exposes and that the novel studies in great detail, most notably once again in the character of Walter. The alternative to this self-deluding reduction of being to a ratio of the self is the humility which Tristram demonstrates in his posture as humble, though sometimes irreverent, enquirer into the mystery of things; "WE live in a world," he says, "beset on all sides with mysteries and riddles——" (IX.xxii.625). In this attitude of humility and its peculiarly appropriate comic mood he declines to violate the essential nature of things by demanding that they conform to the conditions of his own superiority and bend to the demands of the instinct for rational systems. It is this sense in Tristram of mystery in the presence of powers that tran-scend the self that corresponds to the category of the religious in the sermon, the willingness to conform one's actions to a higher principle than the self; in short, to act in accord with the nature of the universal scheme of things, though only partially understood, is the ultimate sanction of moral behavior.

The argument for the superiority of reason over conscience in moral knowledge has important implications for the prob-lem of knowledge in general. It is sometimes argued that Tristram's position finally is a Humean scepticism, where one gets beyond his own subjectivism only by means of customary and habitual beliefs.[14] But whereas Hume never investigates the structure of natural belief, Tristram does. Numerous episodes considered in themselves would seem to justify the claim of scepticism, none more forcefully than when one of Gastriferes's hundred and two hot chestnuts falls into "that aperture of *Phutotorius's* breeches . . . which the laws of decorum do strictly require . . . to be universally shut up." The various interpretations of the outcry "Zounds!" could indicate the impotence of reason to know, but the novel as a whole does not support that conclusion. It is not only the sermon that affirms the possibility of knowledge, on the prior condition that reason be given priority over passion; the episodes of the novel, the materials of Tristram's opinions, demonstrate failures to understand that are not owing to extraneous matters like the nature of words but to the characters' not trying to understand, to their not bracketing their own egocentric inclinations so as to receive what others are saying. What better affirmation of the power of mind to know than the fact that Tristram thoroughly understands the dynamics of the perpetual obscurity that obtains between Walter and Toby and that he conveys that understanding to his audience with precision and clarity? We may be surrounded with mysteries and riddles in "this night of our obscurity," as Tristram calls it (III.xx.198); it is a universe that will not be folded up neatly into the boxes of abstractionist theorizing, but it does not follow that we are doomed to live in complete darkness, that the human desire to know is a surd in the universal scheme. The underlying affirmation of the work resembles that expressed in Locke's image of the tether of the understanding beyond the extent of which we should not, "out of an Affectation of an universal Knowledge," attempt to reach (I.i.4).

Among the passions that mislead the understanding is the

14. Traugott, p. 19.

irrational indulgence in sentiment. The practical effects of Toby's sentiments have already been noticed, but an example from Tristram's own experience in volume VII shows from within how sentiment can mislead judgment. When he meets the ass in his path *en route* to the tomb of the two lovers, he converses with the animal by "framing his responses from the etchings of his countenance———and when those carry me not deep enough———in flying from my own heart into his, and seeing what is natural for an ass to think———as well as a man, upon the occasion." Tristram makes it evident that he understands the anthropomorphism implicit in this sentiment, that his attitude interprets the other as a projection of the self against all the dictates of common sense. He says that he does not talk with parrots and jackdaws who speak by rote, nor with apes who act by it, nor with his dog and cat who "neither of them possess the talents for conversation———I can make nothing of a discourse with them, beyond the *proposition,* the *reply,* and *rejoinder,* which terminated my father's and my mother's conversations, in his beds of justice———and those utter'd———there's an end of the dialogue———." Then he gives the conversation in detail and thereby reduces his sympathy with the ass to absurdity (VII.xxxii.523).

This is not to say that sentiment, emotion, or passion are unnecessary to reason. When Dr. Slop is trying to untie the knots in the bag of obstetrical instruments, the idea crosses his mind that it is a stroke of divine mercy that Mrs. Shandy is having a slow and difficult delivery, else he would never get the bag open in time. "———But here, you must distinguish ———the thought floated only in Dr. *Slop*'s mind, without sail or ballast to it, as a simple proposition; millions of which, as your worship knows, are every day swimming quietly in the middle of the thin juice of a man's understanding, without being carried backwards or forwards, till some little gusts of passion or interest drive them to one side" (III.ix.167). It is the patterns of value and concern, those "little gusts of passion or interest," that provide the incentive or the intentional focus of the whole person and give direction to reason as religion in Sterne's view does to moral judgment. This traditional view, never more forcefully stated than in the myth of the chariot in Plato's *Phaedrus*, provides the solution to the difficult passage where Tristram refers to "getting out of the body in order to think well." He cites the corpulent Bishop Hall's view that "so much motion . . . is so much unquietness; and so much of rest . . . is so much of heaven." The slender Tristram says for his part, "Now, I . . . think differently; and that so much of motion, is so much of life, and so much of joy——and that to stand still, or get on but slowly, is death and the devil——." The state of the body conditions thought; hence the Pythagorean doctrine of " *'getting out of the body, in order to think well.'* No man thinks right whilst he is in it; blinded as he must be, with his congenial humours, and drawn differently aside, as the bishop and myself have been, with too lax or too tense a fibre——REASON is, half of it, SENSE; and the measure of heaven itself is but the measure of our present appetites and concoctions——" (V.xiii.493–94). The critical debate over this passage suggests rival interpretations that can be stated as complementary. It is true as Cash says that the context implies that "the body *distorts* our reason" without completely invalidating it as a means to truth; but it is also true, as Tuveson says, that mind and body are one, not "enemies" as though "the 'natural' man has been divided against himself."[15] It is even accurate to extend Tuveson's view, as New does, to claim that the family, "mounted and galloping, are unable to bring reason to bear on the reality which surrounds them. Their desires (senses) drive

15. "The Sermon in *Tristram Shandy*," p. 410; Ernest Tuveson, "Locke and Sterne," in *Reason and the Imagination, Studies in the History of Ideas, 1600–1800,* ed. J. A. Mazzeo, p. 261. The image of the tether does not serve to restrict the power to know in this case; it suggests the finitude that conditions all knowing.

their reason (ideas) and the bodies (vehicles) far 'faster' than they were made to go—and over the wreckage, the destruction and dissolution which we have everywhere witnessed in *Tristram Shandy* 'breathes forth the disappointment of the soul.' " Thus, he continues, the proposition that "REASON is, half of it, SENSE" is a "source of grief" and of "intellectual blindness."[16] The first thing to notice is that Tristram is "thinking well"; he is analyzing the way in which the body—his own body—conditions thought—his own thought, and he is doing so without putting off the flesh which, the Pythagoreans held, entombs the soul and keeps it from truth. The strategy of Tristram's statement is to assert the Pythagorean position because it contains a truth, and then to contradict it by pointing out that without the body there could be no reason, a notion that Aquinas had developed centuries before the empiricism of Locke. Mind and body must be one if thought is to occur at all. Although the Shandy family epitomizes the distortion of reason by the body, the senses, and the passions, the solution is not in putting off the flesh but putting the soul in order, as Tristram's reflexive strategy demonstrates in this very passage. In the act of reflecting on the influence of relative degrees of corpulency on the thought of the Bishop and himself, he has at once freed his own judgment from or transcended the prejudice inherent in his own physical size and implied that but for their physical presence in the world the direction of his thinking, in this case concern with the effects of motion, whether "unquietness" or "life," would never even arise. The heart of the issue lies in distinguishing clearly between two senses of reason: there is the modern conception of reason, whether the rationalism of the Cartesians, the mechanism of the Newtonians, or the mutilation of human integrity that results from the dream of absolute freedom of action and objectivity of thought, exemplified in Walter's assault upon the

16. *Laurence Sterne as Satirist*, p. 180.

world; and there is the ancient model of reason as the teleology of the integrated life, the capacity for understanding oneself and the world and for guiding one's action in it. The rationality that Tristram can admire and that he clarifies through reflection is one which does not exclude the body and affectivity; it is an agent of a natural hierarchical integration which transforms lower forces into a synthesis with the higher. In rejecting reason divorced from concern or value (Walter *qua* rationalist) and concern without reason (Toby *qua* sentimentalist), he rejects what Max Weber calls the "mechanized petrification" of specialists without spirit, sensualists without heart."[17] Toby, of course, is the repressed version of the voluptuary type, more aptly described as man of feeling without rational discrimination.

The interpenetration of what may best be called "mood" with reason, without sacrificing the superiority of the latter, is one of the superb achievements of Tristram's method and one of the qualities that seems so modern. The patterns of concern constitute a disposition of the total self not easily expressed in the unintentionally rigid and abstract categories of faculty psychology. It is on the basis of such a general state of mind that thought takes its direction. Even in the most abstract of theoretical enquiries that penetration of reason by mood persists without surrendering the process to mere feeling. The most conspicuous example is the underlying concern in Tristram over the condition of his own being which provides the original impulse and the persistent vigor of the whole project.

Another form of dissociation that is a subordinate but related issue throughout the novel is the dualism of mind and body. In the digression on Tristram's failing powers of wit in volume IX, he stresses the unity of mind and body: "soul

17. *The Protestant Ethic and the Spirit of Capitalism,* trans. Talcott Parsons, p. 182.

and body are joint-sharers in every thing they get: A man cannot dress, but his ideas get cloath'd at the same time; and if he dresses like a gentleman, every one of them stands presented to his imagination, genteelized along with him——" (IX.xiii.616–17). The extent to which he rejects and overcomes this dualism by recognizing it as a product of abstraction from a primordial unity is further suggested by his claim that "a Man's body and his mind, with the utmost reverence to both I speak it, are exactly like a jerkin, and a jerkin's lining;——rumple the one——you rumple the other" except among those "good honest, unthinking, *Shandean* people," all thinkers of a stoic bent who pretended that the outside of their jerkins might be "rumpled and crumpled, and doubled and creased, and fretted and fridged . . . all to pieces" without the insides being "one button the worse, for all you had done to them" (III.iv.160–61). Tristram's point is that mind and body do not belong to separate dimensions of consciousness; in fact, the metaphor of the jerkin reminds one of Blake's notion that the body is the perceptible part of the soul, its effective physical horizon.[18] In this regard it is noteworthy that Tristram shows little interest in the naturalistically perceived body except as it reveals the attitudes and dispositions of the whole person as in pose and gesture, and this supports the assumption that physical impotence in the novel is the material articulation of a much larger condition.

The language of mechanism runs at cross-purposes with this effort to rediscover the primitive unity between mood and reason, body and mind. Once nature comes to be conceived of as a collection of objects in simple location and the body is reduced to a physical system conceived in quasi-mathematical terms, the intimate processes of the real world of human experience have been abstracted out of existence, and its abstract replacement has been problematically related to conscious-

18. Cf. Tuveson, "Locke and Sterne," pp. 260–61.

ness. To make matters worse, that mind that Locke proposed to examine by making it "its own object" comes to be another in the collection of mundane objects and subject to the same unidirectional movement of causality. In place of free, rational agency which pulls from in front, as one might say, there is only mechanical, physical force pushing from behind. This sequence of reasoning appears to be implied in the wide use of the language of mechanism in the novel. Tristram seems to grasp intuitively at least that mechanical explanations of animal spirits, humours psychology, or even comedy, make the mistake of judging wholes by parts—specifically by those parts that are their least common denominators. Thus we get accounts like the early explanation of the sequence of ideas in Mrs. Shandy's mind on the first Sunday night of the month in the metaphor of matter and motion. The animal spirits determine "nine parts in ten of a man's sense or his nonsense, his successes and miscarriages in this world. . . . When they are once set a-going . . . by treading the same steps over and over again, they presently make a road of it, as plain and as smooth as a garden-walk, which, when they are once used to, the Devil himself sometimes shall not be able to drive them off it" (I.i.4–5). This is only one among numerous examples in which Tristram uses the language of mechanism although he explicitly claims not to understand a thing about mechanism, as he says in a remark significantly made in contemplating the great clock of Lyons.

Throughout the book he tends to satirize mechanical explanations, but one cannot safely generalize on the basis of his inconsistent tone. The essential and reliable distinction is to be made between the abstract scientific accounts of the workings of things in which he is limited to the language of Newtonian science and his more intimate and concrete accounts of the workings of things as they reveal themselves to reflection. Thus character can be abstractly explained in the vocabulary of mechanistic humors and simultaneously and inconsistently be revealed as an essentially free transcendence whose complex temporal dimensions consist of a conscious-ness given in the present with a residual past and an antici-pated future which gives unity to the whole. The result of setting the empirical and reflexive side by side is to demon-strate how impotent finally the former is, how much it leaves out of what constitutes an adequate understanding. The sequence of reductions that ultimately comes about is, first, nature to mathematical law, second, the body to an object in that mathematicized nature, and third, mind to a function of that body and hence determined by physical causality in which no superior agency acts upon and transforms inferior elements like those forces that push from behind. Thus the soul comes by small degrees to be considered as lacking those very powers of transcendence that distinguished it in less im-potent ages. It is even possible to interpret all the intellectual aberrations of the novel as being in some sense mechanistic in that, as Stedmond says of Toby's view of war, they treat "human beings as 'things' " (p. 60): Walter's efforts to sub-jugate human character to mechanical laws, Mrs. Wadman's inclination to confuse Toby with her chattels, and Dr. Slop's Catholicism as well as his obstetrical theories are represented as mechanical systems that ignore legitimate human needs. The antithesis of the contraction of reality to the Newtonian model is that sense of mystery in which Tristram confronts the rich complexity of his world.

The Power of Play

Most of what has been said in this study has been terribly serious—much to the annoyance no doubt of those readers who correctly regard *Tristram Shandy* as one of the greatest works of comedy in the English language. However, it has been guided by the conviction that Sterne's comedy does not merely provide an alternative to or an escape from serious

concerns, but that its enormous vitality and its greatest significance consists in focusing upon the most serious issues of life
and bringing them under the rule of play. Only by taking the
full weight of those solemn issues can one test the potency of
the comic spirit which relieves them of that weight. It is not
that the novel simply "plays games with ideas," an idiom that
misunderstands the significance of both ideas and play; it
embodies the deepest human meaning of the form comedy as
a way of comporting oneself toward the pains and limitations
of life and brings to light the final dimension of human
ontology as Tristram understands it, namely, freedom. The
Shandy whose name means sorrowful has brought the tragic
sense of life and the most profound sadness under the mood of
joy, and the conditions of his life may accurately be said, as
was said of Vienna during the interwar years, to be desperate
but not serious.

The first point to observe is that Tristram represents his
comedy as exercising a healing influence. In volume IV he says
that his book is written "against the spleen; in order, by a
more frequent and a more convulsive elevation and depression of the diaphragm, and the succussations of the intercostal
and abdominal muscles in laughter, to drive the *gall* and other
bitter juices from the gall bladder, liver and sweet-bread of his
majesty's subjects, with all the inimicitious passions which belong to them, down into their duodenums" (IV.xxii.301–02).
Tristram's physiological explanation of laughter seems satirical of the tendency to reduce an experience of the whole
person to its merely physical dimension; but if the passage
were taken seriously, it would simply indicate once more how
inadequate abstract scientific accounts are of intimate, concrete human experience. The comic procedure exposes the
discontinuity between Tristram's human instincts and his
intellectual equipment which consists of the conceptual tools
of his age. His comedy is his way of being, a superbly balanced
state of mind that repeatedly saves him from absurd or fanat-

ical positions by not allowing him more than a childlike seriousness about himself. That his work aims at more than redistributing the bitter juices of his majesty's subjects is obvious in the passage quoted, but at the end of volume IV he addresses himself directly to his audience and makes the clearest statement of his comic purpose:

> And now that you have just got to the end of these four volumes——the thing I have to *ask* is, how you feel your heads? my own akes dismally——as for your healths, I know, they are much better——True *Shandeism,* think what you will against it, opens the heart and lungs, and like all those affections which partake of its nature, it forces the blood and other vital fluids of the body to run freely thro' its channels, and makes the wheel of life run long and chearfully round.

True Shandeism here is the spirit of Tristram's own work, not that of Shandy Hall, and according to this passage it has the power to correct the very difficulties that marred Tristram's conception and, through it, his whole life. His attitude toward mechanical physiology seems more serious in this passage, as though he believed it to be a true account of the physical dimension of the experience of comedy. The parallel is even clearer in the next paragraph:

> Was I left like *Sancho Pança,* to chuse my kingdom, it should not be maritime——or a kingdom of blacks to make a penny of——no, it should be a kingdom of hearty laughing subjects: And as the bilious and more saturnine passions, by creating disorders in the blood and humours, have as bad an influence, I see, upon the body politick as body natural——and as nothing but a habit of virtue can fully govern those passions, and subject them to reason ——I should add to my prayer——that God would give my subjects grace to be as WISE as they are MERRY; and then should I be the happiest monarch, and they the happiest people under heaven——. [IV.xxxii.337–38]

The passage combines wisdom and cheerfulness as parallel

graces and returns us to an earlier theme of this discussion, namely, the coincidence of comedy and thought which we were then prepared to see only as a happy, but contingent alliance. Tristram repeatedly insists on the combination: "I write a careless kind of a civil, nonsensical, good humoured *Shandean* book, which will do all your hearts good———— ————And all your heads too,————provided you understand it" (VI.xvii.436). Stedmond points the right direction for discovering the exact relation of these two effects when he says that "Sterne's comic 'message' is that man is a being not to be taken too seriously. All that is worst in human history stems from man's tendency to over-value his own importance, to interpret his destiny in terms of gods and angels, heroes and saints. In relation to such paragons, he is a poor creature, but these are not relevant standards against which to measure him" (p. 164). If we take the passages quoted above from the novel at their word, it is obvious that Tristram regards comedy and laughter as a cure for himself and his world. What must be investigated is what power comedy has to work such a healing influence on a world so beset with misfortunes.

In the discussion of temporalism Tristram's life was described as possessing an inner *telos,* an orientation toward the future which provides the unity of all the dimensions of his being. The category of play, by contrast, is usually regarded as necessarily opposed to activities with extrinsic aims: one works *or* one plays, and, as Prince Hal says, "If all the world were playing holidays, to sport would be as tedious as to work." In truth, the categories are not mutually exclusive. The professional actor or athlete who hates his work is a ready example of how play can be subordinated to work or, since work and play are not strict opposites and can be integrated—one should say to necessity. Just as play can be a means to extrinsic aims, so work can be subordinated to play, the extrinsic to the intrinsic, necessity to freedom. Play directly serves ends interior to itself, and even when it includes work and suffering and death within its circle, it offers a respite from the struggle and the intensity that marks one's anxiety about the complex ends of life. Tristram's sorrow is modified by joy as he unites complete intellectual seriousness in the highest sense of the term with a merry mood which affirms that he is under no illusions about the final importance of such things. His game, like most games, proceeds by attempting to master various perplexities, and the profit he has on it is the larger sense of life and invigoration that comes with such sport. In his project Tristram's play dominates his work and is its characteristic spirit. He says, for example, that he is writing according to no rules but his own, an assertion of his independence from external rules and a signal to his reader not to expect traditional form: "in writing what I have set about, I shall confine myself neither to his [Horace's] rules, nor to any man's rules that ever lived" (I.iv.8). His writing is nonetheless an activity governed by many levels of rules, morphological to generic, for he has chosen to write and to write in a given way even if his work is *sui generis*. He creates his own rules, and then by mocking them he raises his whole enterprise out of the realm of the necessary and beyond the "serious." The rules are followed for all that, and the "serious," no less present than in conventional, humorless philosophical discourse, is transformed under the sign of freedom. Among the results are the exclusion in Tristram of both the "gravity" that Yorick detests and the aggressiveness of Walter's rhetoric, and there is a rising above those blows of Fate that he laments in the fifth chapter of the book. The more serious the misfortunes, the more bleak the prospects, the more grave the causes—the more powerful is the spirit of play which liberates them from the realm of necessity, allows the imagination a free hand in transforming them, and affirms the liberty that is concealed in seriousness. It is in a very exalted sense indeed that we are to understand the digressive work as, in Henri Fluchère's phrase, "une exultante affirmation de liberté."[19]

19. *Laurence Sterne, de l'homme à l'oeuvre*, p. 248.

The point wants insisting on because freedom in any important sense has so often been denied in Tristram. Most recently Helen Moglen, commenting on the closing scene of volume VII with the French maid Nannette, says, "Tristram, unlike the other Shandys, is able to recognize the alternatives with which the world confronts him. Understanding and action are limited because objectivity and freedom are impossible. His choice is for art, which represents an escape from death through illusion" (p. 138). It is not completely clear how he recognizes objective alternatives if objectivity is denied, but Moglen seems to have in mind a restricted range of alternatives for action and hence a restriction, at least, of freedom. But there is a more intimate kind of freedom not measured by the number of one's alternatives which grounds the choice among them and leaves aside entirely the old rationalistic debate between voluntarism and determinism that contests the freedom of the will. In this sense the question is not what the protagonist can do to obtain his wishes, to "dance, and sing, and say his prayers, and go to heaven with this nut brown maid," for example. At issue is the structure of the wish. Freedom in this deeper sense refers to the autonomy of choice whereby the incarcerated man, say, chooses himself as escaping, even though he may lack the power to escape. The strength of his bars and the watchfulness of his guard are objects of resistance without which his free project of escaping would not arise and whose significance as obstacles to be overcome arises in turn out of his choice to escape. In this sense freedom is autonomy of choice and is unrelated to the number of alternatives possible and compossible; however restricted Tristram may be in his range of action, he is yet free in the deepest, foundational sense, namely, to choose how he will *be* in relation to what is given. In this free play of mind, furthermore, lies the secret of his own creativity in the midst of a tradition of impotence.

On the basis of this discussion of the power of play to liberate the spirit and guide the understanding the "Author's PREFACE" may be interpreted as a credo for the entire book. It opens with the remark, "when I sat down, my intent was to write a good book; and as far as the tenuity of my understanding would hold out,——a wise, aye, and a discreet,—— taking care only, as I went along, to put into it all the wit and judgment (be it more or less) which the great author and bestower of them had thought fit originally to give me" (III. xx.192–93). His intention contradicts the spirit of his age which not only distinguishes sharply between wit and judgment but, among some represented by Triptolemus and Phutatorius, even holds that "wit and judgment in this world never go together." Even "the great *Locke*" joined in the suspicion of wit as misleading judgment. Locke expresses the standard view of the age that real knowledge is the domain of judgment and that wit (fancy) has nothing to do with the process of arriving at truth beyond dressing it up for popular consumption:

> Since Wit and Fancy find easier entertainment in the World, than dry Truth and real Knowledge, *figurative Speeches,* and allusion in Language, will hardly be admitted, as *an* imperfection or *abuse* of it. I confess, in Discourses, where we seek rather Pleasure and Delight, than Information and Improvement, such Ornaments as are borrowed from them, can scarce pass for Faults. But yet, if we would speak of Things as they are, we must allow, that all the Art of Rhetorick, besides Order and Clearness, all the artificial and figurative application of Words Eloquence hath invented, are for nothing else but to insinuate wrong *Ideas,* move the Passions, and thereby mislead the Judgment; and so indeed are perfect cheat. [III.x.34]

We have seen that Tristram not only does not share Locke's suspicion of "the artificial and figurative applications" of language but also grounds its referential powers in those poetic powers. Likewise, he rejects the suspicion of wit if not the distinction between wit and judgment itself:

> My most zealous wish and fervent prayer in your be-
> half, and in my own too, in case the thing is not done
> already for us,——is, that the great gifts and endowments
> both of wit and judgment, with every thing which usually
> goes along with them,——such as memory, fancy, genius,
> eloquence, quick parts, and what not, may this precious
> moment without stint or measure, let or hinderance, be
> poured down warm as each of us could bear it. [III.
> xx.194]

The play of wit, like Hobbes's and Dryden's nimble spaniel of fancy, is the play of mind limited only by what is conceivable and grounded in the ecstatic nature of the self, the domain of freedom; the solemn exercise of judgment is an act of discrimination and choice among alternatives provided by wit. Wit is therefore granted a certain priority in the process. Tristram's understanding is that the dissociation of wit and judgment in his world precludes creativity either by making an idol of judgment and thereby omitting entirely the faculty of invention or, where there is plentiful fancy, as in Shandy Hall, by omitting entirely the faculty of judgment that must bring that play into harmony with public reality which the mutual understanding between Tristram and his audience demonstrates is knowable.

The analogy of two knobs on the cane chair illustrates how the two powers should cooperate: "they are the highest and most ornamental parts of its *frame*,——as wit and judgment are of *ours*,——and like them too, indubitably both made and fitted to go together, in order as we say in all such cases of duplicated embellishments,——*to answer one another*" (III. xx.200–01). The analogy defends wit and judgment as inseparable, though because of the imbalance caused by the eighteenth-century preference of the latter, he lays a corrective stress upon the former. The position is approximately that of

Pope who combines both the ability to discover resemblances in dissimilar things and the analytic ability to detect differences, under the term *wit,* thereby stressing the importance of wit in the process of arriving at truth. Tristram's effort is to preserve that "wary reasoning by analogy . . . which *Suidas* calls *dialectick induction*" and which brings together the earlier discussion of rhetoric and thought with the present issue of the proximity of comedy and philosophy.

The final issue in understanding the novel is to square the autonomous spirit of the game with the serious ontological issue we have been tracing. The relation between play and the ontological project is that rather than measuring play by the idea of being, that is, play subsumed under ontology, the reverse is the case: being is measured by the activity of play. Tristram is the kind of creature who plays and whose supreme act is the all encompassing play of the being question. William Bowman Piper has argued that Tristram's overriding aim is to establish a permanent importance for the Shandys who, at his death, will become extinct.[20] Piper's evidence leaves little room for doubt that this is one dimension of Tristram's project. But his interest is less in the results, finally (which had to be doubtful at best), than in a way of living his own life which gives central importance to the significance of play as supreme act of the ontology of transcendence, the act whereby the time-bound creature of disappointment and pain and death is recreated by the glimpse of the free realm of possibility. It is in the free play of that splendidly irreverent comic spirit that one can transcend both one's circumstances and one's self and discover the first springs of human creativity. In Schiller's phrase, "in every condition of humanity it is play, and play alone, that makes man complete."[21] Tristram's spirit of the game bears close kinship with the sense of mystery with which

20. *Laurence Sterne,* p. 26.
21. *On the Aesthetic Education of Man,* trans. Reginald Snell, p. 79.

he approaches the universe; it is an experience with echoes of those ritualistic interpretive acts of primitive festival by which one "experienced the proximity of the gods, heroes, the dead, and where he found himself in the presence of all the beneficial and dreadful powers of the universe." In "The Ontology of Play" Eugene Fink goes on to observe that "human play . . . is the symbolic action which puts us in the presence of the meaning of the world and of life." It is a means by which a person may recover "the sense of the infinite, that eludes him, that he might be able to reach the source of his being."²²

There is nothing new or modern about this attitude of playful seriousness; in fact many would say that it is totally antipathetic to the modern spirit. It is an ancient ideal which Plato expresses when he has Theatetus exclaim, "Socrates . . . I am amazed when I think of them [the questions they have been speaking of]; by the Gods I am! and I want to know what on earth they mean; and there are times when my head quite swims with the contemplation of them."²³ Theatetus's experience of wonder derives from contemplating things in new ways. As Josef Pieper says, "To philosophize means to withdraw—not from the things of everyday life—but from the currently accepted meaning attached to them, or to question the value placed upon them."²⁴ It is this power to remove life from the tyranny of ordinary circumstances that gives comedy an inherent propensity toward philosophy: it places the familiar in a new and liberating light as when by the sudden stroke of wit in metaphor two dissimilar grids of meaning converge and new dimensions of reality are unveiled. In the *Nichomachean Ethics* Aristotle names *eutrapelia* ("happy turning") among the moral virtues that cannot be taught. "The eutrapelos is the man of autarkeia, of inner serenity and

22. *Philosophy Today* 18 (Summer 1974), 160–61.
23. *Theaetetus,* 155.
24. *Leisure: The Basis of Culture,* trans. Alexander Dru, p. 98.

self-sufficiency of disposition, who can strike the right note of mingled seriousness and gaiety, who brings a lightness and gracefulness of touch to every situation."[25] This man of inner serenity, the contemplative, marks the mean between the extremes of the boor whose seriousness precludes philosophy and the buffoon whose frivolity is equally foreign to its nature. The true philosopher is the man of leisured mind whose contemplations are the unfettered acts of play, a type to which Tristram has access by means of the example of Yorick.

Earlier, Tristram's project was characterized as an effort to solve the *problem* of his being. That formulation can now be revised in the light of this ancient ideal: problems have solutions and require behavior oriented toward solutions, whereas mysteries have no solutions and invite free contemplation rather than extrinsically directed effort. Tristram tries to understand his being and to write his book, but the motive is intrinsic to the process of his attentive and playful contemplation which allows persons and things to reveal themselves to him in their integrity without suffering the constraints of utilitarian work.

A Work Whole and Unfinished

The thesis of this study has been that the unifying concern of *Tristram Shandy* is human ontology, the conspicuous features of which constitute the wide range of themes that occupy Tristram's reflections: the intentional structure of consciousness, the transcendence and communal nature of the self, the time-forming function of mind, the positive delineating role of human finitude especially the horizon of death, the locus of that being as language, and the primordial unity of cognition and mood, thought and play. The essential unity of these

25. Gavin Ardley, "The Role of Play in the Philosophy of Plato," *Philosophy* 42, no. 161 (July 1967), 229.

themes is Tristram's response to the question of the meaning and topology of his being. Here at last is the inner significance of writing a life which makes its own composition part of its subject. The book is ontological to the core and consists in complexities of design as rich as those of Don Quixote, who is conscious of his own fictional status as a character in a book that has not been written yet, but which, when it comes to be written, will pretend to be copied, though only in part, from an Arabic manuscript about a real person whose name was not "Quixote" at all. Similar, but more recalcitrant to exposition, is the convergence of perspectives that illuminates the human event at the center of Sterne's novel. Tristram reflects upon himself and, in the act of reflection, writes a book about the process. The book includes accounts of its own composition and thereby takes on a relation to itself that parallels Tristram's own self-relatedness. What specifically makes the book become its own subject are the obstacles that arise in the writing such as the need to convey his diachronic, temporal being in synchronic, spatial chains of printed words and the difficulty of making words, so slippery that the characters cannot understand each other, carry all the misunderstood meanings over to the reader with clarity of reference and precision of nuance. Hence, just as the self becomes aware of itself in the encounter with the other or with its own inherent limitations, so the novel becomes related to itself when it encounters intractable material that will not yield easily to its medium. The book thereby becomes an exact image of the finite temporal structure of Tristram's being. To this parallel and potentially infinite self-relatedness of the book with itself and the protagonist with himself, one must add the dimension of each in turn reflecting the full reflecting range of the other. The ontological twist that is left over is the fact that Tristram, like Quixote, is "really"—or almost really—nothing more than a character in his book, the locus of his being is literally words.

This fascinatingly complex relationship raises a final structural question that bears equally upon the form of the book and the being of the hero, namely, in what sense, if any, the work is complete. The question is equivocal where the aesthetic medium has become fully coextensive with its subject. If one means to ask only whether or not the novel is rounded out in shape and unified in design, then Booth's affirmation is compelling. But if one means to ask whether or not the project, the life and opinions it purports to present, is unified, the complexion of the problem changes. The claim here will be that given the thorough coalescence of form and material only a positive response to the second question provides criteria for discussing the first; only if Tristram's life and opinions are unified can his book be a whole. Hence the first consideration is what precisely is meant by Tristram's unity.

A distinction must be made between unity or wholeness and completeness. The protagonist's being as a self is a unity and in one sense complete at any given moment; that is, his open-ended project for becoming draws into a unified whole the three temporal dimensions of his being. Far from precluding change, this view requires the possibility of change which might at any time give the unity of the present quite a different anatomy. The denial of such a dynamics of the self reduces the self-as-act to self-as-object which is the disintegration of the self. That openness toward the future never ceases for Tristram since he never dies, and had Sterne in fact written two volumes a year for forty years, his project was designed in a way that could have accommodated such additions. He might indeed have gotten around to the ontic events of Tristram's own daily life. In this sense the character Sterne has provided is complete and his presentation of the character is complete at whatever point we have grasped the essential unity that he is at any moment.

There is another sense, however, in which Tristram can only be whole when his life is finished, his possibilities for change closed off by death, and no further revision in the design of his life possible. The importance of this sense of completeness for understanding the novel consists in recognizing how Tristram differs from most fictive characters, even from the others in his own life. The elder Shandys are dead, their characters as fixed as alabaster; they are knowable objects, and in that respect Tristram's being is radically dissimilar to those of his genetic community and identical to those of his audience. The ontological intimacy of the second community is demonstrated by our sharing the focus on futurity which is left unresolved by the ending of the book. It is the only appropriate ending in two senses: it is how life ends, with business unfinished, aims still in view, and we actually grasp him as a complete and completed character; in fact, he does not end, the family is not extinct, and his being remains open to revision. So perfectly does the structure of the life reflect the structure of the hero that it is completely impossible for the project to end in any signficantly different manner, for Tristram would have to survive his own death for at least long enough to write about it. Even if that were not contradictory, it would alter radically the phenomenon of the character as a potentiality *toward* wholeness, and it would refocus the meaning of death from the end toward which Tristram lives his life, to an accomplished fact which removes that life from the realm of possibility. The novel, in short, has exactly the kind of unity that its protagonist has, is complete in exactly the same sense, and remains unfinished in the exact degree that his being is unfinished. No more persuasive evidence may be easily conceived that the book is about the domain of potency, freedom, and the future as transcending actuality, necessity, and the past.

If Tristram has succeeded so splendidly in fulfilling his artistic and ontological aim, one should ask whether or not that constitutes proof of his having overcome the Shandy impotence. The impotence is not merely physical, though his artistic achievement is quite as much to the purpose as would be his fathering a family of sons with long and jolly noses; it contrasts as vividly with Walter's stillborn Life of Socrates and Tristrapaedia. The facts require some qualification. To a very substantial degree Tristram has been healed of the wounds sustained at the hand of Fate, and the success of his odd book, the fact that it has pleased many and pleased long, is the proof. But since the symbol of the disorder is physical sterility, complete healing would require, if not progeny, at least a happier resolution to the bedroom scene with dear Jenny. Nor would a claim of complete restoration to psychic health be consistent with the theme of cultural malaise as it is related to the communal dimension of his being. He is no Puritan Crusoe able to transcend completely the historical conditions of his life. He is in the deepest regions of his being *with* others, for better or worse implicated in the life of his age, his destiny bound up with a world whose prospects according to his values are anything but bright. The cultural affliction has not been cured, though the pathology is complete and, it is tempting to argue, the prescription has been given.

If Tristram's journey through the sunlit windings and turnings of his mind has implicated him in the contingencies of history, so too has it implicated Your Honor and Madame reader who have kept him company in those ramblings, for the wish expressed early in the first volume that he and his readers should come not only to understand one another but to be friends has been fulfilled:

> I have undertaken, you see, to write not only my life, but my opinions also; hoping and expecting that your knowledge of my character, and of what kind of mortal I am, by the one, would give you a better relish for the other: As you proceed further with me, the slight acquaintance which is now beginning betwixt us, will grow into familiarity; and that, unless one of us is at fault, will terminate in friendship. [I.vi.10–11]

Whatever attitudes toward the book one chooses to adopt, whether to listen like the characters in the parlor to Yorick's sermon, to the form, the style, and the delivery, without acknowledging the profound kinship that has been established with the protagonist and appropriating the meaning of his work, or whether to join him in the thoughtfully playful conversation that celebrates as it clarifies the mystery of being human, one at least knows him as a unique "thou" who has been given the leisure to reveal himself in his own integrity, and one is inclined to grant his request for "credit for a little more wisdom than appears upon my outside" (I.vi.11). The thesis that has been argued in this study, that Sterne's novel is an incipient phenomenology which clarifies the processes of human be-ing in the person of the protagonist, fully justifies Tristram's retrospective aspiration that his book may offer wisdom as well as pleasure: "ALBEIT, gentle reader, I have lusted earnestly, and endeavored carefully (according to the measure of such slender skill as God has vouchsafed me, . . .) that these little books, which I have put into thy hands, may stand instead of many bigger books" (IV.xxii.301).

Bibliography

Anderson, Howard. "A Version of Pastoral: Class and Society in *Tristram Shandy*." *Studies in English Literature* 7 (1967), 509–29.

Ardley, Gavin. "The Role of Play in the Philosophy of Plato." *Philosophy* 42, no. 161 (July 1967), 226–44.

Aristotle. *The Basic Works of Aristotle*. Edited by Richard McKeon. New York: Random House, 1941.

Augustine, St. *Confessions*. Translated by Vernon J. Bourke. Volume 21 of *The Fathers of the Church*. New York: Catholic University Press, 1953.

Bachelard, Gaston. *The Poetics of Space*. Translated by Maria Jolas. Boston: Beacon Press, 1969.

Bagehot, Walter. *Literary Studies*. 4th ed. 2 vols. London: Longmans, Green, 1891.

Beckett, Samuel. *Watt*. Paris: Olympia, 1958.

Berkeley, George. *A Treatise Concerning the Principles of Human Knowledge*. New York: Bobbs-Merrill, 1957.

Betti, Emilio. *Die Hermeneutik als allgemeine Methodik der Geisteswissenschaften*. Tübingen: J. C. B. Mohr, 1962.

Booth, Wayne C. "Did Sterne Complete *Tristram Shandy?*" *Modern Philology* 48 (1951), 172–83.

Boswell, James. *Life of Johnson*. Edited by R. W. Chapman and J. D. Fleeman. London: Oxford University Press, 1953.

Cash, Arthur Hill. "The Sermon in *Tristram Shandy*." *English Literary History* 31 (1964), 395–417.

————. *Sterne's Comedy of Moral Sentiments: The Ethical Dimensions of the Journey*. Pittsburgh: Duquesne University Press, 1966.

Cassirer, Ernst. *The Philosophy of Symbolic Forms*. 3 vols. New Haven: Yale University Press, 1953.

————. *The Philosophy of the Enlightenment*. Boston: Beacon Press, 1955.

Cervantes Saavedra, Miguel de. *The Adventures of Don Quixote*. Translated by J. M. Cohen. Baltimore: Penguin Books, 1950.

Collingwood, R. W. *The Idea of History*. New York: Oxford University Press, 1956.

"*Der Spiegel's* Interview with Martin Heidegger on September 23, 1966." Translated by Maria P. Alter and John D. Caputo. *Philosophy Today* 20 (Winter 1976), 268–84.

Descartes, René. *The Philosophical Works of Descartes*. Translated by Elizabeth S. Haldane and G. R. T. Ross. 2 vols. New York: Dover Publications, 1955.

Farrell, William J. "Nature Versus Art as Comic Pattern in *Tristram Shandy*." *English Literary History* 30 (1963), 16–35.

Faurot, Ruth Marie. "Mrs. Shandy Observed." *Studies in English Literature* 10 (1970), 577–89.

Fink, Eugene. "The Ontology of Play." *Philosophy Today* 18 (Summer 1974), 147–61.

Fluchère, Henri. *Laurence Sterne, de l'homme à l'oeuvre*. Paris: Gallimard, 1961.

————. *Laurence Sterne: From Tristram to Yorick*. Translated and abridged by Barbara Bray. Oxford: Oxford University Press, 1965.

Foucault, Michel. *The Order of Things*. New York: Vintage-Random House, 1973.

Frank, Joseph. "Spatial Form in Modern Literature." *The Sewanee Review* 53 (Spring, Summer, and Autumn 1945), 221–40; 433–56; 643–53.

Freedman, William, "*Tristram Shandy:* The Art of Literary Counterpoint." *Modern Language Quarterly* 32 (1971), 268–80.

Gadamer, Hans-Georg. *Truth and Method*. New York: Seabury Press, 1975.

Gurwitsch, Aron. *The Field of Consciousness*. Pittsburgh: Duquesne University Press, 1964.

————. "On the Intentionality of Consciousness." In *Philosophical Essays in Memory of Edmund Husserl*, edited by

Marvin Farber. Cambridge: Harvard University Press, 1940.

Hart, Francis R. "The Spaces of Privacy: Jane Austen." *Nineteenth-Century Fiction* 30 (December 1975), 305–33.

Hartley, David. *Observations on Man.* London, 1749. Facsimile, Gainesville: Scholars' Facsimiles & Reprints, 1966.

Heidegger, Martin. *Being and Time.* Translated by John Macquarrie and Edward Robinson. New York: Harper & Row, 1962.

———. *Kant and the Problem of Metaphysics.* Translated by James S. Churchill. Bloomington: Indiana University Press, 1962.

———. *What is a Thing?* Translated by W. B. Barton, Jr. and Vera Deutsch. Chicago: Gateway-Henry Regnery, 1967.

Hirsch, E. D. *Validity in Interpretation.* New Haven: Yale University Press, 1967.

Holtz, William. *Image and Immortality: A Study of "Tristram Shandy."* Providence: Brown University Press, 1970.

Hume, David. *The Treatise of Human Nature.* 2 vols. New York: E. P. Dutton, 1911.

Husserl, Edmund. *Cartesian Meditations.* Translated by Dorian Cairns. The Hague: Martinus Nijhoff, 1973.

———. *The Crisis of the European Sciences and Transcendental Phenomenology.* Translated by David Carr. Evanston: Northwestern University Press, 1970.

———. *Ideas.* Translated by W. R. Boyce Gibson. London: Collier-Macmillan, 1962.

———. *Phenomenology and the Crisis of Philosophy.* Translated by Quentin Lauer. New York: Harper & Row, 1965.

———. *The Phenomenology of Internal Time-Consciousness.* Translated by James S. Churchill. Bloomington: Indiana University Press, 1973.

Ingarden, Roman. *The Literary Work of Art.* Translated by George G. Grabowicz. Evanston: Northwestern University Press, 1973.

James, Henry. *What Maisie Knew.* New York: Charles Scribner's Sons, 1908.

James, Overton Philip. *The Relation of "Tristram Shandy" to the Life of Sterne.* The Hague: Mouton, 1966.

James, William. *The Principles of Psychology*. 2 vols. New York: Dover Publications, 1950.

Johnson, Samuel. *A Dictionary of the English Language*. London, 1755. Facsimile in 2 vols., New York: AMS Press, 1967.

Johnstone, Henry. *The Problem of the Self*. University Park: University of Pennsylvania Press, 1970.

Joyce, James. *A Portrait of the Artist as a Young Man*. New York: Viking Press, 1956.

Kant, Immanuel. *The Critique of Practical Reason*. Translated by Lewis White Beck. New York: Bobbs-Merrill, 1956.

————. *The Critique of Pure Reason*. Translated by Norman Kemp Smith. New York: Macmillan and Co., 1958.

Kierkegaard, Sören. *Fear and Trembling and the Sickness Unto Death*. Translated by Walter Lowrie. New York: Doubleday Anchor, 1954.

Koestler, Arthur. *The Act of Creation*. New York: Dell Publishing Co., 1964.

Kwant, Remy C. *Phenomenology of Language*. Pittsburgh: Duquesne University Press, 1965.

Laird, John. *Philosophical Incursions into English Literature*. New York: Russell & Russell, 1962.

Lanham, Richard. *"Tristram Shandy": The Games of Pleasure*. Berkeley: University of California Press, 1973.

Lehman, B. H. "Of Time, Personality, and the Author: A Study of *Tristram Shandy*." *Studies in the Comic, University of California Studies in English* 8, no. 2 (1941), 233–50.

Lessing, Gotthold Ephraim. *Laocoön: An Essay upon the Limits of Painting and Poetry*. Translated by Ellen Frothingham. New York: Noonday Press, 1963.

Levin, Harry. *Contexts of Criticism*. Cambridge: Harvard University Press, 1957.

Locke, John. *An Essay Concerning Human Understanding*. Edited by Peter H. Nidditch. Oxford: Clarendon Press, 1975.

Lovejoy, Arthur O. *The Reason, the Understanding and Time*. Baltimore: Johns Hopkins Press, 1961.

MacLean, Kenneth. *John Locke and English Literature of*

the Eighteenth Century. New Haven: Yale University Press, 1936.

Maskell, Duke. "Locke and Sterne, or Can Philosophy Influence Literature?" *Essays in Criticism* 23 (1973), 22–39.

Mead, George Herbert. *Mind, Self and Society*. Chicago: University of Chicago Press, 1934.

Merleau-Ponty, Maurice. *Consciousness and the Acquisition of Language*. Translated by Hugh J. Silverman. Evanston: Northwestern University Press, 1973.

———. *The Essential Writings of Merleau-Ponty*. Edited by Alden L. Fisher. New York: Harcourt, Brace & World, 1969.

———. *Signs*. Translated by Richard C. McCleary. Evanston: Northwestern University Press, 1964.

Meyerhoff, Hans. *Time in Literature*. Berkeley: University of California Press, 1955.

Moglen, Helen. *The Philosophical Irony of Laurence Sterne*. Gainesville: University of Florida Press, 1975.

New, Melvyn. *Laurence Sterne as Satirist*. Gainesville: University of Florida Press, 1969.

———. "Sterne and Henry Baker's *The Microscope Made Easy*." *Studies in English Literature* 10 (1970), 591–604.

Ong, Walter. *The Presence of the Word*. New Haven: Yale University Press, 1967.

Palmer, Richard. *Hermeneutics: Interpretation Theory in Schleiermacher, Dilthey, Heidegger, and Gadamer*. Evanston: Northwestern University Press, 1969.

Petrie, Graham. "Rhetoric as Fictional Technique in *Tristram Shandy*." *Philological Quarterly* 48 (1969), 479–94.

Pieper, Josef. *Leisure: The Basis of Culture*. Translated by Alexander Dru. New York: Mentor-Omega, 1963.

Piper, William Bowman. *Laurence Sterne*. New York: Twayne Publishers, 1965.

Plato. *The Dialogues of Plato*. Translated by B. Jowett. 2 vols. New York: Random House, 1920.

———. *The Platonic Epistles*. Translated by J. Harward. New York: Arno Press, 1976.

Pope, Alexander. *The Dunciad*. Edited by James Sutherland.

New Haven: Yale University Press, 1963.

Pound, Ezra. "A Few Don'ts by an Imagiste." *Poetry* 1 (March 1913), 200–06.

Priestly, J. B. "The Brothers Shandy." In *The English Comic Characters*. New York: Dodd-Mead, 1931.

Putney, Rufus D. S. "Laurence Sterne: Apostle of Laughter." In *The Age of Johnson: Essays Presented to Chauncey Brewster Tinker*. New Haven: Yale University Press, 1949.

Rabelais, François. *The Uninhibited Adventures of Gargantua and Pantagruel*. Translated by Samuel Putnam. New York: Viking Press, 1946.

Ricoeur, Paul. "Existence and Hermeneutics." Translated by Kathleen McLaughlin. In *The Conflict of Interpretations: Essays in Hermeneutics*, edited by Don Ihde. Evanston: Northwestern University Press, 1974.

————. *Husserl: An Analysis of His Phenomenology*. Translated by Edward G. Ballard and Lester E. Embree. Evanston: Northwestern University Press, 1967.

————. "Husserl and Wittgenstein." In *Phenomenology and Existentialism*, edited by Edward N. Lee and Maurice Mandelbaum. Baltimore: Johns Hopkins Press, 1967.

————. "Objectivity and Subjectivity in History." In *History and Truth*, translated by Charles A. Kelbley. Evanston: Northwestern University Press, 1965.

Schleiermacher, Friedrich Ernst Daniel. *Hermeneutik*. Translated by Heinz Kimmerle. Heidelberg: Carl C. Winter, 1959.

Shiller, Johann Cristoph Friedrich von. *On the Aesthetic Education of Man*. Translated by Reginald Snell. New York: F. Ungar, [1965].

Sherbo, Arthur. *Studies in the Eighteenth-Century English Novel*. East Lansing: Michigan State University Press, 1969.

Sherover, Charles M. *Heidegger, Kant and Time*. Bloomington: Indiana University Press, 1971.

Shklovský, Victor. "Art as Technique." In *Russian Formalist Criticism: Four Essays*, translated by Lee T. Lemon and Marion J. Ross. Lincoln: University of Nebraska Press, 1965.

Stambaugh, Joan. "Music as a Temporal Form." *Journal of Philosophy* 61 (1964), 265–80.

Stedmond, John. *The Comic Art of Laurence Sterne.* Toronto: University of Toronto Press, 1967.

Sterne, Laurence. *Letters of Laurence Sterne.* Edited by Lewis P. Curtis. Oxford: Clarendon Press, 1935.

————. *The Life and Opinions of Tristram Shandy, Gentleman.* Edited by James A. Work. New York: Odyssey Press, 1940.

————. *A Sentimental Journey Through France and Italy.* Edited by Gardner D. Stout, Jr. Berkeley: University of California Press, 1967.

————. *The Sermons of Mr. Yorick.* Edited by Wilbur L. Cross. 2 vols. New York: J. F. Taylor, 1904.

Sutton, Walter. "The Literary Image and the Reader." *Journal of Aesthetics and Art Criticism* 16, no. 1 (1957–58), 112–23.

Thompson, David. *Wild Excursions: The Life and Fiction of Laurence Sterne.* New York: McGraw-Hill, 1972.

Traugott, John. *Tristram Shandy's World: Sterne's Philosophical Rhetoric.* Berkeley: University of California Press, 1954.

Tuveson, Ernest. *The Imagination as a Means of Grace.* Berkeley: University of California Press, 1960.

————. "Locke and Sterne." In *Reason and the Imagination, Studies in the History of Ideas, 1600–1800,* edited by J. A. Mazzeo. New York: Columbia University Press, 1962.

————. "Locke and 'the Dissolution of the Ego.'" *Modern Philology* 52 (1955), 159–74.

Wasserman, Earl R. *The Subtler Language.* Baltimore: Johns Hopkins Press, 1959.

Watkins, W. B. C. *Perilous Balance: The Tragic Genius of Swift, Johnson, and Sterne.* Princeton: Princeton University Press, 1939.

Watson, Wilfred. "Sterne's Satire on Mechanism: A Study of *Tristram Shandy.*" Ph.D. dissertation, University of Toronto, 1951.

Watt, Ian. *The Rise of the Novel: Studies in Defoe, Richard-*

son, and Fielding. Berkeley: University of California Press, 1957.

Weaver, Richard M. "The *Phaedrus* and the Nature of Rhetoric." In *Philosophy, Rhetoric, and Argumentation,* edited by Maurice Natanson and Henry W. Johnstone, Jr. University Park: University of Pennsylvania Press, 1965.

Weber, Max. *The Protestant Ethic and the Spirit of Capitalism.* Translated by Talcott Parsons. New York: Charles Scribner's Sons, 1958.

Wild, John. "Husserl's Critique of Psychologism: Its Historic Roots and Contemporary Relevance." In *Philosophical Essays in Memory of Edmund Husserl,* edited by Marvin Farber. Cambridge: Harvard University Press, 1940.

Zaner, Richard. *The Way of Phenomenology.* New York: Pegasus, 1970.

Index

267